Confronting Obstacles to Inclusion

Confronting Obstacles to Inclusion uniquely and comprehensively addresses interpretations of inclusive education by drawing upon the experiences and expertise of leading writers and academics who have direct experience of teaching and researching this area around the world.

This landmark publication combines theoretical chapters with practical material demonstrating how the theories can be put into action in the classroom. The contributors, who all have regular contact with pupils and teachers in inclusive settings, provide a broad spectrum of ideas, examine a number of key themes and interpret these in an international context, such as:

- The causes of exclusion, the obstacles to inclusion and how these can be overcome
- Supporting families
- How we can learn from students
- Professional development
- Enhancing teaching and learning
- Support in the classroom

This authoritative text will be of immense interest and use to practitioners, policy makers, researchers and campaigners who are working towards a more equitable and inclusive society. Through a synthesis of theory and practice the book offers readers an opportunity to explore local, national and international perspectives and raises questions with regards to our current understanding of inclusion. Although the interrogation of the concept of inclusion is, in itself, important, the book provides examples of professional approaches to the key questions which are currently challenging the education of a diverse range of learners.

Richard Rose is Director of the Centre for Education and Research at the University of Northampton, UK.

nasen
Helping Everyone Achieve

Other titles published in association with the National Association for Special Educational Needs (nasen):

Living with Dyslexia: The Social and Emotional Consequences of Specific Learning Difficulties/Disabilities, Second edition
Barbara Riddick
978-0-415-47758-1

Dyspraxia 5–14: Identifying and Supporting Young People with Movement Difficulties, Second edition
Christine Macintyre
978-0-415-54397-2 (HB)
978-0-415-54396-5 (PB)

Dyspraxia in the Early Years: Identifying and Supporting Children with Movement Difficulties, Second edition
Christine Macintyre
978-0-415-47684-3

Teaching Foundation Mathematics: A Guide for Teachers of Older Students with Learning Disabilities
Nadia Naggar-Smith
978-0-415-45164-2

A Handbook for Inclusion Managers: Steering your School towards Inclusion
Ann Sydney
978-0-415-49197-6 (HB)
978-0-415-49198-3 (PB)

Beating Bureaucracy in Special Educational Needs
Jean Gross
978-0-415-44114-8

Supporting Children's Reading: A Complete Short Course for Teaching Assistants, Volunteer Helpers and Parents
Margaret Hughes and Peter Guppy
978-0-415-49836-4

Young People with Anti-Social Behaviours: Practical Resources for Professionals
Kathy Hampson
978-0-415-56570-7

Confronting Obstacles to Inclusion

International responses to
developing inclusive education

Edited by Richard Rose

Routledge
Taylor & Francis Group

LONDON AND NEW YORK

nasen

Helping Everyone Achieve

First published 2010
by Routledge
2 Park Square, Milton Park, Abingdon, Oxon, OX14 4RN

Simultaneously published in the USA and Canada
by Routledge
270 Madison Avenue, New York, NY 10016

Routledge is an imprint of the Taylor & Francis Group, an informa business

© 2010 selection and editorial material, Richard Rose; individual chapters, the contributors

The right of the editor to be identified as the author of the editorial material, and of the authors for their individual chapters, has been asserted in accordance with sections 77 and 78 of the Copyright, Designs and Patents Act 1988.

Typeset in Sabon by Prepress Projects Ltd, Perth, UK
Printed and bound in Great Britain by TJ International Ltd, Padstow, Cornwall

All rights reserved. No part of this book may be reprinted or reproduced or utilised in any form or by any electronic, mechanical, or other means, now known or hereafter invented, including photocopying and recording, or in any information storage or retrieval system, without permission in writing from the publishers.

British Library Cataloguing in Publication Data
A catalogue record for this book is available from the British Library

Library of Congress Cataloging-in-Publication Data
Confronting obstacles to inclusion: international responses to developing inclusive education/edited by Richard Rose. — First ed.
p. cm.
Includes bibliographical references and index.
1. Inclusive education. 2. Special education. I. Rose, Richard C.
LC1200.C64 2010
371.9'046—dc22   2010003585

ISBN10: 0-415-49361-7 (hbk)
ISBN10: 0-415-49363-3 (pbk)
ISBN10: 0-203- 84678-8 (ebk)

ISBN13: 978-0-415-49361-1 (hbk)
ISBN13: 978-0-415-49363-5 (pbk)
ISBN13: 978-0-203-84678-0 (ebk)

Helping Everyone Achieve

nasen is a professional membership association which supports all those who work with or care for children and young people with special and additional educational needs. Members include teachers, teaching assistants, support workers, other educationalists, students and parents.

nasen supports its members through policy documents, journals, its magazine *Special!*, publications, professional development courses, regional networks and newsletters. Its website contains more current information such as responses to government consultations. **nasen's** published documents are held in very high regard both in the UK and internationally.

Contents

Illustrations

Figures

Tables

Contributors

Mithu Alur is the Founder Chairperson of The Spastics Society of India and a founder member of The National Resource Centre for Inclusion. She is a long-established campaigner for parents of children with special educational needs and has also been influential in the promotion of teacher education in India. In addition to publishing papers in international journals Mithu is author of 'The Lethargy of a Nation: Inclusive Education in India and Developing Systemic Strategies for Change' in *Policy, Experience and Change: Cross-Cultural Reflections on Inclusive Education* edited by Len Barton and Felicity Armstrong.

Rob Ashdown is the head teacher of St Luke's Primary School in Scunthorpe, UK, having previously been head of a school in Cambridgeshire. He holds a PhD from the University of Wales, is author of *Pupils with Complex Learning Difficulties: Promoting Learning Using Visual Methods and Materials* and was co-editor of *Enabling Access*, which was winner of the TES/nasen academic book award. Rob has more than thirty years' teaching experience, much of it working with children with complex learning needs.

Sheena Bell is senior lecturer in the Centre for Education and Research at the University of Northampton, UK, where she coordinates courses for teachers in the area of dyslexia. Having a particular interest in vocational and post-compulsory education, Sheena is currently engaged in research with colleagues from Ireland investigating transition from school to further and higher education for students with special educational needs. Sheena's commitment to collaborative international research has resulted in the publication of several papers in academic journals.

Erik W. Carter is Associate Professor at the University of Wisconsin-Madison, USA. Erik served as a special education teacher for several years and his research has included investigations into peer relationships and school participation among adolescents with severe disabilities, including the influence of peer-mediated support models within secondary school settings. He has also undertaken research that focuses on equipping youth with disabilities with the skills, services and experiences needed to transition successfully to life after high school. He is co-author of *Peer Support Strategies Improving Students' Social Lives and Learning.*

Meng Deng is Associate Professor in the Department of Education of Central China Normal University, Wuhan, China, and is one of China's leading researchers in the field of special and inclusive education. His work has included a commitment to cross-cultural understanding of the development of inclusive schooling including the study *Meeting Special Education Needs in Mainstream Classrooms in the United States and China: A Cross-Cultural Study on Instructional Adaptations.*

Chris Derrington is an independent researcher whose interests are focused upon the education of young people from marginalised communities. She previously worked as a teacher in schools and advisory teacher for a Local Authority in England. Having previously worked as a researcher for the National Foundation for Educational Research and the University of Northampton, Chris was co-author of *Gypsy Traveller Students in Secondary Schools: Culture, Identity and Achievement*, which reported a three-year study into the lives of Gypsy Traveller students in the UK.

Mary Doveston is senior lecturer in the Centre for Education and Research at the University of Northampton, UK, having previously taught in schools and been an advisory teacher for a Local Authority. Mary's recent research has focused on supporting the development of inclusive classrooms using an appreciative inquiry approach. She has also published work in the area of mentoring support for students with special educational needs. Mary is co-author of *Becoming a Higher Level Teaching Assistant: Primary Special Educational Needs.*

Mary Beth Doyle is Associate Professor at St Michael's College, Colchester, Vermont, USA, where she teaches undergraduate and graduate students who aspire to become secondary education teachers. In addition to researching aspects of the role of paraprofessionals in inclusive classrooms Mary Beth has published and taught extensively in the context of teaching students with severe disabilities in inclusive contexts and is author of *The Paraprofessional's Guide to the Inclusive Classroom: Working as a Team.*

Lani Florian is Professor of Social and Educational Inclusion at the University of Aberdeen, Scotland. Her research interests include categorisation of children, models of provision for meeting the needs of all learners, and teaching practice in inclusive schools. She has written extensively on inclusive education and has consulted on special needs education and inclusion internationally. She is co-author of *Achievement and Inclusion in Schools*, winner of the 2008 TES/nasen academic book award, and co-author of *Disability Classification in Education: Issues and Perspectives.*

Chris Forlin is currently Professor and Director of the Division of Special Education at the Hong Kong Institute of Education, having previously held academic and teaching posts in Australia and the UK. Her research interests include pre-service and in-service education for teachers in the area of inclusion, an area in which she has published widely. She was co-editor of *Reform, Inclusion & Teacher Education: Towards a New Era of Special Education in the Asia-Pacific Region* and is editor of *Teacher Education for Inclusion: Changing Paradigms and Innovative Approaches.*

Michael F. Giangreco is Professor at the University of Vermont Center on Disability and Community Inclusion in the USA. He has researched and published on a wide range of issues in the area of students with disabilities and his work on paraprofessionals in schools has influenced the work of researchers internationally. Between 2000 and 2007 Michael managed Project evolve: expanding and validating options for learning through variations in education. He is author of several books including *Quick-Guides to Inclusion: Ideas for Educating Students with Disabilities* and *A Guide to Educational Planning for Students with Disabilities.*

Ann Gillies has been a Special Education Teacher for eleven years. She taught in Columbus, Ohio, in classrooms for children with labels of multiple disabilities, and is currently in Sarasota, Florida, teaching students with labels of autism. Ann completed her BS and MA degrees in Special Education at The Ohio State University, and is now a doctoral student in Special Education at the University of South Florida.

Beth Haller is Professor of Mass Communication at Towson University in Maryland, USA. She has conducted research on the topic of media images of people with disabilities and disability issues since 1990. Her research has been published in numerous academic publications and as book chapters. She is former co-editor of the Society for Disability Studies' academic journal, *Disability Studies Quarterly*. She holds a PhD in Mass Media and Communication from Temple University in Philadelphia.

Garry Hornby is Professor in the School of Sciences and Physical Education at the University of Canterbury, Christchurch, New Zealand. He has previously held posts at the Universities of Manchester and Hull, UK, and as a Government Consultant on special education in Barbados. Much of Garry's work has been focused upon support for parents, families and young people with special educational needs. He is co-editor of *Counselling Pupils in Schools* and co-author of *The Mental Health Handbook for Schools* in addition to being a regular contributor to journals and other publications.

Phyllis Jones was a teacher and administrator in schools for fifteen years. Her Masters is from Durham University, UK, and her doctoral work was completed at Northumbria University, UK. She is author of *Inclusion in the Early Years: Stories of Good Practice* and *A Pig Don't Get Fatter the More You Weigh It: Classroom Assessment that Works*. Phyllis's research interests are inclusion, low-incidence disabilities, online pedagogy and also teacher education in low-incidence disabilities. She is an associate professor at University of South Florida.

Leena Kaikkonen is Head of Research and Development at Jyväskylä University of Applied Sciences in Finland. In addition to her work in the area of vocational education Leena has experience as a kindergarten teacher working with children with special educational needs. Leena has worked extensively on European projects and has coordinated work in the development of teachers in several of the Baltic states. Leena's research in the area of vocational education has been published in a range of journals and other publications.

Hazel Lawson is senior lecturer in special and inclusive education at the Graduate School of Education, University of Exeter, UK, having previously held posts at the University of Plymouth and Middlesex University after teaching for many years in primary and special schools. Hazel has a particular interest in the education of children and young people with severe learning difficulties and her research in this area has been widely published. She was co-author of *Access to Citizenship*, which addressed the challenges of addressing this curriculum area for students with complex needs.

Thérèse McPhillips is lecturer in literacy education at St Patrick's College in Dublin, Ireland. She has extensive experience in teaching and was principal of a special school for children with specific reading difficulties. Her research and writing has focused on investigations into the nature and provision of support for pupils with dyslexia in primary schools and she is currently involved in collaborative research into aspects of dyslexia with colleagues from the UK.

Cor Meijer is Director of the European Agency for Development in Special Needs Education and was previously based at the Institute for Educational Research at The Hague in the Netherlands. His research has addressed issues of educational policy and its implementation across Europe. Cor is co-author of *Special Needs Education in Europe: Inclusive Policies and Practices* and has been a regular contributor to books and other publications in the area of inclusive education.

Áine O'Neill teaches at Church of Ireland College of Education in Dublin, Ireland, where she is involved in the delivery of courses for both teachers and special needs assistants. Áine previously taught in secondary schools in Ireland. Her research on the development and role of classroom support in Irish schools and through comparative international study has been published in a number of academic journals.

Sue Ralph is visiting Professor at the University of Northampton, UK, having previously held a post at Manchester University. She is editor of the *Journal of Research in Special Educational Needs* and has contributed to a wide range of other academic journals. Sue's research interests and publications have addressed issues of the history of eugenics from a disability perspective, the inclusion of disabled people in mainstream advertising in the UK and the USA, and ethical issues in image-based research.

Sue Roffey is an educational psychologist, writer and academic specialising in social, emotional and behavioural issues. She is currently based at the University of Western Sydney. In addition to having published a number of practical books for teachers she is currently writing *Changing Behaviour in Schools: Relationships and Wellbeing* and editing *Positive Relationships: Evidence Based Practice around the World*, both to be published in 2010.

Richard Rose is Professor of Special and Inclusive Education and Director of the Centre for Education and Research at the University of Northampton, UK. He is currently lead researcher on Project Iris, a three-year longitudinal study of special and inclusive education in Ireland. Richard has published widely in the field of inclusive education and was joint editor of *Strategies to Promote Inclusive Practice* and joint author with Michael Shevlin of *Count me In: Ideas for Teachers to Engage Children in Active Classroom Learning*.

Martyn Rouse is Professor of Social and Educational Inclusion and Director of the Inclusive Practice Project at the University of Aberdeen, Scotland. He has undertaken commissioned research and development work on inclusive education for local authorities in the UK and for several national and international agencies, including UNICEF, in Bosnia and Serbia in the former Yugoslavia. Recent international work includes the Schools for All project in the Republic of Latvia for the British Council/European Social Fund and the Inclusive Practice Project in the Republic of Georgia for UNICEF. He was co-author of *Achievement and Inclusion in Schools* and co-editor of *Special Education and School Reform in Britain and the United States*.

Michael Shevlin is senior lecturer at Trinity College Dublin in the Republic of Ireland. He has researched widely in the fields of disability and special education, with much of his work focused upon the voice of the individual and their experiences of education. This work has been reported in publications which include *Encouraging Voices* and *Hidden Voices: Young People with Disabilities Speak about their Second Level Schooling*, both of which he co-edited. He is also co-author of *Responding to Special Educational Needs: An Irish Perspective*.

Nidhi Singal lectures at the University of Cambridge, UK, having previously trained as a clinical psychologist and worked with children and young adults in clinical, and subsequently a range of different educational, settings. In addition she has worked as a research consultant on a national-level project working towards building inclusive schools across three states in India and has also worked as a consultant for a range of international NGOs. Nidi's research has been reported widely in a range of international journals.

Jesse C. Suter is a Research Assistant Professor at the University of Vermont assigned to the Center on Disability and Community Inclusion in the College of Education and Social Services. His research interests include wraparound, a team-based planning process for meeting the needs of students with serious emotional and behavioural disabilities and maintaining them in their homes, schools and communities, an area in which he has published a number of papers.

Amanda Watkins is Project Manager with the European Agency for Development in Special Needs Education, which provides a platform for collaboration in the field of special needs education across Europe. She has a particular interest in policy and legal frameworks for special needs education, post-compulsory provision for learners with special needs, and learners with severe and profound learning disabilities. Amanda has conducted research into teacher's learning through researching their own practice, and has coordinated several international projects on behalf of the agency.

Zosia Zaks works as a disability adjustment counsellor, teaches courses on disability issues, and conducts workshops, writes and speaks on issues of importance to the autism community. She is the author of *Life & Love: Positive Strategies for Autistic Adults*. Additionally, Zosia is on the boards of several local and national autism advocacy groups and serves on the Maryland Autism Commission. As the parent of two special-needs children, Zosia is particularly interested in how disability and education systems interface.

Acknowledgements

I am grateful to the following colleagues who provided support throughout the production of this book by reviewing chapters and making recommendations for changes:

- Dianne Chambers, Notre Dame University, Perth, Western Australia
- Stella Chong, Hong Kong Institute of Education
- Philip Garner, University of Northampton, UK
- Barry Groom, University of Northampton, UK
- Marie Howley, University of Northampton, UK
- Johnson Jament, University of Northampton, UK
- Kristi Koiv, University of Tartu, Estonia
- Sue Pearson, University of Leeds, UK
- Roger Slee, University of London Institute of Education, UK
- Eileen Winter, The Institute of Child Education and Psychology Europe, Ireland
- Feng Yan, University of Northampton, UK

I am also grateful to Liz Bonnet for administrative support and to Sara Rose for support in too many ways to be calculated.

Chapter 1

Understanding inclusion

Interpretations, perspectives and cultures

Richard Rose (University of Northampton, UK)

Understanding demands effort. Even in an age of increased mass communication when it is relatively simple to share ideas and perspectives it is not always easy to interpret the meaning of the messages we receive. Indeed, although we live in the 'information age', there is probably a greater risk of misinterpretation of the world and its phenomena than at any time in our history. It is tempting to believe that our own perceptions are a fair reflection of the society in which we live, whereas in reality we are limited by our experiences and the narrow confines of our daily lives. In order to ensure that we have an opportunity to understand the world around us we must develop and accrue knowledge on the basis of listening to those whose experiences and lives may differ considerably from our own and respecting their interpretations of the society which we share. Martha Nussbaum has stated the situation and the challenges which face those of us who are attempting to understand changes in the world concisely:

> People from diverse backgrounds sometimes have difficulty recognising one another as fellow citizens in the community of reason. This is so, frequently because actions and motives require, and do not always receive, a patient effort of interpretation.
>
> (Nussbaum 1997: 63)

This profound statement from Nussbaum provides a pertinent summation of many of the issues which have characterised the debates around inclusive schooling. The struggles of society to come to terms with diversity have often led to the imposition of negative labels and stereotypical interpretations of that which we cannot easily understand. It is far easier to judge others by measuring them against our own egocentric self-image than it is to accept that those whom we perceive as different from ourselves are of equal worth. The call for patience and understanding which Nussbaum articulates has not always been in evidence, even within our education systems. All too often in the past our schools have been institutions lacking in the necessary tolerance to recognise, appreciate and address the needs of children who are considered 'different' and are said to challenge existing systems. If this is true of schools, where we would expect tolerance and understanding to be the norm, how much more likely is it that difficulties will be encountered in other aspects of life where respect for individuality receives less attention.

The late twentieth century was a period during which many educators began to confront the issues of inequality and injustice which blight the lives of so many children. A global recognition of the causes of exclusion of children from even the most fundamental aspects of education encouraged increasing numbers of teachers, researchers and writers to challenge the status quo and seek for the means of change which would improve the lives of whole communities. However, as the momentum towards greater inclusion in education and in other aspects of community life has increased, so has our appreciation of the many obstacles which stand in the way of change. Bringing about changes to our education systems continues as a fundamental issue which is central to the development of a more equitable society, but even if it were to be attained this change in isolation is unlikely to yield the results which people who have for so long been marginalised demand. Inclusion requires a holistic and coordinated approach to address the socio-economic, cultural and political barriers which maintain a significant proportion of the world's population in poverty and continue to widen the gap between marginalised individuals and those in positions of authority and power.

Although education alone cannot hope to bring about the necessary change in the lives of disempowered individuals, those within our education systems have a critical role to play. The attention given to issues of social and educational injustice by educators in recent years has certainly maintained a focus upon issues which might otherwise be largely ignored. The challenge now is to ensure that education policy makers, teachers and researchers focus their work and combine their efforts with parents, children and communities whose previous experiences have been those of disenfranchisement and exclusion. Teachers should be natural leaders within their communities, but this demands that their influence be used beyond the classroom in order to ensure that the critical debates around education continue to receive the attention of those in positions to effect change in the lives of disempowered people.

It is appropriate that education, seen as a priority in most countries, should be at the centre of debate and the subject of an extensive body of research. However, whereas most countries have identified national priorities which have become a focus for ongoing discussion, inclusion can be seen to have become an international concern and a catalyst for a long-running discourse both within and across nations. Over the past three decades researchers, policy makers and organisations representing people who previously struggled to find a voice or a place within education systems have taken centre stage in an effort to define and develop fair and sustainable schooling for all learners. In particular, efforts have been made to ensure that the needs of those individuals who have previously been denied opportunities for schooling have been at the forefront of educational initiatives. The call for change has been loud and in many instances well coordinated, yet the endeavours of so many individuals and groups continue to be necessary as progress remains slow and in many societies children continue to fall outside the mainstream of education.

The fact that inclusion has been the centre of attention for such a prolonged period may well be an indication of the complexities and confusions surrounding this topic. A gradual appreciation of the necessity to change schools and education systems, rather than focusing upon perceived deficits in individual children, has led to a reappraisal of previously established special education pathways. Medical models have given way to social interpretations of the needs of individuals and the communities in which they live and have encouraged researchers to take a broader perspective of the causes of marginalisation and the ways in which these may be addressed. Although an increased understanding of the needs of individual pupils and the characteristics associated with some forms of disability can be helpful, where this has led to stereotyping and a lowering of expectations such an approach has done a considerable disservice to the very individuals that our education system has identified as being in need of support. It is now apparent that simplistic solutions imposed upon schools have often been found wanting and in many cases have led to the kind of compromise which leaves individuals frustrated and angry.

As the debates surrounding schooling have intensified it has become increasingly clear that interpretations of inclusion require an understanding of the established cultures and traditions upon which societies have been founded. The imposition of western models of schooling upon countries that have a long and proud history of education simply serves to perpetuate a cultural imperialism that throughout the late twentieth and early twenty-first century has been shown to fail. If inclusive schooling is to be achieved it will be built upon an appreciation and respect for the established social and cultural values of unique societies rather than on introduced systems which have their origins in countries with significantly different values and ideals. In an age which has seen increased international collaboration between educational researchers a first principle must be to recognise that in relation to inclusive education there may be many different perspectives of a shared issue of concern.

The scrutiny to which moves towards providing a more equitable education system have been subjected in recent years has to an extent been the result of a mobilisation of individuals and organisations who have been marginalised within society throughout history. If advances are to be made in confronting those iniquities which continue to pervade schooling it is essential that we not only listen to the voices of these individuals and groups, but engage with them as equal partners to become agents for change. Societies having chosen to identify individuals according to their abilities, income, ethnicity, sexuality or gender have been forced to reappraise the ways in which they interpret the needs of individuals and to come to terms with an international movement which seeks justice for those who have been forced to the margins. Whereas in the past individuals and groups have found difficulties in establishing a voice that could be heard beyond their immediate vicinity, in an era of global communication it has become easier to mobilise ideas and actions in order to ensure that the injustice of exclusion is at the forefront of the minds of politicians and policy makers. In coordinating action for social justice it will be necessary to deploy the skills and expertise of many players. Policy makers, politicians, teachers and researchers all have important roles to play. However, all of these need constantly to attend to their own personal motivations for involvement and in so doing to ensure that their commitment to marginalised individuals takes full account of the opinions and expertise of the very people they claim to support. The principles of 'nothing about us without us' (Shevlin and Rose 2003; Johnson 2009) have become enshrined in disability politics and needs to inform the actions of all who work towards a more inclusive society. Whereas in the past researchers have at times made efforts to consult with people who have been denied their rights of access to education and other services, we must now move beyond this to ensure that partnerships are established based upon inclusive principles which may serve as a model for other service providers. Observations made by researchers need to be tempered with a recognition that the majority of those undertaking such investigations are from social and economic backgrounds which differ greatly from those of marginalised people. Judgements made by researchers and activists need to be made on the basis of an understanding that their personal beliefs and lifestyles may be at variance with those whom they intend to support or represent through their work.

Bourdieu (1977) in establishing his theory of practice and symbolic power suggested that individuals become either dominant or subservient within society according to the distribution of resources. In identifying four forms of capital – economic, cultural, social and symbolic – he demonstrated how each of these impacts upon both the image of individuals held by those in positions of dominance and the self-perception of those in positions of weakness. In order to address situations of marginalisation Bourdieu saw the necessity to empower those individuals whose capital is currently low. The links between poverty and exclusion are well established (Penn 2005; Gray 2007; Terzi 2008) and it is clear that inclusion, if it is to be achieved, will be dependent upon significant changes to the current socio-economic and political structures which maintain large numbers of individuals at a distance from the mainstream of society. The necessity for such wholesale changes to the very fabric of the systems which we have created within our societies is most certainly a reason why progress towards inclusion has often been slow and in some instances faltering. In times of upheaval including natural disaster, economic recession or international conflict it is the most vulnerable who suffer. They do so not only because of the events that immediately surround them but also because such events lead to a shift in national priorities and a redistribution of resources away from those in greatest need. A holistic approach to tackling issues of social injustice and to formulating new structures which ensure inclusive practices not only in schools but within communities will demand a broader focus from researchers and activists than has often been in evidence to date.

This book brings together writers who have made a commitment to investigate inclusive education and its many dimensions. They do so from a range of perspectives, each bringing to their writing a breadth of experience from their own country and often from their work internationally. Each writer provides an independent interpretation of inclusion and its many dimensions. Whereas some are concerned with deepening our philosophical understanding of the influences upon inclusive schooling, others are more concerned to explore those responses from schools or within communities to a challenging and at times contended movement. Each of these authors has, over several years, demonstrated an ongoing commitment to enquiry from a broad range of experiences as teachers, researchers, parents and advocates. The varying dimensions of the debate around inclusion are articulated by individuals who bring insights to an issue which continues to challenge our understanding of how schools can become more equitable and supportive from the point of view of all learners. The writers represented in this book do not speak with one voice. Each has made a commitment to explore those everyday impediments which restrict access to schooling for a significant number of learners. The fact that they address this challenge from different perspectives is a strength rather than a weakness in terms of our understanding of inclusion.

Discourses of inclusion are set to continue. This is inevitable so long as exclusion from an education that is appropriate and fair persists for so many individuals. By sharing our understanding and experiences, but most importantly by listening to individuals whose experiences differ from our own, we may improve our appreciation of how educational systems can be developed for the benefit of all. Only when this level of appreciation has been achieved will we be in a position strong enough to confront the injustices which continue to be a feature of the lives of so many people.

Bibliography

Bourdieu, P. (1977) *Outline of a Theory of Practice*. Cambridge: Cambridge University Press.

Gray, H. (2007) Diversity, inclusion and education: the educational needs of children from severely disadvantaged socio-cultural groups in Europe. In G. K. Verma, C. R. Bagley and M. M. Jha (Eds) *International Perspectives on Educational Diversity and Inclusion*. London: Routledge.

Johnson, K. (2009) No longer researching about us without us: a researcher's reflection on rights and inclusive education in Ireland. *British Journal of Learning Disabilities*, 37 (4): 250–256

Nussbaum, M. (1997) *Cultivating Humanity*. Cambridge, MA: Harvard University Press.

Penn, H. (2005) *Unequal Childhoods*. London: Routledge.

Shevlin, M. and Rose, R. (2003) *Encouraging Voices: Respecting the Insights of Young People who have been Marginalised*. Dublin: National Disability Authority.

Terzi, L. (2008) *Justice and Equality in Education*. London: Continuum.

Section 1

Causes of exclusion and obstacles to inclusion

Chapter 2

Confronting obstacles to inclusion

How the US news media report disability

Beth Haller (Towson University, MD), Sue Ralph (University of Northampton, UK) and Zosia Zaks (Maryland Autism Commission, USA)

The news media act as a major source of information about the society in which we live. Much research has confirmed the place of news media as agents in the social construction of reality (Gamson 1992) and in the creation of a societal worldview (Cohen & Young 1982). The reporting of disability issues has tended to follow the medical model of disability and such themes as medical and other controversies, causes, cures, symptoms and associated behaviors have been reported. Disabled people are generally "talked about" rather than being able to speak for themselves. We argue that the attitudes perpetuated in the news media act as barriers towards the inclusion of disabled people in mainstream society. In this research we have analyzed stories about autism from four major US publications to demonstrate what is written about disabled people and ask how the news media are creating the "reality" about a particular disability, autism, for their audiences.

In the past few years, autism has become much discussed in the US news media. Both *Newsweek* (2006, Nov. 27) and *Time* (2008, June 2) magazines recently devoted cover stories to the topic, and scholars are beginning to assess the representation of people with autism spectrum disorders in film (Schwartz 2007), the news media (Robertson 2009), and narrative fiction (Murray 2006; Berger 2007).

Inclusive education topics are rarely reported in the US news media. (A search of *New York Times* stories found only eight stories with the keywords "inclusive education" from 1991 to 2007.) Consequently, this chapter focuses on a specific disability associated with children, autism, to see what news audiences are learning about this neurological disability and to determine if children with autism are reported in the context of inclusive education.

This chapter proposes to add to the body of knowledge about news representations of autism but provide something unique by assessing what kind of media messages educators are receiving. It is based on a qualitative analysis of two years of the coverage of autism in the major US news media that reaches the general public, the *New York Times* ($n = 107$), *Time* magazine ($n = 13$), *Newsweek* ($n = 7$), and a publication directed toward educators, *Education Week* ($n = 28$).

By assessing the themes, called news frames (Entman 1993), present in these publications' coverage of autism, the research can ascertain what information educators are receiving. The recent popularity of autism-related stories could be the result of the sensational headlines claiming there is an "autism epidemic" in the US and the UK, as the numbers of children being identified as "autistic" has dramatically increased. For example, *Newsweek* reported in 2008 that the Centers for Disease Control and Prevention (CDC) said there has been a tenfold jump in autism disorders in the last decade (Kalb and Springen 2008). This research was based on reports from parents about what health care providers had told them about their children, namely that they had autism (Samuels 2006, May 17). The CDC is a very reputable US government agency but the way this survey was conducted does not account for health care providers who may not be competent to make a diagnosis and parents who are desperate to put a name to their child's symptoms.

In contrast, educational research into autism's supposed increase shows that the numbers are growing only because of changes in labels and definitions. The pediatric researcher Paul T. Shattuck's study of US Department of Education data shows that the increased numbers of children with autism in US schools can be accounted for by "diagnostic substitution" (Shattuck 2006; Osterweil 2006).

> My research indicates that the increase in the number of kids with an autism label in special education is strongly associated with a declining usage of the mental retardation and learning disabilities labels in special education during the same period. Many of the children now being counted in the autism category would probably have been counted in the mental retardation or learning disabilities categories if they were being labeled 10 years ago instead of today.
>
> (Osterweil 2006)

Although written about education and autism, Shattuck's article was published in the medical journal *Pediatrics*, and the mainstream news media seem to be mostly unaware of his research, which clearly indicates an "autism epidemic" may not be an accurate characterization.

The news media use a variety of definitions for autism possibly because it is, as the Autism Society of America says, "a complex developmental disability" (2009). Autism is a disability with a spectrum of symptoms.

> The word "spectrum" is used because, while all people with autism share three main areas of difficulty [social, communication, social integration, and social imagination], their condition will affect them in very different ways. Some are able to live relatively "everyday" lives; others will require a lifetime of specialist support.
>
> (National Autistic Society 2009)

Additionally children with Asperger's and other high-functioning forms of autism were often not diagnosed at all in the past and just seen as "weird kids." But many of these facts about autism are absent in the media and public discourse about it, so autism takes on huge significance because of the many mysteries and controversies associated with it. One film researcher has watched the increasing societal interest in autism foster numerous fictional portrayals. "As diagnosis has become more accurate and the autistic spectrum more fully understood, the figure of the autistic individual has become a narrative marker of fascination for much cultural production across different media," Murray (2006: 25) says.

This chapter analyzes news narratives or frames that may wrongly and inaccurately characterize autism for news audiences that include US teachers who are educating children with autism.

Framing and the news coverage of autism

We argue that news frames within the coverage of autism and education present narratives that ignore, devalue, or misrepresent disability issues and we illustrate how news content is shaped by dominant societal beliefs about a disability such as autism. Our hypothesis is that these news frames are imbued with the power of the dominant able-bodied culture, which defines and classifies disability. When these dominant beliefs ignore or represent disabled people negatively, disability studies scholars call this phenomenon "ableism" (Hehir 2005; Campbell 2008).

This narrative frame presents people with autism as inferior to able-bodied people, as "defective" or as having a worthless status (Weeber 1999). Ableism creates a societal meta-narrative in which "society perceives disabled persons to be damaged, defective, and less socially marketable than non-disabled persons" (Phillips 1990: 850). Because of the ableism frame, people on the autism spectrum are presented as disadvantaged persons who must look to the state or to society for economic or social support, which is considered a gift, not a right.

Another news frame comes from the medical model. Within the medical model, autism is presented as an illness/disorder dependent on health care professionals for cures or maintenance. In the United States and the United Kingdom, the disability rights movement has created an oppositional frame to these mainstream media presentations, arguing that ableism and the medical model lead to the oppression of disabled people (Fallon 2007). The disability rights perspective views disability as a phenomenon created by external factors, such as architectural, occupational, educational, communication, and attitudinal environments that fail to accommodate people who are physically different (Scotch 1988). "Disability scholars locate disability in the oppression of a given culture and historical period rather than in the impairments per se" (Sticker 2000, cited in Reid and Knight 2006: 18). In the rights perspective, physical difference is acknowledged, and even celebrated as an ethnicity might be by some, but the focus is away from the disabled individual as the problem and on society's structures instead (Shakespeare and Watson 2002).

Similarly, a growing autistic rights movement in the US also confronts the medical model and ableism in favor of a rights model. A profile of US leaders in the autistic rights movement in 2008 explained it this way: "Rather than advocating for a cure, or seeking research into the cause of the much-publicized 'autism epidemic,' these activists argued that society needed to change, not autistic people" (Solomon 2008, May 25).

In terms of inclusive education in US schools, it is still more the exception rather than the rule. The National Council on Disability found in 2000 that three-quarters of American schools did not have integrated education for children with disabilities, despite legislation to the contrary. The 1975 law, the Individuals with Disabilities Education Act (IDEA), guaranteed disabled children "free and appropriate public education," which should take place in the "least restrictive environment" and be held with their peers (Johnson 2004: 16). Johnson says that the media have long perpetuated the myth that "special education took money away from normal children and gave it to disabled children" (2004: 100).

Qualitative content analysis

This qualitative content analysis seeks to understand the news narratives in the framing of stories about autism. This analysis looks at two years' (2006–2008) coverage of autism in the major US news media that reaches the general public, the *New York Times* ($n = 107$), *Time* ($n = 13$) magazine, and *Newsweek* ($n = 7$), and a publication directed toward educators, *Education Week* ($n = 28$). The *New York Times* and the two major news magazines, *Time* and *Newsweek*, were chosen because they are elite and agenda-setting publications in the US. *Education Week* was chosen because it is a publication specifically directed at American teachers.

This study follows Christians and Carey's notion (1981) that the qualitative researcher should assess all aspects of the media texts so this analysis looked at story sources, direct and indirect quotes, language/terminology used, pro or con narratives about autism, and missing perspectives about the issue. Qualitative content analysis (Altheide 1996) allows us to assess how ableist cultural beliefs about disability may be imbedded in the news frames of stories about autism.

A number of studies have already shown how these beliefs make their way into general representations of disability in news media (Clogston 1990; Haller 2000a; Haller and Ralph 2001; Lellis 2009). Additional studies of journalism revealed that disability issues were too frequently misunderstood and misrepresented by journalists (Bonnstetter 1986; Keller, Hallahan, McShane, Crowley, and Blandford 1990; Haller 2000b).

Many of these analyses, however, were quantitative studies that looked at general disability coverage, rather than a specific disability issue such as autism. For this study, a qualitative assessment was chosen because it fits well with the analysis of frames in news texts. A news frame is defined here as a "central organizing idea or story line that provides meaning to an unfolding strip of events, weaving a connection among them. The frame suggests what the controversy is about, the essence of the issue" (Gamson and Modigliani 1987: 143).

> News frames are almost entirely implicit and taken for granted. They do not appear to either journalists or audiences as social constructions but as primary attributes of events that reporters are merely reflecting. News frames make the world look normal. They determine what is selected, what is excluded, what is emphasized.
>
> (Gamson 1985: 617)

These news frames are crucial in autism coverage because autism has become one of the most talked about disabilities of school-age children. Bird and Dardenne (1988) assert that news frames provide understanding of the values and symbols in a culture. Because negative news frames actively stigmatize people with autism, such people may be seen as "invalid" in society and many adults with autism receive no support for independent living, employment, proper health care, and equipment.

These frames have significant implications for news coverage of a disability issue such as autism because many journalists continue to represent disability as a medical problem or social deviance (Clogston 1990). Also, the media ethics scholar Deni Elliott reports that journalists do not see the analogy between a minority group status and disabled people because they say "there is something abnormal about being disabled" (Elliott 1994: 77). This belief in the "abnormality of disability" can lead to misrepresentative or negative news frames and, in turn, these frames can and do influence public understanding of autism. This type of reporting can create barriers for American and British educational institutions trying to become more inclusive for people with autism.

Frames about autism

The 155 news articles read for this study were analyzed to find prominent themes, also known as news frames. Several frames quickly became clear thanks to the controversy surrounding autism in the US. The following section shows the identified frames and gives examples from the news articles.

Frame 1: Autism is about conflict, controversy, and tragedy, for example, with parents who think vaccines ruined their children on one side and scientists who say that's not true on the other side

The news media have provided wide coverage of the discussions concerning the measles, mumps, and rubella vaccine (MMR) since the British physician Andrew Wakefield's paper in the prestigious medical journal *The Lancet* in 1998 suggesting a link between inflammatory bowel disease, autism in children, and the MMR vaccine. His research has been discredited over the years and as recently as February 2009 *The Times* in London reported that he had changed and misreported the data used in his study (Deer 2009). Many studies around the world have confirmed that there is no link between the MMR vaccine and autism (Johnson 2009), and a special court in the US found no autism–vaccine link (Freking and Neergaard 2009). However, many parents of children on the autism spectrum still believe in the link, as do 25 percent of Americans, according to a study by Florida Tech University (Ubanis 2008). Mulholland says, "The belief that routine childhood vaccines can lead to autism remains one of the more stubbornly enduring" (2008). Despite the mainstream medical community saying there is no link, "the Internet is filled with groups and organizations who insist that vaccines are causing children to become autistic" (Mulholland 2008).

Some of the stories (17 percent) mentioned the vaccine controversy, even though it had been disproven many times. For example, a story in the *New York Times* in 2007 reported on the debate over the causes of autism that have strained a family and caused a split in the charity they run. The founders of Autism Speaks tried to end the "autism internecine warfare in the world of autism" (Gross and Strom 2007). Katie Wright, mother of a child with autism, and daughter of Autism Speaks founders Bob and Suzanne Wright, has taken the side of "the mercurys" (who believe the preservative, thimerosal, present in MMR vaccine until 2001, is the cause of autism). Autism Speaks and those aligned with it support the side of finding cures from genetic testing.

Another *New York Times* story highlighted a controversy over flu shots in New Jersey, which is the first state to "mandate flu shots for preschoolers" (Capuzzo 2007). There, parents were seeking ways to opt out. The article cites some parents' belief in the link between autism and thimerosal. In the story a mother who has a child with autism says her child's autism was linked to having had childhood vaccinations. In arguing against the NJ requirement for flu shots for children, she says "try having a child bite chunks of skin out of herself, or tell you she's going to chop your head off, or smear feces over the wall . . . Something's going on with these vaccines, and we don't want any more" (Capuzzo 2007). The following year the *New York Times* had another story that reported that more parents are saying no to inoculations for their children (Silverman 2008).

What is interesting about the vaccine controversy in the news media is that the media continue to include references to it in many stories, even though it has been disproven many times. Some of the controversy comes from US autism organizations that persist in believing that vaccines caused their children's autism. On many occasions they publicly attack anyone who disputes the vaccine-as-cause theory. In fact, an American vaccine researcher, Dr. Paul Offit, who wrote the book *Autism's False Prophets* in 2009, had to forgo a book tour because of the many death threats he received (McNeil 2009). It is unclear whether the journalists still believe the vaccine-as-cause theory or are just frightened of attacks from autism organizations.

Other controversies about autism rose during the time of this media study. An advertising campaign for a child study center at New York University (NYU) used ransom notes to present the "awfulness" of autism. The advertisement about autism read: "We have your son. We will make sure he will no longer be able to care for himself or interact socially as long as he lives." The note was signed "Autism." The campaign caused much controversy and the autistic rights movement and parents groups were successful in getting the campaign stopped just a few weeks after it started (Kaufman 2007a,b).

In the summer of 2008, a well-known conservative talk show host, Michael Savage, said on air that nearly every child with autism was "a brat who hasn't been told to cut the act out," and that in "99 percent of the cases" autism is caused by poor parenting. He said: "They don't have a father around to tell them, 'Don't act like a moron. You'll get nowhere in life.'" He said children with autism should be told, "Straighten up. Act like a man. Don't sit there crying and screaming, idiot" (Steinberg 2008a,b). Even when he lost advertisers and parents protested to his radio show's parent company, he insisted he stood by his comments.

In October 2008, the actor and comedian Denis Leary made negative comments about autism in his new book. Leary called his book *Why We Suck: A Feel-Good Guide to Staying Fat, Loud, Lazy and Stupid.* In a chapter titled "Autism Schmautism," he wrote: "There is a huge boom in autism right now because inattentive mothers and competitive dads want an explanation for why their [expletive] kids can't compete academically, so they throw money into the happy laps of shrinks" (Levenson 2008). He added that these parents are looking for "diagnoses that help explain away the deficiencies of their junior morons" (Sweet 2008). Leary ended up issuing a formal apology about his comments concerning autism.

As horribly misunderstanding of autism as many of these controversies were, some of the non-vaccine controversies probably ended up contributing to more positive coverage of autism because the media had to go to a variety of autism groups to get their "side of the story."

For example, protests against the NYU ransom notes advertising campaign brought the autistic rights movement to the attention of major media. The most prominent of these groups, the Autistic Self Advocacy Network (ASAN), led the fight against the campaign and got it removed in two and a half weeks. ASAN, unlike most autism groups, which are run by parents and focused on cure, is run by and for people on the autism spectrum. It

> was created to provide support and services to individuals on the autism spectrum while working to change public perception and combat misinformation by educating communities about persons on the autism spectrum. Our activities include public policy advocacy, community engagement to encourage inclusion and respect for neurodiversity, quality of life oriented research and the development of autistic cultural activities and other opportunities for autistic people to engage with others on the spectrum.
>
> (ASAN 2009)

ASAN's response to the NYU advertising campaign was featured in articles in the *New York Times, Washington Post*, and *New York Daily News*. The recognition ASAN received led to an in-depth story in *New York* magazine about the autistic rights movement. ASAN's founder and president, Ari Ne'eman, says that ASAN was founded under the principles of disability rights and rejects the medical model. "We bring the traditional focus of disability rights to the autism community," he said (Ne'eman 2009).

Ne'eman says the NYU advertisements followed a "tragedy-centric paradigm" that sees people with autism as less than human. He says many other autism groups, usually led by parents, reinforce this same notion with their emphasis on cures, the vaccine controversy, and the medical model. He calls the narrative the "stolen child phenomenon," which "tells parents their children (with autism) are not there" (2009). However, Ne'eman explains that these parents groups, especially those that mistakenly believe that vaccines cause autism, are the loudest about their issues. This current study seems to confirm that phenomenon; journalists are latching onto the narratives that come from many parents groups that their children have been "ruined" by autism.

For example, during the Michael Savage controversy, ASAN continued its narrative of rights when countering Savage, but the parents group, Autism Speaks, countered him with a frame of pity for their children: "There are those who are apparently incapable of feeling compassion. They (children with autism) deserve our pity, not our scorn" (*Time* 2008: 18).

ASAN embraces the neurodiversity movement, which accepts that many people have neurological differences and don't need to be "cured" of them. Ne'eman says the focus should be on supporting people with autism and helping to integrate them into society. The *New York* magazine article explained the term "neurodiversity" in the popular press. The term comes from Judy Singer, an Australian who is on the autism spectrum and has several family members on the spectrum. "I was interested in the liberatory, activist aspects of it—to do for neurologically different people what feminism and gay rights had done for their constituencies," Singer said (Solomon 2008).

Ne'eman explains that some characteristics of autism are not negative. (Many in the autism community cite people such as Charles Darwin and Albert Einstein, both of whom were believed to be on the autism spectrum.) He also likens the autistic rights movement to the early gay rights movement, which rejected the medical model whereby homosexuality was diagnosed as a psychiatric disorder, in favor of civil rights for gay and lesbian people.

The narrative of rights for autistic people and neurodiversity still receives little coverage in the news media, and many in the general public believe the narrative that autism is a "tragedy" that needs to be "cured." A writer for *Education Week*, a US publication for teachers, expressed skepticism about neurodiversity in her blog.

Christina Samuels, who covers special education for *Education Week*, reflected on what Ne'eman said about neurodiversity in an ABC TV news story:

> a young man with Asperger's Syndrome (Ne'eman) who would like people to stop treating him as if he has a disability, and start recognizing autism as an acceptable neurological difference that does not need to be "cured." What would that mean for educators, I wonder? "Anti-cure doesn't mean anti-progress," said one of the leaders of this movement, Ari Ne'eman. And a mother quoted in the story says that some of the treatments her son has undergone are a waste of time, and she'd like to see better services for him. But Thomas Insel, director of the National Institute of Mental Health, cautions against "romanticizing" and "trivializing" mental disorders. Children with autism are not merely shy loners, he says. I think we can all get behind the idea of treating a child as something more than a bundle of defects that must be fixed. Is the idea of neurodiversity and groups like the Autistic Self Advocacy Network moving too far in a direction that leads away from appropriate treatment?
>
> (Samuels 2008)

As the news frame of controversy and tragedy indicates, the news media only rarely give the public counternarratives from groups such as ASAN, which show people on the autism spectrum living engaged and satisfying lives.

Frame 2: Language use about autism misinterprets it and/ or stigmatizes it, i.e. it is linked to other disabilities, such as intellectual disabilities, or a sense of hopelessness for families

Autism can be devastating for some families, especially those with fewer economic resources. But some of the language used about autism in the news stories projects an undercurrent of hopelessness in the situation that may not even be present. For example, in one story middle-class parents complained they can't live their lives the way they want because of issues such as not being able to find a babysitter for their child with autism. Finding child care is a problem that families across the USA face and is not specific to families with a child with autism (Luongo 2008).

Some news stories collapsed autism with other disabilities, such as intellectual disabilities, which is often not the case. In a *Newsweek* article, "The Puzzle of Hidden Ability," the author writes "it is torture to try and engage with someone on even this interpersonal level, so it's no wonder so many wind up with IQ scores just above a carrot's" (Begley 2007: 50). In addition to a possibly incorrect connection between autism and IQ, the reference to someone's IQ as that of a vegetable is extremely offensive.

Some articles made sweeping generalizations about children with autism, reinforcing the notion that all people with autism are the same, which is not correct. In a *New York Times* story about the bat mitzvah of a teenager with autism, the author suggests the teenager's behavior is typical of all people with autism. "Jami is autistic, which means she lacks a whole quiver of intellectual and social skills and might create some awkward moments by whining or jumping up and down on the bimah, the stage where the Torah is read" (Berger 2007: WE1). The article ends in a patronizing manner. Readers are told all the potential difficulties which could arise during Jami's bat mitzvah but all went well and "after she finished, she skipped once around the stage and let out a whoop of pleasure. No one minded." The reporter even references her own perceived credibility by mentioning that at her synagogue a teenager with Down syndrome is one of the Hebrew Torah readers.

In other stories, people with autism are called "abnormal" (Rabin 2007) and autism is called an "affliction" (Bazelon 2007). In a *New York Times* story, a film director asked "what is wrong with him?" Another source in the story, Mrs. Vendditti, explained, "We've been conditioned to think if we don't understand something, we need to put a name on it to understand" (Lim 2007: 27).

Some of the headlines about families with a child with autism presented an underlying narrative of hopelessness. One *New York Times* headline said, "Hopes Diminish but She Still Pursues an American Dream." In discussing the background of the mother, the story gives an example of her financial "hopelessness" because she is "separated from her husband and does not receive financial help from him (Mitchell 2007). Another headline says autism and disability cause "Tough, Rewarding Days Caring for Four Children" (Haskell 2007). But the story is actually about necessary supports for families that should come from the US welfare system.

Frame 3: Autism causes bizarre behavior

Many stories used descriptions of autism that perpetuated a narrative of people with autism always behaving bizarrely. There is rarely a counternarrative that indicates that many children do things that society considers "inappropriate" because they are children, not because they have autism. In a story about New York police receiving training to better understand autism, several examples of "bizarre behavior" are placed first in the story in an effort to add more "drama" to the story. "An autistic boy is discovered standing in the middle of a busy road, on his way to the beach. A young girl with autism outsmarts a number of locks, leaves the house before her mother wakes up and is found, naked but alive, in a neighbor's pool" (Kelley 2007a: 5).

These examples read as a kind of "scare tactic" for police about why they need to know more about autism. The article does contain some useful information about autism that police should know, such as how many people on the autism spectrum understand word meanings in a literal sense. "If they [police] asked someone with autism if they wanted to waive their rights, they might find that the person waved back at them" (Kelley 2007a: 5).

The majority of stories examined about autism, whatever the topic being covered, have a section that gives examples of "bizarre behavior," usually to introduce the story. Thus, the story focuses the reader's attention on the "negative" characteristics of children with autism. This news frame links to the medical model of disability, which is concerned with "what is wrong with them," what are the causes, whom society can blame, and the media's obsession with finding a cure.

One story, which has as part of its title "Separating Fact from Fear as the Courts and Hollywood Wade in," begins with a description of a young boy with autism. "You wonder what he thinks. The little boy who flaps his arms and bangs his head. Who bristles at the touch of wool, and covers his ears when balloons go 'pop!' The boy who doesn't respond to his name and will never say, 'I love you'" (Kalb and Springen 2008: 64). Despite the positive title, the usual topics are covered, such as increasing numbers of children in the US with autism, the refueled controversy about the relation of autism to vaccines, the causes, and finding a cure.

On a more inclusive note, the story does give voice to Ari Ne'eman of the Autistic Self Advocacy Network, who has Asperger's syndrome. In the story he voices his concern about research that could locate "genes and other markers" that would enable doctors to test for autism and allow for abortion of fetuses with the "autism gene." He says his fear is, "That autism will become like Down syndrome – essentially selected out of the population" (Kalb and Springen 2008: 64). But even an articulate advocate such as Ne'eman is painted with the "bizarre behavior" frame. Preceding his comments is a description of his behavior. Readers are told that he is part of a high-functioning subgroup. The article says, "Ne'eman says he has never struggled with speech, but he has always had difficulty understanding non-verbal forms of communication, like sarcasm. He also flaps his hands occasionally and he can't stand the feel of certain fabrics, especially velvet" (Kalb and Springen 2008: 64). A person with autism is used as a source in the story, but the reporter makes sure we know he is "different."

Frame 4: People with autism functioning in society

This is not a particularly prevalent news frame, but occasionally the media did cover people with autism as they engaged with society. A feature in the *New York Times* reported on a theatre workshop for adults with autism organized by a joint project of the Autism Center of the New Jersey Medical School and Montclair State University, wrote positively of the programme and let a person with autism speak for himself (Kelley 2007b).

"It is designed to build on the participants' strengths and interests rather than focusing on their deficits," Madeline Goldfarb, director of outreach and education at the Autism Center said in the article. " 'They were all sitting in their own little worlds, not communicating with one another around a big conference table, not making eye contact or engaging.' But she asked them what their passions were, and the atmosphere quickly became charged as consensus grew around theatre" (Kelley 2007b: 6).

Tyler, a member of the group, spoke about a book he was writing about his "life with learning difficulties" and said, "it is about how some of the staff members and teachers treat me differently, or kids treat me differently, or anybody else. They have sick minds and should know better than that" (Kelley 2007b: 6).

An excellent documentary about autism appeared in the USA in spring 2008, when it was broadcast on the paid cable channel, HBO. Called "Autism: The Musical," it received many positive reviews from mainstream media critics. The documentary describes itself this way:

> one woman's (Elaine Hall) optimistic pledge to lead a group of autistic children in defying diagnosed expectations by writing, rehearsing and performing their own full-length musical. Following five Los Angeles children over the course of six months, director Tricia Regan captures the struggles and triumphs of their family life and observes how this musical production gives these performers a comfort zone in which they can explore their creative sides.

The documentary is even more in-depth than this description indicates: it presents the children as multifaceted human beings with many of the same problems kids without autism face. But, most importantly, the children and their parents tell their own stories openly and with sometimes brutal honesty through their numerous interviews in the documentary.

"Autism: The Musical" allowed some more nuanced news frames to enter the media's reporting on autism because it showed children with autism functioning well in society. In a quote from the theatre project's creator, Elaine Hall, in the *New York Times*, narratives of struggle and success are paired:

> "The first 11 weeks were so chaotic, kids were literally hiding under tables and spinning around in circles," she [Hall] said, and whispered: "Then all of a sudden they start coming together as a group. We wrote a play. We learned songs. We wore costumes. We no longer talked about Steven hiding under tables. We were saying, 'O.K., what role do you think Steven should play?'"
>
> (Hart 2008)

The film's director, Tricia Regan, explained the importance of incorporating all perspectives into the documentary: "The Miracle Project is this oasis where the kids come to relax, but the film wouldn't be successful unless we also saw how painful it can be for the parents of these kids. When you show both sides, it's not so scary anymore."

However, even with the more empowering news frames that came from news coverage of "Autism: The Musical," some who saw the documentary questioned where the screaming, uncontrollable kids with autism were. Some viewers could not put aside their preconceived notions about children with autism. Also, this misunderstanding did not acknowledge the benefits that the children were receiving in controlling some symptoms of autism by participating in the theatre project. The *New York Times* TV critic showed his own skepticism with this comment in his review:

> Ms. Hall's troupe is not very representative of the spectrum of autism – the most difficult types of children are not in evidence here – and for the first two-thirds of the film, viewers unfamiliar with the condition might be thinking, "These kids don't look so bad off." But around the one-hour mark, when Ms. Hall's 12-year-old slams a smaller child to the ground for no reason, the film begins to show some of autism's more disturbing manifestations. And you start to see why these parents are so frazzled.
>
> (Genzlinger 2008)

Finally, even though the USA elected a new president after the time of this study, autism has made the news by being the only disability singled out in the new president's disability agenda. President Barack Obama says he is "committed to supporting Americans with Autism Spectrum Disorders ('ASD'), their families, and their communities." Although much of what he plans connects to the mission of parents' groups, i.e. prevention and treatment of autism, President Obama says he does have a plan for people living with autism. He "supports improving life-long services for people with ASD for treatments, interventions and services for both children and adults with ASD" (2009). So, as negative as some of the news frames about autism are, the constant drumbeat about the "tragedy" of autism and the controversy swirling around it seems to have been very effective in getting this specific disability special attention from the US government.

Education Week stories

Stories about autism were analyzed in a publication specifically for teachers in the US, *Education Week* (*n* = 28). With a circulation of 50,000, it is known as "American education's newspaper of record." Established in 1981, it describes its mission as helping to "raise the level of awareness and understanding among professionals and the public of important issues in American education" (*Education Week* 2009). A number of the *Education Week* stories were written by the special education reporter Christina Samuels, who had revealed on her blog her skepticism about the idea of neurodiversity, which is the foundation of the autistic rights movement in the US (2008, June 12).

Many of the news frames of the *Education Week* stories were similar to that of the news media, focusing on the growing numbers of children with autism, the cost of educating them, and the causes and cures of autism. However, in *Education Week*, the debate about the autism epidemic was continued but with a much more in-depth analysis of what the figures really meant (Samuels 2006, April 19).

For example, unlike the *New York Times*, which did not cover Shattuck's research, *Education Week* did a story about his analysis of US Department of Education data that shows most of the growth in autism numbers is likely to be due to "diagnostic substitution." His research surmises that since 1993, when autism was first used as a diagnostic category, "the number of children diagnosed with autism spectrum disorders has increased at the same time as the number of children diagnosed with mental retardation and learning disabilities has declined" (p. 8). However, Samuels's article also contained attacks on Shattuck from a vaccine-as-cause group, Safeminds, even though Shattuck's research makes no mention of vaccines or any possible environmental causes of autism. The story is a good example of how journalistic norms sometimes feed controversies on disability topics. Journalists are trained to cover "all sides" of a story so they will include the vaccine-as-cause theory because that is what many of the spokespeople of US parent-run autism organizations say. Consequently these articles become the conduit for the autism organizations to keep the misinformation alive.

Because *Education Week* focuses specifically on education issues across the US, it also reported an important 2007 court case from parents wanting to represent their own children in court to ask for control over the type of education they might receive (Walsh 2007, May 25). The case went to the US Supreme Court and was finally decided in favor of the parents of children with autism. The *New York Times* did cover the case (Greenhouse 2007), but *Education Week* followed it more closely and in more depth (Walsh 2007, June 6).

Education Week also reported on some of the innovative educational programs available for children with autism. For example, Samuels reported on these pre-school programs in an in-depth manner, looking at a number of initiatives across the US (2007). The story contains a wide variety of sources and includes references so teachers could gather even more information about the programs if they wished. Another story provides a good discussion on teacher's CPD, a study day in which teachers are encouraged to read. The article includes references to books describing how children with autism live their lives (Keller 2008). However, despite a few good in-depth articles about autism, it is surprising that *Education Week* covered so few stories about an important educational issue such as autism. From two years of coverage, an estimated 104 issues for the weekly publication, *Education Week* wrote only 28 stories about autism.

Mostly, *Education Week* covered autism similarly to the *New York Times*. Some articles contained much of the same misinformation about autism, especially over the vaccine debate, and few people with autism were speaking for themselves. Little insight was given into people living with autism and managing their daily life.

Education Week misses an opportunity to inform and educate American teachers about autism and inclusive education issues. Instead of repeating the same old stories about autism, *Education Week* should be focused on the significant issue of inclusive education and how schools are dealing with their growing numbers of students with autism in innovative ways. For example, a teacher in Florida won a national award for her inclusive education methods in 2008. In Kate Schau's first-grade class, she teaches children with Down syndrome, autism, and other learning disabilities alongside non-disabled students. Her model of how to integrate disabled children in elementary schools was named the best in the US by the American Federation of Teachers (O'Donnell 2008). *Education Week* did no story on Kate Schau.

Conclusions

Many in American society believe it is in the midst of an "autism epidemic." Whether this is true or not, it is reinforced by sensational media coverage of "controversies" surrounding it. Murray (2006) says, "autism . . . currently occupies a place in the public consciousness that is akin to a phenomenon. The increased rate of diagnosis . . . has suggested to some that we live in a time of an autism 'epidemic.'" And, except for parents of children with autism, those in American society with the most contact with autism are probably educators. American educators, like many in society, gain much of their understanding of a topic such as autism from popular news media.

Therefore, it is crucial that educators look critically at the information they receive from the news media and their own specialty publications. This study aimed to reveal many of the underlying themes/news frames that inform media coverage of autism.

A major theme in the news media reports is how the media perceive a constant swirl of controversy surrounding autism. They constantly reinforce this narrative of controversy, despite the scientific evidence, which has never shown any link between the MMR vaccine and autism. Other "controversies" arise when American celebrities begin making comments about autism, as in the cases of Jenny McCarthy, Michael Savage, and Denis Leary. James says that "autism has become to disorders what Africa is to social issues, the celebrity cause du jour" (2007: 18).

Many of the news articles in this study embody the medical model, in which people with autism are presented as having a disorder that causes them to engage in bizarre behaviors and as needing to be "cured." In terms of inclusive education, this study illustrates the continuing ableism that informs much news media coverage of a disability such as autism. Because ableism is embedded in many US special education classrooms, this reinforcement within the media fuels any anti-inclusion attitudes in American classrooms.

The Harvard University education scholar Thomas Hehir explains the ableist assumptions that already plague the education of disabled children in the US.

> From an ableist perspective, the devaluation of disability results in societal attitudes that uncritically assert that it is better for disabled students to do things in the same manner as nondisabled kids. Certainly, in a world that has not been designed with the disabled in mind, being able to perform like nondisabled children gives disabled children distinct advantages. However, ableist assumptions become dysfunctional when the focus of educational programs becomes changing disability. School time devoted to activities associated with changing disability may take away from the time needed to learn academic material. The ingrained

prejudice against performing activities in ways that are more efficient for disabled people may add to educational deficits.

(Hehir 2003)

Schools, the media, and American society must begin to understand the dire consequences of ableism in public discourse such as the media and in classrooms. Put bluntly, Hehir says, "the most damaging ableist assumption is the belief that disabled people are incapable."

The *New York Times, Newsweek, Time* and *Education Week* spent so much of their coverage of autism focused on controversies, cures, tragedies, and causes that news audiences receive little information about the abilities of people with autism. To find the stories of capable people with autism that confront notions of ableism, we have to go to the other forms of media, such as the documentary "Autism: The Musical," which showed children with autism as capable of creating their own musical, and the Internet, where many adults with autism have shown their own view of the world through blogs and online videos. Amanda Baggs, an autistic woman who uses a speech synthesizer, has been blogging and creating videos about her life experiences since 2005. Her YouTube video called "In My Language" captures how she interacts with the world. She says she creates her videos because:

It's one thing to describe the way I interact with my surroundings, it's another to actually show people, as in "In My Language," the ways that have always (whether I've had words or not at the time) come more naturally to me than standard language has. Also, a lot of people online tend to think that I and other autistic bloggers all somehow magically "look normal". Videos counteract that impression quite well, I've found.

(Baggs 2007a)

Her "In My Language" video has had more than 750,000 views on YouTube and, seeing the video directly, her viewers are able to bypass the traditional news media and see how an autistic person makes the world inclusive on her own terms.

Bibliography

Altheide, David L. (1996) *Qualitative Media Analysis*. Thousand Oaks, CA: Sage.
Autism Society of America website. (2009) About autism. Accessed 19 January 2009 at http://www.autism-society.org/site/PageServer?pagename=about_home
"Autism: The Musical." (2007) About the film. "Autism: The Musical" website. Accessed 17 January 2010 at http://www.autismthemusical.com
Autistic Self Advocacy Network (ASAN). (2009) About us. Accessed 20 February 2009 at http://www.autisticadvocacy.org/modules/smartsection/category.php?categoryid=8

Baggs, A. (2007a) How I make my videos. Amanda Baggs blog, Ballastextenz. Austistics.org. Accessed 20 February 2009 at http://ballastexistenz.autistics. org/?page_id=405

Baggs, A. (2007b, January 14) In my language. [YouTube video]. Accessed 20 February 2009 at http://www.youtube.com/watch?v=JnylM1hI2jc

Bazelon, E. (2007, August 5) What are autistic girls made of. *New York Times*, Section 6, p. 38.

Begley, S. (2007, August 20) The puzzle of hidden ability. *Newsweek*, p. 50.

Berger, J. (2007a) Alterity and autism: Mark Haddon's *Curious Incident* in the neurological spectrum. In Mark Osteen (Ed.) *Autism and Representation*. New York: Routledge.

Berger, J. (2007b, August 5) A faith's embrace leaves no one on the outside. *New York Times*, Section WE, p. 1.

Bird, S. Elizabeth and Dardenne, Robert W. (1988) Myth, chronicle, and story. In James W. Carey (Ed.) *Media, Myths, and Narratives*. Newbury Park, CA: Sage.

Bonnstetter, Cathy Meo. (1986) Magazine coverage of the mentally handicapped. *Journalism Quarterly*, 63 (3): 623–626.

Campbell, F. K. (2008) Refusing able(ness): a preliminary conversation about ableism. *M/C Journal*, 11 (3). Accessed 19 January 2009 at http://www.media-culture.org.au

Capuzzo, J. P. (2007, December 11) New Jersey is expected to require flu shots for preschoolers. *New York Times*, Section B, p. 1.

Christians, Clifford and Carey, James. (1981) The logic and aims of qualitative research. In G. H. Stempel and B. H. Westley (Eds) *Research Methods in Mass Communication*. Englewood Cliffs, NJ: Prentice-Hall.

Clogston, John S. (1990) *Disability Coverage in 16 Newspapers*. Louisville: Advocado Press.

Cohen, Stanley and Young, Jock (Eds). (1982) *The Manufacture of News: Social Problems, Deviance & the Mass Media*. London: Constable.

Deer, B. (2009, February 8) MMR doctor Andrew Wakefield fixed data on autism. *The Times*. Accessed 8 February 2009 at http://www.timesonline.co.uk/tol/life_and_style/health/article5683671.ece

Education Week website. (2009) Editorial projects in education – a history. Accessed 20 February 2009 at http://www.edweek.org/info/about/history.html

Elliott, Deni. (1994) Disability and the media: the ethics of the matter. In Jack Nelson (Ed.) *The Disabled, the Media, and the Information Age*. New York: Greenwood Press.

Entman, Robert M. (1993) Framing: toward clarification of a fractured paradigm. *Journal of Communication*, 43: 51–58.

Fallon, A. (2007) My thoughts on my disability studies degree. *Beyond the Social Model of Disability*. Accessed 19 January 2009 at http://enabledisability.wordpress.com/2007/02/27/beyond-the-social-model-of-disability

Freking, K. and Neergaard, L. (2009, February 13) Vaccines don't cause autism, special court says. *Associated Press*. Accessed 14 February 2009 at http://www.google.com/hostednews/ap/article/ALeqM5i5qHH2OdrDMQkErloXqYD-HZAcHwD96A8SO05

Gamson, William A. (1985) Goffman's legacy to political sociology. *Theory & Society*, 14: 605–622.

Gamson, William. (1992) *Talking Politics*. Cambridge: Cambridge University Press.

Gamson, William A. and Modigliani, A. (1987) The changing culture of affirmative action. In R. G. Braungart and M. M. Braungart (Eds) *Research in Political Sociology*. Greenwich, CT: JAI Press.

Genzlinger, N. (2008, March 28) A different sort of "hey kids, let's put on a show!" *New York Times*. Accessed 2 March 2009 at http://www.nytimes.com/2008/03/25/arts/television/25genz.html?scp=1&sq=autism:%20the%20musical&st=cse

Giles, J. (2004) Media attack prompts editorial backlash against MMR study. *Nature*, 427: 765.

Greenhouse, L. (2007, May 22) Legal victory for families of disabled students. *New York Times*. Accessed 20 February 2009 at http://www.nytimes.com/2007/05/22/washington/22scotus.html?scp=2&sq=jacob+winkelman&st=nyt

Gross, J. and Strom, S. (2007, June 18) Debate over cause of autism strains a family and its charity. *New York Times*, Section A, p. 1.

Haller, B. (2000a) If they limp, they lead? News representations and the hierarchy of disability images. In D. Braithwaite and T. Thompson (Eds) *Communication and People with Disabilities*, Mahwah, NJ: Lawrence Erlbaum.

Haller, B. (2000b) How the news frames disability: print media coverage of the Americans with Disabilities Act. *Research in Social Science and Disability*, 1: 55–83.

Haller, B. and Ralph, S. (2001) Content analysis methodology for studying news and disability: case studies from the United States and England. *Research in Social Science and Disability*, 2: 229–253.

Hart, H. (2008, March 23) A season of song, dance and autism. *New York Times*. Accessed 2 March 2009 at http://www.nytimes.com/2008/03/23/arts/television/23hart.html?_r=1&scp=3&sq=autism:%20the%20musical&st=cse

Haskell, K. (2007, December 11) Tough, rewarding days caring for four children. *New York Times*, Section B, p. 2.

Hehir, T. (2003, May) Beyond inclusion: educators' "ableist" assumptions about students with disabilities compromise the quality of instruction. *School Administrator*. Accessed 20 February 2009 at http://www.kidstogether.org/BEHeard/Beyond%20inclusion-ableist.doc

Hehir, T. (2005) *New Directions in Special Education*. Cambridge, MA: Harvard Educational Press.

Individuals with Disabilities Education Act (IDEA). (1975) U.S. Department of Education. [Federal legislation].

James, C. (2007) Hollywood finds its disorder du jour. *New York Times*. Accessed 28 March 2010 at http://www.nytimes.com/2007/04/29jame.html

Johnson, C. K. (2009, January 25) Study adds to evidence of vaccine safety. *Associated Press*. Accessed 26 January 2009 at http://www.google.com/hostednews/ap/article/ALeqM5jp7ZD1RFVm7yOzgaB04Ra4dY_ZuQD95UKPPG0

Johnson, M. (2004) *Make Them Go Away*. Louisville, KY: Advocado Press.

Kalb, C. and Springen, K. (2008, March 24) Mysteries and complications: autism is everywhere—once again: separating fact from fear as the courts and Hollywood wade in. *Newsweek*, 151 (12): 64.

Kaufman, J. (2007a, December 14) Campaign on childhood mental illness succeeds at being provocative. *New York Times*. Accessed 23 February 2009 at http://www.

nytimes.com/2007/12/14/business/media/14adco.html?_r=2&adxnnl=1&oref=slogin&ref=media&adxnnlx=1197648897-hj0nSc0taFO1WwuerPEf8Q

Kaufman, J. (2007b, December 20) Ransom-note ads about children's health are canceled. *New York Times*. Accessed 23 February 2009 at http://www.nytimes.com/2007/12/20/business/media/20child.html?_r=2&ref=health&oref=slogin

Keller, B. (2008, May 21) "Book study" helps teachers hone skills. *Education Week*, 27 (38): 1.

Keller, Clayton E., Hallahan, Daniel P., McShane, Edward A., Crowley, E. Paula, and Blandford, Barbara J. (1990) The coverage of persons with disabilities in American newspapers. *Journal of Special Education*, 24: 271–282.

Kelley, T. (2007a, December 21) Helping police officers understand the autistic. *New York Times*, p. 5.

Kelley, T. (2007b, November 4) Theatre workshop embraces those with autism. *New York Times*, Section 14NJ, p. 6.

Leary, D. (2009) *Why We Suck: A Feelgood Guide to Staying Fat, Loud, Lazy and Stupid*. London: Viking.

Lellis, J. (2009) Local news coverage of disability: current themes and the role of nonprofit organizations as sources. In K. Yamamura (Ed.) *Research that Matters to the Practice*, 11th International Public Relations Research Conference, 6–9 March 2008, University of Miami.

Levenson, M. (2008, October 23) Leary's comments on autism anger Emerson alumni. *Boston Globe*. Accessed 23 February 2009 at http://www.boston.com/news/local/breaking_news/2008/10/learys_comments_1.html

Lim, D. (2007, December 9) It's his world; she was just filming it. *New York Times*, Section 2, p. 27.

Luongo, M. T. (2008, August 12) Travel complicates special needs. *New York Times*, p. C6.

McNeil, D. G. (2009, January 12) Book is rallying resistance to the antivaccine crusade. *New York Times*. Accessed 20 February 2009 at http://www.nytimes.com/2009/01/13/health/13auti.html?_r=2&emc=tnt&tntemail0=y

Mitchell, E. V. (2007, November 15) Hopes diminish but she still pursues an American dream. *New York Times*, Section B, p. 5.

Mulholland, A. (2008) Controversy over vaccine–autism link endures. *CTV News*. Accessed 2 January 2009 at http://www.ctv.ca/servlet/ArticleNews/story/CTVNews/20080201/thimerosal_080202/20080202?hub=Specials

Murray, S. (2006) Autism and the contemporary sentimental: fiction and the narrative fascination of the present. *Literature and Medicine*, 25 (1): 24–45.

National Autistic Society website. (2009) What is autism? Accessed 19 January 2009 at http://www.nas.org.uk/nas/jsp/polopoly.jsp?d=211

National Council on Disability. (2000, January 25) *Back to School on Civil Rights: Advancing the Federal Commitment to Leave No Child Behind*. Washington, DC: National Council on Disability.

Ne'eman, A. (2009, February 28) Presentation to "Disability and Mass Media" class, City University of New York Disability Studies Master's program, Graduate Center, New York.

Newsweek. (2006, November 27) A terrible mystery. [Cover story].

Obama, B. (2009) The agenda: disabilities. Accessed 2 March 2009 at http://www.whitehouse.gov/agenda/disabilities/

O'Donnell, C. (2008, December 5) Bradenton teacher's work with disabled students wins national honor. *Sarasota Herald-Tribune.* Accessed 7 December 2008 at http://www.heraldtribune.com/article/20081205/ARTICLE/812050373/–1/ NEWSSITEMAP#

Osterweil, N. (2006, April 4). Autism "epidemic" in schools called illusory. *MedPage Today.* Accessed 20 February 2009 at http://www.medpagetoday.com/Neurology/Autism/2985

Phillips, Marilyn J. (1990) Damaged goods: the oral narratives of the experience of disability in American culture. *Social Science & Medicine,* 30: 849–857.

Rabin, R. (2007, February 27) It seems the fertility clock ticks for men, too. *New York Times,* Section F, p. 1.

Reid, K. and Knight, M. G. (2006) Disability justifies exclusion of minority students: a critical history grounded in disability studies. *Educational Researcher,* 35 (6): 18–23.

Robertson, J. W. (2009) Informing the public? UK newspaper reporting of autism and Asperger's syndrome. *Journal of Research in Special Educational Needs,* 9 (1): 12–26.

Roper, L. (2003) Disability in media. *Media Education Journal.* Accessed 19 January 2009 at www.mediaed.org.uk/posted_documents?Disabilityinmedia.htm

Samuels, C. (2006a, April 19) Research questions use of autism data. *Education Week,* 25 (32): 8.

Samuels, C. (2006b, May 17) CDC surveys confirm that autism is a "major public-health concern". *Education Week,* 25 (37): 9.

Samuels, C. (2007, June 20) Project to probe preschool programs for autistic children. *Education Week,* 26 (42): 19.

Samuels, C. (2008, June 12) Neurodiversity. On Special Ed blog. *Education Week* online. Accessed 2 March 2009 at http://blogs.edweek.org/edweek/speced/2008/06/neurodiversity.html

Schwartz, P. (2007). Film as a vehicle for raising consciousness among autistic peers. In Mark Osteen (Ed.) *Autism and Representation.* New York: Routledge.

Scotch, Richard K. (1988) Disability as the basis for a social movement: advocacy and politics of definition. *Journal of Social Issues,* 44: 159–172.

Shakespeare, T. and Watson, N. (2002) The social model of disability: an outdated ideology? *Research in Social Science and Disability,* 2: 9–28.

Shattuck, P. (2006) The influence of the media on the MMR debate. *Autism 2006 Conference,* AWARES.org Conference Centre (online), October 2006. Accessed 27 January 2010 at http://www.awares.org/conferences/show_paper.asp?section =000100010001&conferenceCode=000200020034&id=107&full_paper=1

Silverman, F. (2008, March 2) More families shunning inoculations. *New York Times,* Long Island Weekly section, p. 3.

Solomon, A. (2008, May 25) The autism rights movement. *New York* magazine. Accessed 28 May 2008 at http://nymag.com/news/features/47225/

Steinberg, J. (2008a, July 22) Savage stands by autism remarks. *New York Times.* Accessed 23 February 2009 at http://www.nytimes.com/2008/07/22/business/media/22sava.html?scp=1&sq=michael%20savage%20autism&st=cse

Steinberg, J. (2008b, July 23) Savage loses advertisers. *New York Times.* Accessed 23 February 2009 at http://www.nytimes.com/2008/07/23/arts/23arts-SAVAGELOSESA_BRF.html?scp=4&sq=michael%20savage%20autism&st=cse

Sticker, H. (2002) *A History of Disability*. Ann Arbor: Michigan Press.

Sweet, L. J. (2008, October 28) Denis Leary tells parents: I'm sorry. *Boston Herald.* Accessed 23 February 2009 at http://news.bostonherald.com/news/regional/view/2008_10_28_Denis_Leary_Tells_Parents:_I_m_Sorry:_%E2%80%98Raising_Children_With_Autism__Deserves_Admiration__Comic_Says/srvc=home&position=0

Time. (2008, June 2). The truth about vaccines. [Cover story].

Ubanis, L. (2008) New poll takes pulse on autism. TV 10 News, Tampa Bay. Accessed 4 October 2008 at http://www.tampabays10.com/news/health/story.aspx?storyid=91327&catid=12

Walsh, M. (2007a, May 25) High Court backs parents' rights to argue cases under IDEA. *Education Week*, 26 (38): 1.

Walsh, M. (2007b, June 6) Experts ponder whether parents will rush to court. *Education Week*, 26 (39): 18.

Weeber, Jo. (1999) What could I know of racism? *Journal of Counseling & Development*, 77: 20–24.

Chapter 3

'They say the grass is blue'

Gypsies, Travellers and cultural dissonance

Chris Derrington (independent researcher)

Why do Gypsy and Traveller[1] pupils continue to underachieve in UK schools? What causes so many of them to drop out of school well before the statutory leaving age? Historically, a nomadic lifestyle was perceived to be the main barrier to educational access but, increasingly, as more Gypsy and Traveller families become sedentary, other cultural reasons are typically used to explain educational non-engagement. This chapter draws on the findings of a major longitudinal study, which examined the experiences of young Gypsies and Travellers in school and exposed evidence of psychological discomfort. Subsequent analysis of psycho-cultural effects offers an alternative perspective on obstacles to inclusion for this group of pupils.

It has been recognised officially that Gypsy and Traveller children are the group 'most at risk' in the British education system (Ofsted 1999: 7). With a history of underachievement and limited access to schooling being repeatedly flagged up in the literature, their predicament has been slow to improve despite the effects of an 'inclusion agenda' that has driven and shaped UK education policy for the past thirty years. The Plowden Report *Children and their Primary Schools* first highlighted the plight of Gypsy children, describing them as 'probably the most deprived group in the country' and estimating that fewer than 10 per cent accessed school (Department for Education and Science 1967: Appendix 12). A discussion paper *The Education of Travellers' Children* (HMI 1983)further exposed their continuing underachievement and, two years later, the problem was reiterated yet again in the Swann Report, which suggested that the degree of racism, discrimination and stereotyping directed at Gypsies in school exceeded that experienced by other minority ethnic groups (Department for Education and Science 1985).

In the 1990s, educational opportunities and prospects for all Traveller children improved thanks largely to the introduction of a centralised funding stream that gave Local Educational Authorities the opportunity to bid for a specific grant. This funding was earmarked for provision made above and beyond support available for all children and it resulted in the growth of dedicated Traveller Education Services (TESs) employing peripatetic teachers, classroom assistants and welfare officers (Derrington and Kendall 2008).

This policy development brought increasing numbers of Traveller students into the primary phase of schooling but access to school for secondary-age children remained 'a matter of grave concern' (Ofsted 1996). In the same inspection report, it was suggested that up to 80 per cent of secondary-age Traveller children could be out of the education system altogether.

Under the last national census (conducted in 2001) neither Romany Gypsies nor Irish Travellers were included as minority ethnic groups. Consequently, there are no reliable, official figures available in relation to the overall Gypsy Traveller population in Britain (Department for Communities and Local Government 2004). Local Authorities are required by the Department for Communities and Local Government (CLG) to conduct twice-yearly counts of caravans in their area but figures generated from this exercise are little more than a crude proxy measure as they fail to take account of housed families. This results in a gross underestimate of the total Gypsy and Traveller population (Niner 2004). The Council of Europe estimates the figure to be in the region of 300,000 Gypsies and Travellers, with approximately 200,000 of those being in settled housing (Crawley 2004: 6).

If accurate, this would make the Gypsy Traveller population similar in size to the Bangladeshi community in the UK, which could usefully provide a benchmark in the comparison of school attendance and educational attainment data. Although these indicative demographics reveal little about the age distribution within populations, there is evidence to suggest that both populations present with a younger age profile than the national picture (Department for Communities and Local Government 2004; Home and Greenfields 2006:40).

Recent statistical analysis by the Department for Children, Schools and Families (2007a) indicates fewer than 4,000 Gypsy/Roma and Irish Traveller pupils (combined) attending English secondary schools during the academic year 2006/7 (representing 0.1 per cent of the secondary school population). In the same period, there were 33,370 pupils of Bangladeshi origin enrolled in secondary schools (representing 1.0 per cent of the total secondary school population).

In view of the (apparently) analogous populations, this suggests that either only around one in eight young Travellers between the ages of 11 and 16 are attending school or there is a very low incidence of ascription by Gypsies and Travellers on ethnic monitoring forms. Evidence suggests that it is likely to be a combination of the two. Recent guidance for schools aimed at increasing the number of Gypsy, Roma and Traveller (GRT) parents and pupils declaring their ethnicity acknowledges only a very small percentage of the estimated cohort currently doing so (Department for Children, Schools and Families 2008). The former hypothesis appears to be reinforced by government statistics, which show three times as many Gypsy and Traveller pupils attending school in Key Stage 1 (5- to 7-year-olds) than in Key Stage 4 (14- to 16-year-olds) (Department for Education and Skills 2005a). The same document indicates that Gypsy and Traveller pupils are also four times more likely than any other ethnic group to be excluded for unacceptable behaviour. Unsurprisingly, therefore, this disproportionate representation is mirrored in the published data on secondary school achievement. For example, in 2004, the national analysis of KS3 SATs results is based on a total cohort of only 515 Gypsy and Traveller students compared with 5,757 Bangladeshi students (Department for Education and Skills 2005b). This said, Gypsy and Traveller pupils are reported as having the lowest achievement of all minority groups at both KS3 and KS4. For example, in 2006, 9 per cent of Gypsy pupils achieved five A*–C grades at GCSE compared with the national average of 56.9 per cent. Gypsy pupils also have lower value-added scores in both primary and secondary sectors, and make less progress than pupils with similar prior attainment (Department for Education and Skills 2006). Because of the low numbers identified, the relative position of Gypsy Traveller pupils in terms of their attainment, attendance and exclusion is often understated or even left out of the executive summaries in official reports. Troyna and Vincent argue that, although this practice may be defended in statistical terms, such an oversight has the effect of depreciating the problem and effectively 'robs pupils and their families of the right to challenge injustice' (1996: 8). It may also help to explain why education policy (and political will) has been slow in accepting and addressing the gravity of the situation (Lloyd and McCluskey 2007).

> The vast majority of Traveller pupils linger on the periphery of the education system. The situation has persisted for too long and the alarm bells rung in earlier reports have yet to be heeded.
>
> (Ofsted 2003: 6)

In 2003, the government launched its Aiming High strategy for raising the attainment of black and minority ethnic (BME) pupils but Gypsy, Roma and Irish Traveller children were conspicuously absent from the guidance document (Department for Education and Skills 2003a). Strong objections from support groups such as the National Association of Teachers of Travellers (NATT) led to the subsequent publication of targeted guidance for schools (Department for Education and Skills 2003b). However, neither *Every Child Matters* (Department for Education and Skills 2003c) nor *The Children's Plan* (Department for Children, Schools and Families 2007a), which set out the government's policies for improving the life chances and well-being of all children, acknowledges explicitly the inauspicious predicament of young Gypsy Travellers. The only isolated reference to Gypsy, Roma and Traveller pupils in *The Children's Plan* pertains to their eligibility for the Education Maintenance Allowance (EMA), implying a causal link with social disadvantage (p.115) and reflecting the stereotyped assumption that was prevalent thirty years ago.

In England, *The Children's Plan* includes the expectation for 90 per cent of young people nationally to achieve the academic benchmark of five GCSEs at A*–C grade by the age of 19 and a commitment to raise the participation (in education and training) age to 18 by 2015. As already noted, only 9 per cent of Gypsy Traveller pupils met this academic objective in 2006 and the overwhelming majority of young Gypsy Travellers already opt out of the education system by the age of 14 or apply for elective home education (Department for Education and Skills 2007). According to a recent research study the number of Gypsy children recorded as registered for elective home education increased year on year by approximately 40 per cent between 2000 and 2004 (Ivatts 2006).

Understanding the reasons for Gypsy Traveller children's disengagement and underachievement has exercised educationalists and policy makers for many years. As previously suggested, discourse around barriers to their access and attainment has historically been linked to a nomadic or highly mobile lifestyle. However, this no longer carries weight, as the vast majority of Gypsy Travellers in Britain today are housed or are settled on established, authorised sites (Office of the Deputy Prime Minister 2004). Other 'pathological' forces such as cultural expectations or a desire to preserve a separate identity by maintaining cultural boundaries have also featured prominently in discourses and similarly locate culpability within the Traveller community rather than looking at ways in which schools themselves may be inadvertently creating and compounding barriers to inclusion. Just as popular notions of nomadism representing the principal barrier to educational achievement are no longer sustainable, previously entrenched patterns of non-transfer between primary and secondary school are also showing signs of reversal and challenging the maxim that Gypsy Travellers do not wish to engage in or do not value secondary education (Bhopal 2004). So what exactly is going wrong once these children get to secondary school?

A phenomenological longitudinal study of forty-four 'settled' Gypsy Traveller students was conducted in England between 2000 and 2005 (Derrington and Kendall 2004; Derrington 2005, 2007). The research team tracked and recorded the progress, experiences, attitudes, expectations and aspirations of the students from the age of 11 to 16. Data were collected on six occasions throughout the five-year study, including four rounds of interviews with the students as well as their parents and teachers. The study found that more than half of the students dropped out of school by the age of 14 and that fewer than a third of the original sample (thirteen) remained in school until the statutory leaving age.

One of the key aims of the research project (which was supported by the Nuffield Foundation) was to identify various 'pull and push' factors that might influence or determine the students' continued engagement with secondary education. These variables were then explored in greater depth using componential analysis to see if any commonality or pattern could be discerned within and across groups of retained and non-retained students.

One of the key 'pull' factors was related to cultural perceptions of childhood and adulthood. In the UK, young people generally are now expected to continue their engagement in full-time education or training beyond the age of 16 and raising young people's engagement in education and training has become a central aim of the Labour government at the time of writing. With the loss of the youth labour market and the increase in higher education engagement, the period of financial dependency of young people on their parents/carers has necessarily been extended and many young people do not achieve financial independence until their mid-twenties. Unsurprisingly, the age at which young people marry and become parents themselves is also increasing. The average age of new fathers is now around 31 years, and is 29 years for first-time mothers (Jones 2005). Within Traveller communities, these adult markers of marriage, autonomy and financial independence arrive significantly earlier (Derrington and Kendall 2004).

Allied to this expectation, priorities associated with the maintenance of family-based learning and traditional patterns of practical self-employment are thought to be weighed against a perceived irrelevance of a gauje[2] secondary education, with its emphasis on gaining academic qualifications as a prerequisite for further or higher education and professional employment (Reynolds et al. 2003; Bhopal 2004). Although a number of the parents articulated high aspirations for their sons and daughters, vocational skills were given a greater priority by most and the achievement of a functional level of literacy was the determining factor of a 'good education' and was commonly associated with being a 'scholar'. However, upon closer examination, expectations about racism in the wider community and its impact on employability often underpinned these parental 'scripts'. Thus, parents may aspire for their children to work alongside relatives because it offers a safer option than exposing them to the prejudice and social exclusion they would inevitably encounter in the wider world of work. Such deep-seated anxiety about their children's moral, emotional and physical well-being feature regularly in the literature, especially in relation to the perceived hostile and threatening environment of the secondary school, but is this a 'pull' factor shaped by irrational cultural attitudes or a 'push' factor grounded in reality?

Ivatts's pioneering case study of twenty-two housed Gypsy Travellers (1975) certainly pointed to negative attitudes and inflexible approaches in schools that offered Gypsy Traveller pupils neither dignity nor self-respect. Lloyd et al.'s (1999) study of Travellers in Scottish secondary schools drew a similar conclusion that the racist behaviour of other pupils often lay at the root of imposed and self-initiated exclusion from school. Warrington (2006) found that racism was the single largest problem facing Gypsy children and young people in school and many expected to encounter it on a daily basis, a finding that supports the evidence garnered from our own longitudinal study (Derrington and Kendall 2004). Whereas racist behaviour from non-Traveller peers has featured in a number of studies, less overt racist attitudes communicated by teachers and other staff have been discussed in only a handful of studies conducted in America (Anderek 1992), Scotland (Lloyd *et al.* 1999), Ireland (Kenny 1997) and Wales (Clay 1999). Overt expressions of teachers' underlying stereotyped beliefs are exposed clearly in Anderek's (1992) study of Irish Travellers in the USA. This ethnographic researcher observed how teachers began labelling students as 'Travellers' in the later primary school years, viewing them as products of their culture rather than as individuals. Teachers often referred to pupils' ethnicity during conversations about unacceptable behaviour and absences were discussed in front of the whole class, although they did not perceive their behaviour to be discriminatory. In the longitudinal study (Derrington and Kendall 2004) more than a quarter of the students (fourteen) felt that certain teachers held racist attitudes towards them and in a few cases this was corroborated by visiting support teachers who observed:

> 'Frankly, they don't want Travellers there. It's an uphill struggle.'
> 'It's not a supportive environment . . . I don't think they feel valued.'
> 'You're fighting prejudice. They talk about "them". It's hard work!'
> (Derrington and Kendall 2004: 131)

Cultural influences present themselves at different levels ranging on a continuum from unconscious habits and routine behaviour to values and belief systems, traditions, customs, social rules and established laws (Larcher 1993 cited in Allan 2003). Some cultural variables such as dress code are overt and immediately observable whereas others are more subtle and difficult to discern. Dissonance is likely to be experienced when these subtle differences in behaviour and expectations are unexplained and unexpected, leaving the individual in a state of ambiguity and confusion (Allan 2003). Gordon and Yowell (1999) develop the concept further, emphasising that dissonance is more likely to breed under conditions of cultural hegemony. In previous work (Derrington and Kendall 2004; Derrington 2007) I have suggested that this phenomena is likely to affect Gypsy and Traveller pupils whose daily contact with the settled community is significantly restricted through a combination of geographical and socio-cultural factors. Although the term 'cultural dissonance' had not been used previously in the literature on Traveller education, the concept has been alluded to. Kiddle (1999) observed that some teachers misunderstood certain behaviours exhibited by Traveller children and their parents. Clay (1999) warned of the potential challenge Gypsy Traveller children face in navigating their way through cross-cultural interference in order to meet conflicting expectations from home and school, and Levinson and Sparkes referred to 'an intrinsic discord' that should not be ignored (2006: 91).

One 13-year-old Gypsy girl articulated her sense of cultural dissonance at school to me in this metaphoric way:

> It can be difficult because, like, you know one thing but then they [non-Travellers] try to teach you another. It's like when you grow up, you learn that the grass is green don't you. But then, you gradually find out that other people say the grass is blue and then they try to teach you that the grass isn't green at all, it is actually blue! And you kind of know deep down that it really isn't – it's green. But no-one else seems to agree.
>
> (Derrington and Kendall 2004: 89)

Although the literature on cultural identity and dissonance is currently limited as far as Gypsy Travellers are concerned, there are parallels with the experiences of other indigenous communities (Coxhead 2007) and a number of cross-cultural studies offer transferable insights. For example, the theory of cultural dissonance has been applied widely to studies of under-achievement and disaffection of Indigenous American and Indigenous Australian students (LaFramboise *et al.* 1993; Nicholls *et al.* 1996; Long *et al.* 1999; Schwab 1999). This body of research suggests that, where children in education systems experience cultural dissonance, they become vulnerable to educational disadvantage. Allan (2003) asserts that cultural dissonance is a prerequisite for developing a bicultural identity, a condition described by Berry *et al.* (1986) that is correlated with psychological adjustment and well-being. LaFromboise *et al.* (1993) use the term 'alternation' to describe bicultural competency in which individuals are able to switch their perception and behaviour accordingly without having to commit to that cultural identity. Cheng *et al.* (2006) found evidence that Chinese-American students who were more adept at cultural frame switching were retained in school longer.

Two influential studies demonstrate the part that parents play in helping their children to adjust in culturally conflicting worlds. A longitudinal study of children from immigrant families in the USA (Suarez-Orozco and Suarez-Orozco 2001) found that children whose parents were themselves adept at straddling two cultural worlds adapted and achieved better at school than those whose parents resisted the process of acculturation. In the second study of Indigenous American students' experiences in mainstream schools, Whitbeck *et al.* (2001) lend credence to the theory that a positive cultural identity is important for academic success but found that those students who had most difficulty adjusting were those whose parents and community members reacted with greater anxiety to change and who resisted mainstream influences. Acton's cultural adaptation typology, cited in Hawes and Perez (1995), describes four sets of responses that Gypsy parents adopt in relation to schooling (conservative, culturally adapting, culturally disintegrating and passing). The 'conservative' response describes parents who are outwardly opposed and resistant to the prospect of schooling. Acton's fourth adaptation response, referred to as 'passing,' is applied to Gypsy parents who believe that their children will be able to compete on an equal footing in school only if their ethnic identity is hidden. This theoretical position is referred to later on in this chapter as 'Playing White' (Derrington 2007); a term adopted from Cline *et al.* (2002) who coined it to describe BME pupils in mainly white schools who resisted their home language or tried to keep cultural traditions hidden from their white friends in an attempt to achieve social acceptance.

Dealing with cultural dissonance and trying to reconcile conflicting values and belief systems is an encumbrance that many young Gypsy students have to contend with. Operating within a dual cultural framework can regularly bring them into conflict with both their families and Traveller peers as well as with their teachers and non-Traveller peers as they attempt to balance loyalties (Derrington 2007). Interviews with teachers, parents and Traveller pupils identified tensions, mutual disrespect, conflicting expectations and crossed transactions probably stemming from culturally determined differences about the adult–child relationship, acceptable communication styles and responsibility for discipline. Additionally, conflicting messages about the value of the secondary curriculum (including extra-curricular activities) and acceptable career aspirations (including the prospect of further and higher education) could similarly create a degree of discord.

Levinson and Sparkes (2006) suggest that this intrinsic discord can cause psycho-social difficulties for those young Gypsies and Travellers in the education system who have not developed effective coping strategies to assuage the discomfort. Coping strategies are cognitive and behavioural responses that help individuals to deal with the person–environment relationship and can be functional or non-productive (Frydenberg and Lewis 1993). As part of my previous analysis, I identified three broad coping strategies that Gypsy and Traveller pupils were found to adopt; 'Fight', 'Flight' and 'Playing White' (Derrington 2007). 'Fight' coping included combative resistance such as deliberate acts of non-compliance as well as the overt challenging of authority and spontaneous physical or verbal attacks. Seventeen students (ten male and seven female) exhibited coping strategies associated with the fight response, of whom three-quarters left school before they were 16. 'Flight' refers to the coping strategy of temporary or permanent self-exclusion from school. Overall, more than three-quarters of the students in the study were, at some point, considered by their teachers to have unsatisfactory school attendance although interviews revealed that the causes were usually contested. Whereas teachers attributed sporadic attendance to home factors and peer pressure, pupils and parents were more likely to refer to school-related social or emotional difficulties (including instances of bullying).

Camouflage and concealment are well-known survival strategies in the natural world. In human social behaviour, the counterpart coping response involves inhibiting the public expression of thoughts and feelings as well as masking identity markers such as address, customs, faith, relationships with others and home language, to gain acceptance from the majority group and minimise threat. In cultural psychology this phenomenon is known as 'passing' (Tajfel 1978). According to some commentators such as Acton (1974) and Hancock (1997), it is a fairly common institutionalised response adopted by Gypsies to cope with deep-rooted racism. As a coping strategy 'Playing White' is probably more accessible to Travellers than to other minority ethnic groups who are ethnically distinct, although in some cases identity markers such as accent and name effectively ruled out this strategy. The concealment of identity, either partially or completely, was the least common strategy of the three, being adopted by ten students (seven female and three male). Half of these went on to complete their education, suggesting that this may have been an effective coping strategy for them. However, as Tajfel (1978) points out, 'passing' identity is essentially a maladaptive coping strategy as its roots are in denial and repression and may have negative psychological consequences manifesting in anxiety and depression.

Comparative research drawn from studies of other minority ethnic groups in the UK and how they cope with the secondary school experience include Shain's study of forty-four Asian girls in eight secondary schools across Manchester and Staffordshire (cited in Shain 2003). In a similar approach, Shain critically examines the cultural pathology discourse, which positions Asian females as the victims of oppression and illustrates how new cultural identities are constantly shaped through bicultural experiences. Shain identified four main categories of coping: resistance through culture, passivity and working within stereotypes, rebellion against own culture, and promotion of religious identity. A fifth and less common strategy was described as resistance against culture, whereby some Asian girls exhibited a preference for white friends, saw themselves as distinct from other Asian pupils and defended western values. The strategies identified by Shain share certain common features with the coping responses identified in Gypsy and Traveller students (Derrington 2007). For example, the 'resistance against culture' group were similar to those Gypsy Travellers that 'played white'; and Shain's 'gang girls', who consciously disassociated themselves from the dominant culture like the 'Fight' Travellers, were likely to have more difficult relationships with teachers, often believing that they were treated unfairly. Shain's analysis also exposes the simplicity of the view that Asian girls' educational careers are limited by cultural constraints and suggests more complex reasons that have more to do with dissonance-related parental anxiety than low expectations. The girls that achieved most highly in Shain's study were those who adopted strategies such as working hard, avoiding trouble, avoiding peers with bad reputations, not fighting back, making friends with pupils from all ethnic groups and holding high aspirations. Crucially:

they did not view the worlds of home and school as fundamentally opposed. Although they did not automatically receive support from either
their families or the school, support was won through a carefully worked
out strategy, which involved a series of negotiations.

(Shain 2003: 85)

This approach also reflects the conclusions of Gordon and Yowell (1999),
who recognise that an individual student's *perception* of events is more
important than the event itself in becoming a 'risk factor' to educational success. This suggests that a cognitive approach could be usefully developed as
an adaptive coping strategy. According to Frydenberg and Lewis (1993) the
most effective coping strategies adopted by adolescents include seeking social
support, working hard, cognitive reframing and positive reappraisal. There
are messages here for parents as well as teachers. Gypsy parents who model
and encourage their children to cultivate bicultural adjustment (whilst maintaining pride in their cultural roots) may help to minimise social isolation in
school and lessen the effects of cultural dissonance. For schools to be more
inclusive towards this group, there is a need to develop a greater understanding of the subtle and overt effects of cultural hegemony on the attendance
and subsequent attainment of Gypsy and Traveller pupils (Derrington 2007).
This includes heightened awareness in relation to racism, the manifestation
of maladaptive coping strategies and ways we can support young people to
cope more effectively through cognitive approaches such as coaching, anger
management, role play and solution-focused methods.

Notes

1 English Romany Gypsies and Irish Travellers are (unlike New Travellers and
Show-people) recognised in law as ethnic groups, with ethnicity ascribed at birth
and each with its own geographical origin, shared language, sense of kinship and
traditional customs.
2 A Romani term to describe a non-Traveller/non-Gypsy.

Bibliography

Acton, T. A. (1974) *Gypsy Politics and Social Change*. London: Routledge and Kegan
Paul.
Adams, B., Okely, J., Morgan, D. and Smith, D. (1975) *Gypsies and Government
Policy in England*. London: Heinemann.
Allan, M. (2003) Frontier crossings: cultural dissonance, intercultural learning and
the multicultural personality. *Journal of Research in International Education*, 2
(1): 83–110.
Anderek, M. E. (1992) *Ethnic Awareness and the School*. New York: Sage.
Balls Organista, P., Chun, K. M. and Marin, G. (Eds). (1998) *Readings in Ethnic
Psychology*. New York: Routledge.

Berry, J., Trimble, J. and Olmedo, E. (1986) Assessment of acculturation. In W. Lonner and J. Berry (Eds) *Field Methods in Cross-cultural Research*. Newbury Park, CA: Sage.

Bhopal, K. (2004) Gypsy Travellers and education: changing needs and changing perceptions. *British Journal of Educational Studies*, 52 (1): 47–64.

Cheng, C.-Y., Lee, F. and Benet-Martinez, V. (2006) Assimilation and contrast effects in cultural frame switching. *Journal of Cross-Cultural Psychology*, 37 (6): 742–760.

Clay, S. (1999) *Traveller Children's Schooling*. PhD thesis, University of Wales.

Cline, T., Abreu, G. de, Fihosy, C., Gray, H., Lambert, H. and Neale, J. (2002) *Minority Ethnic Pupils in Mainly White Schools* (RR 365). London: DfES.

Commission for Racial Equality. (2004) *Gypsies and Travellers: A Strategy for the CRE, 2004–2007*. London: CRE.

Coxhead, J. (2007) *The Last Bastion of Racism: Gypsies, Travellers and Policing*. Stoke-on-Trent: Trentham Books.

Crawley, H. (2004) *Moving Forward: The Provision of Accommodation for Travellers and Gypsies*. London: Institute of Public Policy Research.

Department for Children, Schools and Families. (2007a) *The Children's Plan: Building Brighter Futures*. London: DCSF.

Department for Children, Schools and Families. (2007b) *Statistical First Release: Pupil Characteristics and Class Sizes in England* (SFR 30:2007). London: DCSF.

Department for Children, Schools and Families. (2008) *The Inclusion of Gypsy, Roma and Traveller Children and Young People*. London: DCSF.

Department for Communities and Local Government. (2004) *Gypsies and Travellers – Facts and Figures*. London: HMSO.

Department for Education and Science (DES). (1967) *Children and their Primary Schools* (The Plowden Report). London: HMSO.

Department for Education and Science. (1985) *Education for All: The Report of the Committee of Enquiry into the Education of Children from Ethnic Minority Groups* (The Swann Report). London: HMSO.

Department for Education and Skills. (2003a) *Aiming High: Raising the Achievement of Minority Ethnic Pupils*. London: DfES.

Department for Education and Skills. (2003b) *Aiming High: Raising the Achievement of Gypsy Traveller Pupils. A Guide to Good Practice*. London: DfES.

Department for Education and Skills. (2003c) *Every Child Matters*. London: DfES.

Department for Education and Skills. (2005a) *Ethnicity and Education: The Evidence on Minority Ethnic Pupils* (Topic paper RTP01–05). London: DfES.

Department for Education and Skills. (2005b) *Statistical First Release: National Curriculum Assessment, GCSE and Equivalent Attainment and Post-16 Attainment by Pupil Characteristics in England 2004* (SFR 08:2005). London: DfES.

Department for Education and Skills. (2006) *Statistical First Release: National Curriculum Assessment, GCSE and Equivalent Attainment and Post-16 Attainment by Pupil Characteristics in England 2005/06* (SFR 46:2006). London: DfES.

Department for Education and Skills. (2007) *Elective Home Education: The Situation Regarding the Current Policy, Provision and Practice in Elective Home Education for Gypsy, Roma and Traveller Children*. London: DfES.

Derrington, C. (2005) Perceptions of behaviour and patterns of exclusion: Gypsy Traveller students in English secondary schools. *Journal of Research in Special Educational Needs*, 5 (2): 55–61.

Derrington, C. (2007) Fight, flight and playing white: an examination of coping strategies adopted by Gypsy Traveller adolescents in English secondary schools. *International Journal of Educational Research*, 46 (6): 357–367.

Derrington, C. and Kendall, S. (2004) *Gypsy Traveller Students in Secondary Schools: Culture, Identity and Achievement*. Stoke-on Trent: Trentham Books.

Derrington, C. and Kendall, S. (2008) Challenges and barriers to secondary education: the experiences of young Gypsy Traveller students in English secondary schools. *Social Policy and Society*, 7 (1): 1–10.

Frydenberg, E. and Lewis, R. (1993) Teaching coping to adolescents: when and to whom? *American Educational Research Journal*, 37 (3): 727–745.

Gordon, E. and Yowell, C. (1999) Cultural dissonance as a risk factor in the development of students. In E. Gordon (Ed.) *Education and Justice: A View From the Back of the Bus*. New York: Teachers College Press.

Hancock, I. (1997) The struggle for the control of identity. *Patrin Web Journal*, 4 (4). Accessed 2 July 2006 at http://www.geocities.com/~Patrin/identity.htm.

Hawes, D. and Perez, B. (1995) *The Gypsy and the State: The Ethnic Cleansing of British Society*. Bristol: SAUS Publications.

HMI. (1983) *The Education of Travellers' Children*. London: HMSO.

Home, R. and Greenfields, M. (2006) *Cambridge Sub-Region Traveller Needs Assessment*. Cambridge: Cambridgeshire County Council.

Ivatts, A. (1975) *Catch 22 Gypsies*. London: ACERT.

Ivatts, A. (2006) *The Situation Regarding the Current Policy, Provision and Practice in Elective Home Education (EHE) for Gypsy, Roma and Traveller Children*. London: DfES.

Jones, G. (2005). *Young Adults and the Extension of Economic Dependence*. Policy Discussion Paper. London: National Family & Parenting Institute.

Kenny, M. (1997) *The Routes of Resistance: Traveller and Second-level Schooling*. Ashgate: Aldershot.

Kiddle, C. (1999) *Traveller Children: A Voice for Themselves*. London: Jessica Kingsley.

LaFromboise, T. D., Coleman, J. S. and Gerton, J. (1993) Psychological impact of biculturalism: evidence and theory. *Psychological Bulletin*, 114 (3): 395–412.

Levinson, M. P., and Sparkes, A. C. (2006) Conflicting value systems: Gypsy females and the home–school interface. *Research Papers in Education*, 21 (1): 79–97.

Lloyd, G. and McCluskey, G. (2007) Education and Gypsies/Travellers: contradictions and significant silences. *International Journal of Inclusive Education*. DOI: 10.1080/13603110601183065. Accessed 10 January 2008 at http://www.informaworld.com/smpp/content~db=all~content=a781884854

Lloyd, G., Stead, J. and Jordan, E. (1999) Teachers and Gypsy Travellers. *Scottish Educational Review*, 31 (1): 48–65.

Long, M., Frigo, T. and Batten, M. (1999) *The School to Work Transition of Indigenous Australians: A Review of the Literature and Statistical Analysis*. Canberra: Department of Employment, Education, Training and Youth Affairs.

Nicholls, C., Crowley, V. and Watt, R. (1996) Theorising Aboriginal education: surely it's time to move on? *Education Australia*, 33: 6–9. Accessed 19 May 2005 at http://www.edoz.com.au/educationaustralia/edoz/archive/features/abed1.html

Niner, P. (2004) *Counting Gypsies and Travellers: A Review of the Gypsy Caravan County System*. London: ODPM.

Office of the Deputy Prime Minister. (2004) *Gypsy and Traveller Sites: Thirteenth Report of Session 2003–4 Vol. 1*. London: HMSO.

Office for Standards in Education (Ofsted). (1996) *The Education of Travelling Children*. London: Ofsted.

Office for Standards in Education. (1999) *Raising the Attainment of Minority Ethnic Pupils*. London: Ofsted.

Office for Standards in Education. (2003) *Provision and Support for Traveller Pupils*. London: Ofsted.

Reynolds, M., McCartan, D. and Knipe, D. (2003) Traveller culture and lifestyle as factors influencing children's integration into mainstream secondary schools in West Belfast. *International Journal of Inclusive Education*, 7 (4): 403–414.

Schwab, R. G. (1999) *Why Only One in Three? The Complex Reasons for Low Indigenous School Retention*. Research Monograph 16, Centre for Aboriginal Economic Policy Research. Canberra: The Australian National University. Accessed 20 September 2007 at http://www.anu.edu.au/caepr/Publications/mono/CAEPR_Mono16.pdf

Shain, F. (2003) *The Schooling and Identity of Asian Girls*. Stoke-on-Trent: Trentham Books.

Suarez-Orozco, C. and Suarez-Orozco, M. M. (2001) *Children of Immigration*. Cambridge, MA: Harvard University Press.

Tajfel, H. (1978) *The Social Psychology of Minorities*. New York: Minority Rights Group.

Troyna, B. and Vincent, S. (1996) The ideology of expertism: the framing of special education and racial equality policies in the local state. In C. Christiansen and F. Rizvi (Eds) *Disability and the Dilemmas of Education and Justice*. Buckingham: Open University Press.

Warrington, C. (2006) *Children's Voices: Changing Future – The Views and Experiences of Young Gypsies and Travellers*. Ipswich: Ormiston Children and Families Trust.

Whitbeck, L. B., Hoyt, D. R., Stubbon, J. D. and LaFromboise, T. (2001) Traditional culture and academic success among American Indian children in the Upper Midwest. *Journal of American Indian Education*, 40 (2): 48–60. Accessed 4 January 2006 at http://jaie.asu.edu/v40/V40I2A3.pdf

Chapter 4

Including 'children with special needs' in the Indian education system

Negotiating a contested terrain

Nidhi Singal (University of Cambridge, UK)

Exclusion of children from and within the education system has been a primary concern in many countries of the South. Efforts have traditionally focused on providing increased access; however, lately there has been a greater awareness of the need to examine the quality of education being delivered. The discussions in this chapter will take India as an example to examine how various variables and resultant intersectionalities of caste, gender, abilities and socio-economic status have resulted in the continued marginalisation of certain groups from the education system. It will critically examine contemporary developments in the Indian government's efforts to respond to the educational needs of children with disabilities – arguably the most marginalised group in the Indian context. Discussions here will address how certain efforts have become barriers to the development of a more inclusive and better quality education system.

The Indian education system

The Indian education system is marked by extreme contrasts and contradictions. On one hand it trains millions of graduates each year, many of whom have been the backbone of Silicon Valley in the United States, but on the other hand it masks deep-seated problems of lack of relevant and high-quality education for millions, leaving them with skills that are of little use in a thriving economy. Not only are the outcomes of education experienced differentially by people who have progressed through the system, but the discrepancies in educational provisions are also greatly varied. For example, some students hardly ever leave the air-conditioned and hi-tech environment of their school setting, while others work in makeshift classes which are at the mercy of the natural elements. These somewhat simplified extremes, which can be regarded as the paradox of many economically developing and developed societies, do not adequately capture the breath and magnitude of the Indian education system.

India has by far the largest number of school-aged children in the world. The population aged 6–10 years was 146.4 million in 2005, whereas the comparable figure for China was only 108.9 million (UNESCO 2008).[1] Moreover, the country is poised to reap the benefits of a 'youth bulge' (World Bank 2006), as approximately 51 per cent of its population of 1.1 billion is under 25 years (Registrar General of India 2001). In such a scenario the role of education in national development cannot be underestimated.

India has had a long-standing constitutional commitment to universalisation of elementary education (UEE). Article 45 of the Indian Constitution states that 'The State shall endeavour to provide, within a period of ten years from the commencement of this Constitution, for free and compulsory education for all children until they complete the age of fourteen years'. However, this commitment has remained unfilled, though each of the subsequent policy statements have re-emphasised it. More recently, in December 2002, elementary education was made a fundamental right. The new Article 21A (incorporated in the 86th Constitutional Amendment) reads: 'The State shall provide free and compulsory education to all children of the age of six to fourteen years in such manner as the State may, by law, determine.' However, the phrase 'in such manner as the State may, by law, determine' has attracted the hostility of activists as it gives power to the government to control or dilute the scope of provision. Moreover, it is not clear how its implementation will be monitored.

Despite all these efforts, nearly 7.5 million primary school-age children (2.8 million boys, 4.7 million girls) remain out of school, making India one of the thirty-five countries most unlikely to meet Education for All (EFA) goals by 2015 (UNESCO 2008). These numbers do not reflect those who have repeated years or dropped out before completing the primary cycle. However, the system has been successful in terms of increased student enrolments, greater improvements in the number of schools and an increasing concern with the quality of teaching and learning imparted.

Even though India has been historically committed to UEE, it is still struggling to achieve universal school access and completion. Educational exclusion is most evident in relation to particular groupings, such as scheduled caste (SC)/scheduled tribe (ST),[2] gender, location (rural–urban divide) and indeed disabilities. Although all these dimensions are important they have received different priorities in policy development; and the interfaces – where multiple disadvantages overlap – are not necessarily accounted for in such ways that they can be overcome.

Although differing combinations of structural factors, such as gender, caste, religion, poverty, location and disability, impact on educational participation of children, there are some who are at a greater risk of marginalisation, namely children with disabilities. Majumdar (2001: 123), analysing educational provisions for various disadvantaged groups across different states, sums up the scenario for children with disabilities as:

Apparently, nothing is available other than a few government scholarships, facilities in the form of a couple of institutions for boys and girls and institutes for training teachers for the disabled . . . for the mentally disabled, no conscious developmental scheme is focused on by any of the states.

Though various efforts have been made in the recent past, both the rates of educational participation and outcomes of education remain very poor for children and young adults with disabilities.

A recent study by the World Bank (2007) noted that children with disabilities are five times more likely to be out of school than children belonging to SC/ST. Moreover, when children with disabilities do attend school they rarely progress beyond the primary level, leading ultimately to lower employment chances and long-term income poverty. This study also notes that 'it is very clear that both educational attainment of all people with disabilities and current attendance of children with disabilities are very poor and far below national averages' (p. 64). People with disabilities have a 52 per cent illiteracy rate against a 35 per cent average for the general population. Equally, the share of children with disabilities who are out of school is around five and a half times the general rate and around four times even that of the ST population. Figures also indicate that, across all levels of severity, children with disabilities very rarely move into secondary-level schooling. Thus, the exclusion faced by children with disabilities is most marked and India is unlikely to make much progress on its commitment towards EFA if it does not address the needs of this group.

In this chapter I will critically examine key assumptions underpinning efforts aimed at achieving educational equality for children with disabilities. In India efforts under the umbrella of inclusive education have been largely aimed at bringing 'children with special needs' into the education system. It is therefore useful to deconstruct this concept to enable a better understanding of the government efforts. In the final section I will examine how some deeply ideological issues, such as assumptions about difference/disabilities, undercut even the most genuine reform measures and render them incapable of delivering promises of an equitable and quality education.

Children with special needs (CWSN): working within a medical discourse

According to estimates made under the Sarva Shiksha Abhiyan (SSA)[3], around 1.5 per cent of children in the 6–14 age groups have special needs, whereas the 2001 census data indicate the proportion to be around 2.2 per cent. Although these discrepancies could be attributed to perceptions or training of the enumerators, they do raise concerns about the effectiveness and reliability of the identification procedures and indeed issues around definitions. Even though documents refer to the category 'children with special needs' (CWSN), the term is not defined, rather is seen as being synonymous for 'children with disabilities' (CWD). A background paper presented at the Rehabilitation Council of India workshop stated that 'every disability gives rise to special educational needs' (RCI 2001: 6).

SSA documentation lists CWSN as encompassing the following kinds of disabilities: visual impairment,[4] hearing impairment, mental retardation, locomotor impairment, learning disability, cerebral palsy, multiple disabilities and others. The current emphasis is on increased identification of this group of children, as reflected in Table 4.1.

Although it is argued that these increased numbers suggest that there is a growing awareness of the concerns relating to CWSN, the deterministic assumptions underpinning the process of identification and assessment remain unexamined. These rigid and child-centric assumptions about ability highlighted in the SSA list draw further support from the existing socio-cultural constructions of disability.

In India, understandings of disability are largely dominated by a medical perspective, whereby it is regarded as inherent in the individual's mind and body, and a condition that must be diagnosed, cured or catered for, so that the person can function like 'others'. This understanding draws further support from prevalent religious norms, according to which disability is regarded as retribution for past *karmas* (bad actions or deeds) and punishment for sins committed in a previous life. However, it is important to note that the dominance of a medical perspective is reinforced by the fact that a high proportion of disabling conditions are the result of poor nutrition, limited access to vaccination programmes, poor hygiene, bad sanitation etc. Nonetheless, such medicalised thinking has resulted in a complete neglect of the social dimensions and consequently a failure to respond effectively to the needs of people with disabilities. This thinking resonates at the micro level where teachers view the 'problem' as being situated in the child with disabilities. The natural recourse in such a scenario is to respond to their perceived needs by 'fixing' the problem through additional resources aimed at making them as normally functioning as others, or to exclude the child to a 'special' (different) setting. Both these approaches are evident in the Indian context.

A report from the Ministry of Human Resource Development (MHRD) provides a list of disabilities which can be integrated in the 'normal school system – formal as well as in non-formal schools'. These include:

> children with locomotor handicaps; mildly and moderately hearing impaired; partially sighted children; mentally handicapped educable group (IQ 50–70); children with multiple handicaps (blind and orthopaedic, hearing impaired and orthopaedic; educable mentally retarded and orthopaedic, visual impaired and mild hearing impaired.

Table 4.1 Identification of CWSN

Year	Total numbers identified as CWSN
2005–6	2,017,404
2006–7	2,399,905
2007–8	2,621,077

Source: Sarva Shiksha Abhiyan (2007).

The assumption is that those with other disabilities need to attend special schools.

The naturalness of this grouping, of those identified as CWSN, is further reinforced by the immense faith placed in the knowledge of the 'expert'. SSA (2007: 13) makes a distinction between formal and functional assessment, and states that these should be 'done by a competent team comprising of doctors, eye specialist, ENT specialist, resource teachers and general teachers'. Here the complete absence of the voices of parents and the child is noteworthy. Such a belief in the 'expert' for CWSN is further supported by the existing structures of educational delivery and professional training. The assumption thus holds that within-child factors, such as her/his IQ, result in her/his legitimate exclusion from the mainstream. This overly medicalised view of CWSN takes the focus away from the learning needs of the child.

Alternative systems: responding equitably or reinforcing inequalities

The assumption underpinning the construction of the category of CWSN has far-reaching implications: framed in the discourse of difference it reinforces a belief that the needs of this category of children are qualitatively different from the needs of others. Thus, the approach in the field has been to assume that because of this difference these children can be legitimately denied entry into the mainstream, as they cannot function in it. Historically, Indian policies have adopted a dual approach, wherein it was noted that 'many handicapped children find it psychologically disturbing to be placed in an ordinary school' and in such cases they should be sent to special schools (Education Commission 1966: 109). This stance is reiterated in the National Policy of Education (MHRD 1986) and more recently in the People with Disabilities (PWD) Act, which states that 'it endeavours to promote the integration of students with disabilities in the normal schools' and also promotes the 'establishment and availability of special schools across the nation' (Ministry of Law, Justice and Company Affairs 1996: 2). This multiplicity of provisions has been further extended under the SSA with the government adopting a 'multi-option model of educating CWSN', with the objective of providing 'appropriate need based skills, be it vocational, functional literacy or simply activities of daily living . . . in the most appropriate learning environment'. This has more recently meant the introduction of 'home based education (HBE) for children with severe- profound disabilities' (SSA 2006: 23).

The tendency to place people with disabilities in a separate category is alarming, especially when it is accompanied by a significant narrowing of their perceived purpose of education. For example, advocating inclusive education, Sharma (2002: 407) notes:

> Education of the handicapped children should be an inseparable part of the general education system so that it can prepare them for adjustment to a socio-cultural environment designed to meet the needs of the normal.

Moreover, there seems to be a complete lack of perceptiveness with regard to the economic and social inequalities that special education and other alternative systems can produce. Even though there has been a lack of systematic collection and analysis of data, anecdotal experience from the field suggests that the skills, especially vocational skills, taught in many special school classrooms have little or no relevance outside the classroom (especially in a rapidly changing market place).

A central aspect of the government's efforts towards addressing the needs of various marginalised groups has been its policy to adopt a targeted approach. Over the last few decades it has implemented many different schemes and programmes specifically targeted for children from SC/ST groups, the girl child etc., and also distributed responsibilities across different ministries and departments. For example, the education of children belonging to SC/ST groups is under the purview of the Ministry of Social Justice and Empowerment (MSJE), the Department of Education (DoE) (which is under the MHRD) and the Ministry of Tribal Affairs. Additionally, a Non-Formal Education (NFE) scheme, introduced in 1978, was established to meet the requirements of children from weaker sections who were unable to attend formal schooling. However, various studies have accused NFE of diluting learning achievement, and its characteristics of flexibility, localisation and need-specific strategy have often been used as loopholes for offering second-track, sub-standard education (Nambissan 2000).

Nonetheless, this approach has been extended to the education of children with disabilities, with the involvement of both the MSJE and the DoE. The former caters to the education of children with disabilities in special schools and the latter focuses on those deemed suitable for the mainstream. However, this approach has been highly inefficient, internally conflicting and financially draining. While, on one hand, the DoE, which is under the

MHRD, is allocating substantial funds through SSA to develop an inclusive system, the MSJE with its focus on special schools has increased its budgetary allocations to 2.1 billion rupees, of which 700 million rupees were given to NGOs (MSJE 2003). The rapid rise of special schools and HBE for children with disabilities, it can be argued, is another attempt at addressing difference by building alternative educational systems with little regard to their effectiveness.

National Sample Survey (NSS)[5] data indicate that, although an overwhelming majority of children with disabilities attend a regular school, there is significant variation in terms of location. In urban areas around 11 per cent of those with disabilities in the 5–18 years age group were enrolled in special schools, whereas this was less than 1 per cent in rural areas. This reflects the recent growth in the number of special schools, especially in urban areas. In the early 1990s there were about 1,035 special schools and nearly a decade later it was estimated that their numbers had risen to 2,500.[6] The majority of these are located in urban areas, with Mumbai having the highest number (Mukhopadhyay and Mani 2002). Quoting somewhat higher figures, a 2003 report stated that there are more than 3,200 special schools throughout India. Interestingly, it further notes:

> However, these special schools have certain disadvantages which became evident as the number of these schools increased. These institutions reached out to a very limited number of children, largely urban and they were not cost effective. But most important of all, these special schools segregated CWSN from the mainstream, thus developing a specific disability culture.
>
> (Janshala 2003: 1)

Such reflections are very rare in government documents, which have largely propagated the development of special schools and reinforced professional boundaries at the micro level through teacher training.

Reinforcing rigid professional boundaries: deskilling mainstream teachers

Swarup (2001) draws attention to the current paradox in teacher training programmes whereby, on one hand, the thrust is on mainstreaming children with disabilities but, on the other, teacher preparation is categorised as either general education or special education *The Tenth Five-Year Plan* (Planning Commission 2002: 31) encourages the 'appointment of special teachers for mildly handicapped children' and provide 'special in-service training to teachers in schools for the disabled children'. A review of the syllabus for pre-service teacher training reveals that mainstream teachers are offered 'inclusive education' as an optional paper, in which the focus is on issues concerning diagnosis and identification of CWSN and on awareness building. The training of teachers for CWSN is regulated by different departments and the inadequacy of its quality has come under increased scrutiny.

In the complete absence of any pre-service training, the focus remains on providing in-service training. Under SSA this training is being conducted using a range of different models, from 1–2 or 3–5 days to 45- to 90-day orientations. Analysis of the short courses highlights their very basic nature, covering only issues of identification and management, but this remains the most preferred medium in preparing teachers. As of 2005, fewer than 0.2 per cent of all SSA teachers had been through the longer programme (quoted in World Bank 2007).

Although there is a lack of research evaluating the effectiveness of these programmes, various studies in the field suggest that teachers do not feel confident in teaching CWSN (Singal 2006, 2008). Moreover, it can be argued that this model is further deskilling mainstream teachers by assuming that the needs of these children are not the primary concern of the general teacher. Rather they need to be taught by resource teachers or special educators. This deskilling of teachers is recognised in the National Council of Educational Research and Training (NCERT) (2005) paper, which recommended that there is a need to 'gear all teacher education programmes (both pre-service and in-service) to developing the pedagogical skills required in inclusive classrooms' (p. 29). The document goes on to categorically recommend:

> Make the class teacher responsible for all the children in the class. In case special support is required on account of SEN, this should be in the form of assistance to the class teacher.
>
> (p. 30)

However, this has not been the case in practice. Based on teacher interviews and classroom observations, Singal (2006) noted that teachers and special educators held very rigid and fixed views about their roles and responsibilities, which shaped their perceptions of the appropriate place for some children to study. One of the teachers aptly summed up the existing perceptions towards mainstream by observing that it is 'more like the real world'. Driven by pragmatic concerns about existing mainstream pressures, teachers and heads unanimously argued for the continuing role of special schools. Special educators were perceived as having more time, and being under no pressure to complete the set curriculum. The quality of education being imparted in special schools was thus not regarded as being of the same level as in mainstream classrooms, where children had to do well in a highly competitive environment in order to succeed later in life.

Even when children with disabilities do attend mainstream classrooms, research suggests that teachers do not regard them as their primary responsibility. The onus of their participation is laid on either the child or others, such as a private tutor at home (especially in the case of families from middle-class urban homes) or the parents (Singal 2008). Similar experiences of being neglected by mainstream teachers were recounted by young people with disabilities and their parents (Singal *et al.* 2008), who had been asked to withdraw their children because teachers expressed their inability to teach them. The few young people in the sample who had attended secondary school spoke favourably of their experiences in special schools. For instance, Rajkumar, a visually impaired man who had completed fourteen years of schooling and had experienced both mainstream and special settings, described the difference between his experiences in these schools as follows:

> the difference is that in the special school everyone was like us . . . everything was taught according to our levels . . . there was no problem of blackboards and so on . . . there everything used to be explained orally and practically . . . there were teachers . . . who were in touch with us . . . they knew Braille also . . . and whatever we could not be understood through Braille, they used to touch and hold with their hands and explain . . . but in a normal school what happens is that the teacher explains on the board.

However, what is remarkable in many of these accounts is that, even though these young people tended to find learning in special schools much easier and conducive to their needs, they continued to highlight the need and desire for more mainstream engagement and participation, which was seen as a way into mainstream society.

Working towards inclusion

The above discussion sets out some of the key factors impacting on the educational participation of children with disabilities in the Indian context. Exclusion of this group has been marked, despite government efforts aimed at increasing their participation. In the concluding section of this chapter, I will focus on two fundamental ideological issues which need to be critically re-examined in the current approach in order to develop a more inclusive system.

Re-examining assumptions about difference: deconstructing CWSN

As noted earlier, the notion of CWSN in India is anchored purely in a medical model of disability, which is highly deterministic in its approach. The dominant thinking in such a context is that each child has a fixed (dis/in)ability and efforts must be directed at identifying these and then placing her/him in a suitable learning environment. The government's focus has thus been on diagnostic measures, whereby success is measured by highlighting the increasing numbers of CWSN. The discourse here has become conflated by a lack of understanding of the difference between impairment and a child's learning needs. Thus, the focus is not necessarily educational; rather it is more medicalised in nature. This is reflected in the efforts of SSA whereby the focus is on providing CWSN with various aids, appliances and other assistive devices. Efforts here are marked by the absence of a focus on teaching and learning processes.

This thinking also underpins current teacher training programmes, which are marked by a clear division between the perceived roles and responsibilities of mainstream and special teachers. Similar to the medicalised model of relying on the expert for diagnosis of the child's abilities (as discussed previously), such dual training further strengthens the belief in specialised knowledge. This further deskills the mainstream teacher, whose tacit knowledge is ignored, and in the absence of professional collaborations the chasm between the mainstream and special education further increases.

Even though the quality of teaching is becoming a concern for all children, and there is growing international research evidence to suggest that pedagogical practices adopted for children with disabilities are primarily good teaching practices for all children, the Indian government continues to largely neglect this area. NCERT (2005: 33) provides useful reflections when it notes that:

> In India, the concept of Inclusive Education has not yet been linked to a broader discussion of pedagogy (Anita, 2000) and quality education (Taneja, 2001). Any broad reform in education cannot be implemented without taking the inclusion of learners with SEN into consideration.

Although this is a powerful assertion, implementation in practice remains a distant reality.

Need to recognise and reorganise rather than relying solely on redistribution

Historical and current efforts towards the education of children with disabilities have been largely shaped by a focus on redistribution of resources and access. The government has developed schemes and programmes which provide children with disabilities with aids, appliances and other assistive devices, or an increased provision in terms of access to schools – special, home-based or mainstream. The focus is on providing equality in terms of resources and access. Although such efforts are important they are inherently limiting in nature, as there is a danger that they will be shaped by individualistic assumptions. In this scenario the assumption that disability is inherent in the individual and hence must be addressed through redistribution of resources is dominant. As Christensen and Dorn (1997) argue it is the deficit that becomes the target of redistribution, which detracts attention away from a critical examination of existing and *dis*abling social structures and institutional contexts, which uphold patterns of injustice in society.

Although this redistribution of resources is desirable and important, as children with disabilities are disproportionately represented in the lower economic strata, and without these special schemes they are unlikely to receive basic essentials, it is not necessarily adequate. Such a focus addresses only 'first generation' concerns of inclusive education, wherein access does not automatically deliver equality. Evidence from efforts aimed at education of girls suggests that, although ensuring basic conditions such as infrastructure is essential, there is also a need to focus on transformations in the curriculum and pedagogy. Research in this field has continually challenged the role of schooling in reinforcing gender inequalities of socialisation and social control. This focus has been very useful in developing more nuanced debates around issues of quality of provision alongside concerns of addressing gender equity. These 'second generation' concerns, focused on curriculum and pedagogy, need to become an integral part of deliberations on the education of children with disabilities in India. The focus cannot be simply about building more special schools, or shifting children to the mainstream; rather we need to be concerned about what they are being offered in these schools and its relevance to the lives they would like to lead (rather than the kind of lives which we think are appropriate for them).

This focus is even more pertinent at a time when the quality of education being offered in Indian schools is coming under scrutiny; flagging teacher morale, pedagogical inadequacies, rigid and irrelevant curriculum, and high drop-out and repetition rates highlight a pressing need which demands a critical engagement and re-examination of a general education system that has failed to deliver its promise of greater equality. Finally, it is important to acknowledge that all these issues cannot be addressed in isolation from the larger socio-cultural context of education. Any attempt to develop a truly equitable and inclusive system ultimately requires systemic reform. Here not only does an emphasis on society's conception of difference become important, but it also brings into critical focus the need to reflect on the responsibilities of schools, the role of teachers and indeed the vision of education for a developing society. In this regard academic debates and educational efforts must address issues of equity in consonance with quality – two integral dimensions in the concept of inclusion.

Notes

1 In Indian terminology, the primary sector is grades 1–5, with admission to grade 1 usually around the age of 5 (admission is often delayed to age 6 or 7, or accelerated at age 4). As birth registration is not universal, pupils may be given a birth date when they first attend school, often one or two years later than

a real birthday. This gives the child more time to pass the final school exams (which have an age restriction) and to appear in competitions for public sector jobs. Upper primary schooling is grades 6–8; these two together constitute elementary education. Not all Indian states (which have constitutional priority in educational matters) follow this pattern, however.

2 The Constitution recognises a list of castes (those previously regarded as 'untouchable') and tribes in one of its attached Schedules (hence the legal terms, scheduled castes [SC] and scheduled tribes [ST]). SC (16.2 per cent of total population) and ST (8.2 per cent of total population) groups are also known as 'Dalits' and 'Adivasis' respectively. Dalits can be found throughout the country, often in segregated hamlets away from main villages, whereas Adivasis are concentrated in more remote parts of central India and the north-east.

3 SSA (or Education Movement for All) is the largest government programme in education currently being implemented.

4 There is no clarification of the assumed difference between impairment and disability.

5 The National Sample Survey data set is one of the most comprehensive educational data sets available in India.

6 The Second Five-Year Plan in 1956 noted only 118 special schools across the country.

Bibliography

Christensen, C. A. and Dorn, S. (1997) Competing notions of social justice and contradictions in special education reform. *Journal of Special Education*, 31 (2): 181–198.

Education Commission. (1966) *Education and National Development*. New Delhi: Ministry of Education.

Janshala. (2003) *Perspectives in Special Needs Education in India: A Journey from Isolation to Inclusion*. Jan.–March.

Majumdar, S. (2001) Educational programmes for the disadvantaged groups. In M. Mukhopadhyay and R. S. Tyagi (Eds) *Governance of School Education in India*. New Delhi: NIEPA.

MHRD. (1986) *Ministry of Human Resource Development: National Policy of Education 1986*. New Delhi: Government of India.

MHRD. (2004) *Education for All: India Marches Ahead*. New Delhi: Government of India.

Ministry of Law, Justice and Company Affairs (1996) *The Persons with Disabilities (Equal Opportunities, Protection of Rights and Full Participation) Act, 1995*. New Delhi: Government of India.

MSJE. (2003) *Notes on Demands for Grants, 2002–2003*. New Delhi: Government of India.

Mukhopadhyay, S. and Mani, M. N. G. (2002) Education of children with special needs. In R. Govinda (Ed.) *India Education Report: A Profile of Basic Education*. New Delhi: Oxford University Press.

Nambissan, G. B. (2000) Dealing with deprivation. *Seminar*, 493: 50–55.

National Council of Educational Research and Training (NCERT). (2005) *The National Focus Group on Education of Children with Special Needs: Position*

Paper. Accessed 30 September 2005 from http://www.ncert.nic.in/sites/publication/schoolcurriculum/Position_Papers/

National Council of Educational Research and Training. (2007) *Position Paper: National Focus Group on Work and Education*. New Delhi: NCERT.

Planning Commission. (2002) *Tenth Five-Year Plan, 2002–2007*. New Delhi: Planning Commission, Education Division.

Registrar General of India. (2001) *Census of India*. Accessed 6 November 2007 from http://www.censusindia.net.

Rehabilitation Council of India. (RCI). (2000) *Status of Disability in India*. New Delhi, India: Author.

Rehabilitation Council of India. (2001) *Draft National Policy on Special Education*. Workshop on appropriate models of education for children with special needs. New Delhi: Author.

Sarva Shiksha Abhiyan. (2006) *Discovering New Paths in Inclusion: A Documentation of Home Based Education Practices for CWSN in SSA*. Delhi: Department of EE&L (MHRD).

Sarva Shiksha Abhiyan. (2007) *Inclusive Education in SSA*. Accessed 4 March 2010 from 164.100.51.121/inclusive-education/Inclusive_Edu_May07.pdf

Sharma, K. (2002) Education of children with special needs: policy perspectives. In S. Rao (Ed.) *Educational Policies in India: Analysis and Review of Promise and Performance*. New Delhi: NIEPA.

Singal, N. (2006) An ecosystemic approach for understanding inclusive education: an Indian case study. *European Journal of Psychology of Education*, Special issue: Ten years after Salamanca, 21 (3): 239–252.

Singal, N. (2008) Working towards inclusion: reflections from the classroom. *Teaching and Teacher Education*, 24: 1516–1529.

Singal, N., Jeffery, R., Jain, A. and Sood, N. (2008) *Exploring the Outcomes of Schooling for Young People with Disabilities*. Paper presented at the RECOUP mid-term dissemination workshop, New Delhi.

Swarup, S. (2001) *Teacher Preparation Policy*. Paper presented at the workshop on Appropriate Models of Education for Children with Special Needs, Rehabilitation Council of India, New Delhi.

UNESCO. (2008) *EFA Global Monitoring Report: Statistics*. Accessed 20 October 2008 from http://portal.unesco.org/education/en/ev.php-URL_ID=49630&URL_DO=DO_TOPIC&URL_SECTION=201.html

World Bank. (2006) *Development and the Next Generation: World Development Report 2007*. Washington, DC: World Bank.

World Bank. (2007) *People with Disabilities in India: From Commitments to Outcomes*. New Delhi: Human Development Unit, South Asia Region.

Section 2

Supporting families

Chapter 5

Family perspectives

Parents in partnership

Mithu Alur (The Spastics Society of India)

Introduction

This chapter provides a practical account of how parents have been critical forces in the inclusive process with reference to the services we have established in India. This did not happen overnight but had to be built up over three decades. It began by enabling parents to become critical partners in the management of their disabled child and later developed structures so that they continued this with a transformed role in an inclusive framework. Although I am writing about inclusion of disabled children into regular schools, we have adopted a concept of inclusion which engages with socially and economically disadvantaged children as well as culturally disadvantaged children, for example girls who have had limited access to schooling.

Indian society has an exclusive hierarchical structure based on class and caste. However, within this there is a social structure of dependency on families. Despite a socio-cultural context that does so much to maintain exclusion, we found that attitudes can be changed. Parents' attitudes were a critical factor, as they have been among the most sceptical and hesitant about the transition from special schools to regular schools. They saw our special schools as providing a caring and supportive environment and did not want to risk losing this. Most parents admitted to being anxious initially about their child's inclusion. Their fears pertained mainly to apprehensions about the reactions of non-disabled peers, the teasing and adjustments their children might confront, the attitudes of teachers and how their children would be supported in the regular school, and whether they would be able to cope academically. However, after inclusion, the overall attitude of parents was extremely positive and they took ownership of the transfer from special schools to regular school and finally to the sustainability of their child in a regular school. In this chapter I write about the methods we used to effect the change through two processes: first, how we introduced a new process of partnering with parents in the management of their children, thus building up trust, and second, how we made them key resource members in the continuum of support needed in the inclusive process.

What was the *raison d'être* for doing this work?

I begin with my own empowerment. My story is really a story of many journeys. The first journey began when I became a parent of a child with a disability. That event changed my life and she became my greatest teacher.

I came from one of those privileged highly educated families of Kolkata, where there was a strong combination of British and Indian influence. My parents were staunch nationalists as many people were during the historic pre-independence and immediate post-independence period. It was culturally very strong too; my mother loved singing Tagore songs and Indian hymns, my father loved reciting poetry, Shakespeare and Tagore: he was a *littérateur* and published a college newsletter in which he could give vent to his passionate feelings against the British occupation of India. The oft-repeated phrases one heard were 'you must serve India' and 'the service must go beyond self' and then the approach to service was 'the right should be to work only and not to the fruits.'[1]

It was 1966 and Calcutta, when my daughter Malini was born with cerebral palsy. Knowledge of cerebral palsy was virtually non-existent in India at that time. Neither I nor my husband had any idea of what cerebral palsy was. In India's premier institute in Delhi, in front of a group of young interns staring at me and my weeping daughter, the doctors examined Malini and said brusquely: 'Your child is a spastic. She will not be able to achieve very much as her brain is damaged. She will be "a vegetable" and there is nothing much you can do about it . . . Once the brain gets damaged, it is irreversible.' We did not accept what they said. My husband and I were young parents, 22 and 24, and we ran from pillar to post in desperation trying to understand what had happened to her. My husband, who was very educated and had just returned from finishing a Tripos in Cambridge, was very dynamic in his decision-making ability and, finding nobody who understood her, decided to go to England in search of treatment for Malini.

In England, Malini was assessed as above average in her intelligence. Their whole approach to her changed our lives. My daughter progressed and I became a professional special educator.

For us, the time in England was key. I met people who treated my daughter and me with great care and great sensitivity. I decided to study more on the subject and did my first course at the Institute of Education in London. That is how my life became an east–west journey, living and serving in India, returning to England to get recharged and as a respite from the apathy and indifference that always confronts us here, and returning again to serve India!

Because of those early days the fight and the battle against ignorance proved challenging. However, in England, because of appropriate and effective management, Malini flourished. Today she has done her double Masters, one in Gender Studies and the other in Information Technology.

She is presently a Senior Events Manager at the Oxford Bookstore, in downtown Bombay. It is her own courage and grit and determination, combined with the best services she was exposed to, that got her there.[2]

In 1972, when we returned from England after six years, there were still no special schools for children with cerebral palsy in India. The situation was exactly the same as when I had left. My first thought was: what about the other Malinis? What was happening to them and how to educate other children like her? They should get the same kind of services as Malini, who was privileged enough to go to England. However, it was easier said than done. The situation was fraught with negative responses from prominent people. The first question I was confronted with was 'Why educate them?' An eminent citizen of the city said 'Why bother, Mithu, there are hundreds of normal children needing education'. The Health Minister met me and asked me 'are you talking about plastics?' He had not heard of spastics. A Vice Chancellor said when Malini was ready for her degree, 'Why do you want to bother to make her do a BA? . . . it is such a useless examination.' Entrenched mindsets needed change and such questions made me more than determined to change the scene.

How did we change the situation between 1972 and 1998?

Fortunately the late prime minister Indira Gandhi did not have such a mindset. I was fortunate to have good contacts so I began, as things usually do in India, at the top. Mrs Gandhi, the then prime minister, met me, heard my traumatic story and reacted with great compassion. Through her intervention, we were given a beautiful bungalow overlooking the Arabian Sea to start the first experimental school and later a plot of land to build the larger National Centre. Our first patron was Nargis Dutt, the famous actress and social worker. She was the queen of Bollywood and her presence added glamour to a situation fraught with despair, gloom and negativity.

In 1972, together with a few like-minded friends and parents of disabled children, the Spastics Society of India (SSI) was established. It became the first innovative model for the education of children with disability (specifically children with neurological and physical disabilities), combining education and treatment under one roof within a social setting.

Recalling the tortuous clinical examination to which Malini had been subjected in hospitals in India, I decided that one of the first areas that the new organisation should develop was 'care and assessment'. Infant clinics were set up for high-risk babies and holistic programmes run within a context-specific environment. I had learnt that it is not possible to assess children with multiple disorders such as cerebral palsy in a single examination; it needs a team of specialists who understand the difficulties of the children and their parents. Most importantly it is a time of immense trauma and crisis for a mother and needs the full attention of doctors. Specialists were trained not to lose their compassion while assessing families and the child, and we began with a new humane approach. The team undertaking the assessment interacted with the child not as a 'handicapped person' but as a child first. This model of assessment and identification combined with professionalism and humanity was a way not previously practiced in India.

Parent support system: parents in partnership

Being a parent, I gave a strong focus to parents as important members of the team and launched a new partnership with parents. Parents began to be empowered. They were trained to understand techniques of management of their child and their family at home. In addition to managing their children at home, parents were encouraged to become professionals and help as teachers, therapists and principals of schools, and are now in management positions. In the Indian cultural context it is not enough only to train the parent; there are large joint families consisting of parents-in-law, aunts and grandparents. All these family members need training.

The centre slowly became equipped with paramedics, special educators, social workers and psychologist doctors, and an important member of the team was the parent. A leading filmmaker, Shyam Benegal from India, made a film on the SSI entitled *The Love They Give for Nothing, the Care Costs Money*.

What were our achievements in the first phase?

* SSI made a technical contribution providing a very strong base for children and youth with cerebral palsy and other physical disabilities. Holistic programmes combining education and treatment under one roof, and early infant clinics where high-risk babies were assessed, helped to create an awareness that children must have early detection and management. More than 5,000 babies, children and young people have come for assessment and remedial programmes over the last thirty-five years.
* Parents in partnership in the management of their children was a key outcome which gave us a strong base to build on. It introduced the concept that expertise and specialist knowledge is certainly necessary to achieve the desired progress, but that it should be given with a humane compassionate approach.
* Professionalism combined with care changed the lives of families with severely disabled children and the new approach of treating parents as important voices to listen to helped to change the situation for hundreds of parents in the subcontinent.

- A major outcome of SSI is that neurological disability and cerebral palsy, which had previously not been recognized amongst the government's classifications, is now recognised as one of the eleven official classifications accepted by the Government of India's Ministry of Social Justice & Empowerment.
- Similarly students have been able to pursue higher education and technical education and careers in accounting, journalism, finance and computing. They have pursued academics at the Masters and PhD level. Some have set up their own successful businesses. Over 300 models of employment have been developed. Looking back at the last thirty-five years of work, we take pride at the number of our students who have become accountants, journalists, teachers and professionals in many other areas.
- Pedagogy training of manpower on a national level has helped to decentralise the services. This we did by sharing our knowledge through the curriculum and training workshops and seminars around the subcontinent.
- A major outcome has been a profusion of regionally based and autonomous societies that have grown with help from SSI. Nationally SSI has promoted the growth of services at Kolkata (1974), Delhi (1977), Bangalore (1980) and Chennai (1985). These centres in turn have spun off peripheral services in their regions. Eighteen of the thirty-one Indian states have replicated the same model combining education and treatment under one roof. These organisations are all based on our first model and were initiated by parents and family members such as aunts, great-aunts and grandmothers. They were initially helped by us and then encouraged to be autonomous. It has essentially been a women's movement. A survey of the services indicates that between 100,000 and 1 million people have been reached out to around the country.

How did we change the situation between 1998 and 2008?

An agenda for change was established and progress was made. However, all this happened on a micro level. Although the Spastics Societies have had phenomenal outreach we soon found out that their valuable contribution was only the tip of the iceberg. Statistics now show that there are 70–80 million disabled people in India. The government's own statistics for disability report that 98 per cent of disabled people and children are out of the ambit of services. During my own work at Dharavi (Asia's largest slum) over sixteen years I too noticed that children with disabilities were not included in the government's Integrated Child Development Scheme (ICDS)(India) programmes, one of the world's largest pre-school services providing basic welfare and psycho-social services through their nurseries or anganwadis for women and children. Children with disabilities were not included nor were they entitled to even basic health care and nutrition. This is a violation of human rights and unacceptable.

It was important at this juncture in our lives to examine the broader framework in which policy gets embedded and question this so I moved to do doctoral research which would further inform work in this area. The questions at the heart of my research were: how was a government policy (perhaps inadvertently) excluding children with disabilities from their programmes resulting in a 90 per cent exclusion of vulnerable disadvantaged children in the poorest areas? Why had nobody raised an objection?

Therefore I began another journey of discovery. In 1994 I examined the ICDS and the larger policy for disabled people in the country in which it had been embedded.

What emerged from my research was that no clear data, no stratified sample details about age groups and locations, were available about the disabled groups. The most crucial finding of all was that until the last census disability was not included. The surveys being done regularly by primary teachers as part of the universal education programme did not include the disabled child as part of the programme of EFA (Education For All). The finding that none of the government's teacher education syllabi included pedagogic issues concerned with the teaching of disabled children is another key issue. Leaving out disability from the Census of India has relegated the group to the wilderness, in which they were perceived by many to belong, not to be seen or heard. Invisible groups do not need policy or financial allocations.

The findings showed substantively that the ICDS policy of non-inclusion of disabled children seems to be symptomatic of the wider malaise that exists in India where, without a clear-cut policy, massive exclusion has been happening at the ground level. 'Education For All' could remain an empty promise on the part of the Government of India, if there are no plans for operationalisation of policy into practice for the inclusion of this large segment of the child population.

To address this became critical and two major projects which made the paradigm shift in policy framework a reality were taken up by SSI. They were the National Resource Centre for Inclusion, India (NRCI) and the Early Intervention in Inclusive Education, an SSI/UNICEF project. Both projects were supported by the Canadian International Development Agency (CIDA) and launched in Bombay.

The National Resource Centre for Inclusion, India

In 1999 a National Resource Centre for Inclusion was set up in Bombay. The NRCI has a macro–micro-level agenda of changing policy at one level and changing services at another level.

NRCI has focused on how the mechanism of implementation can be operationalised through change at three levels:

- micro level of school and classroom, culture/policies/practice;
- mezzo level of community: to study the mechanism or intervention strategies needed to put children with disabilities into the existing government's framework of services;
- macro level of policy, ensuring change in the legislative, structural and political culture at the local, state, national and global levels.

Our definition of disability, which began with children with cerebral palsy, became more inclusive and expanded to cover the girl child, the socially disadvantaged caught in the grip of poverty and all children with other disabilities. Our admission policies had to be changed and reoriented to include *all* disabilities. Pedagogy was transformed, and ecologically appropriate and differentiated curricula with multiple teaching and learning styles, community involvement and cooperative and collaborative learning were introduced.

Poverty and disability: inclusive education practice in early childhood

We moved to the community, in this case the slums of Mumbai. There has been a steady rural–urban migration into the cities of India and the result is ghettoes of slums in the inner cities. Most metropolitan cities have somewhere between 50 and 60 per cent of people living in shanty town, slum settlements. We had moved into Dharavi, Asia's largest slum, and begun work. To begin the concept of inclusion (as mentioned above) a two-year action research project in the community was also begun with UNICEF, entitled Inclusive Education Practice in Early Childhood in Mumbai, combining two elements of research and intervention. The intervention aspects demonstrated *how* inclusion can be operationalised and the research methodology tracked the development, providing an ongoing evaluation by external independent researchers.

Six demonstration sites based on the ICDS model were set up in the slums. The preparation for inclusive education in the slums, which we called 'a whole community approach', involved:

- strengthening the six communities that were within the development sites;
- building the capacity of the anganwadi (nursery) teachers and transforming them to become multipurpose workers;
- building support from among community members.

How did we involve parents as partners in the inclusion process?

In both the projects parents were the key people we began working with. The aim was to involve parents as decision makers, to involve them as auditors and evaluators of the services, to acquire feedback on the functioning of the nurseries and to transform parents into resource people in order to facilitate the sensitisation process in the community. We evolved a Plan of Action and changed our school culture according to the new philosophy and ideology. Other strategies carried out and detailed below also proved to be valuable.

Deprofessionalisation

The three new 'Rs' for deprofessionalisation

Inclusion of children need not only be done by professionals. But it usually is. It is dominated by a highly professional attitude that has its roots in a specialist approach cloaked in the medical model. This creates a barrier. In a context where there were few professionals, the aim became to introduce a more cooperative and collaborative partnership instead of an authoritarian and hierarchical one. Professionals had to be retrained in approaching the new context and culture where they were operating. A system and process of deprofessionalisation began which I have called the three R's:

- retraining into a new context and culture of the community;
- relocation away from the institute to the community, which meant developing more community-based initiatives;
- redeployment of time: in the institute several jobs were chalked out; these had to be worked out and another set of priorities introduced into their agenda.

Professionals had to understand that they, too, had a great deal to learn. Professionals learned to listen to the voices in the community before giving advice. They were encouraged to reframe the context of their own expertise in a way that acknowledged the expertise of parents, community members, and others playing a role in the inclusive classroom and community. They became less arrogant, authoritative and hierarchical. They learned to accept the expertise of parents, and to listen more than to speak. A change in the balance of influence took place, resulting in a more equal approach.

Deinstitutionalization

Rather than providing primary interventions in specialised settings, inclusion involved moving away from specialised settings to the community setting involving parents. Moving from an institutional base to a community base was not easy. Many trained specialists have a bio-medical approach and are used to well-resourced rooms, beds for examinations and technical aids, and find it difficult to shed their aura of professionalism. Professionals moving from an institutional base to a community base needed training and understanding to appreciate that the usual well-resourced institutional-based equipment was never going to be available in places where there were no services for anyone. All professionals were taught to take up multifaceted roles. They did not limit themselves to only their area of expertise but also provided broad-based inputs to all fields of intervention that the child may need.

Ecological inventory

It was important to know about the children's background: what a child saw, smelled, tasted, heard, felt. My team did what is known as an ecological survey of the area, which I have called the *Ecological Inventory*. The Ecological Inventory gave us the knowledge we needed about the children's environment, the various recreational and routine activities and tasks the children performed and how they went about it, the variety of objects, animals, people they saw and were familiar with and the cultural diversity and the social mores of the community: their regional, caste and religious differences. The Ecological Inventory led us on to the design of a *culturally appropriate* enrichment programme.

Demystification of 'disability'

It was necessary to demystify the processes framed by the 'specialist approach'. Simple methods of handling their children at home and at inclusive schools were introduced. Workshops for regular teachers continue. We took a number of steps to build support and engage parents and community leaders. We trained the sisters of the children attending our pre-school.

Parents as partners in the inclusion process

Initially, parents were apprehensive about inclusion after experiencing a safe environment at a special school, such as the one SSI had provided. They said:

- Disabled children are best in special schools.
- The teachers will not know how to deal with our children's needs.

We met with parents of children with and without disabilities. In both cases, they were negative. Initially when the parents were introduced to the concept of inclusion by the social worker, the first response was 'How will our child cope?'

Parents of children with disability felt:

> How will my child study with normal children? Will the normal children not hit him, if they push him, he will fall, and won't they tease him?

Parents of children without disabilities said:

> How will they study with the disabled? They will lag behind and learn the habits of the disabled. He/she will imitate the mannerisms of the disabled.

A few had their reservations about including children with severe disability, intellectual deficits or epilepsy. They felt that, at a very young age, the children without disability would be scared or upset when they watched a child getting a seizure, or the unusual behaviours exhibited by the severely challenged. About girls they said:

- Boys and girls should have separate schools

> How could the teacher give attention to my child when she has twenty-five students in the class now as against eight earlier, my child will surely be neglected!

Parent support groups for inclusion

Regular 'Parent–Teacher–Therapist' meetings were held at the outset to understand parents' fears about the transition to a regular school, address them and keep a continuous check on parental support and needs, mainly those of mothers. It took a series of meetings to convey the concept of inclusion, its benefits of peer learning and social development, to parents. These kinds of meetings were very familiar to the team because of their earlier experience in the Spastics Society. We began by elucidating how inclusive education would work for the child, and putting everything in very simple terms so that parents and volunteers could understand. I decided to meet them and speak to them as a mother. I told them that I had no options when my daughter was young and had to put her in a special school, but today the world had moved on and there was a choice. Children with disabilities were being accepted in regular schools. We would have to do a great deal of preparation. We were ready to do this new experiment if the parents became our partners. It appeared to work. *Parent support groups for inclusion* were created. Parents were asked to introduce the idea of inclusion into a mainstream school to their children, and over time many became very confident ambassadors of inclusive education. We worked with their fears, respecting them. Then we began empowering them to give their children a *continuum of support*. Instead of having a specialist resource member of our staff provide all the ongoing support to children, we began preparing the parents and mainstream teachers to provide the additional support required. The changing role of parents was stressed and their dependency on NRCI gradually reduced. At some of these meetings, students included earlier were invited along with their parents to share their initial apprehensions and strategies that worked for them.

Parents undertook the majority of initial preparatory work for inclusion. This approach resulted in a direct interaction of parents with the heads with no middleman coming between them; this facilitated making a relationship between parents, teachers and heads of regular schools, thus enabling these actors *to take ownership* of the inclusion process. Parents soon took over and got their friends and neighbours to help. Eventually, it was they who took ownership of the inclusion process, sorting out any barriers that came in the way of their child. The availability of parents to provide support in the classroom and outside has proved indispensable.

Parents became a critical resource for the successful growth and sustainability of inclusive education. Seventy per cent of parents managed to secure admission for their children into the neighbourhood schools, through their own efforts coupled with the support we provided them. This transfer of leadership from professionals to parents was key to reaching a greater scale of inclusion.

In India not having enough specialists can help. The services are not too compartmentalized and are much more broad-based than is the case in the west. Professionals become multitasking, multifaceted. For instance we spoke to parents on family planning, referred mothers who had suffered domestic violence and alcoholism to counsellors, got other siblings admitted into mainstream schools, provided aids and adaptations, linked our students to the nutrition programme of the hospital and also provided a nutritious breakfast every day for children who came to the nurseries. All of these actions helped build trust towards us in the community.

In conclusion one can say that the involvement of the whole community in a bottom-up approach is critical in creating an inclusive environment. Inclusive schools assume more responsibility for children with disabilities in the community if one works closely with families and the local community. This strengthens the cooperation, making inclusion a collaborative effort. Community-based programs based on the community's cultural mores and strengths helps to build a community-based mechanism enabling growth and development, especially for families and children at risk. Engaging the community strengthens the community to take ownership of the programme.

Parents in India have been built up to become a critical resource for the successful growth and sustainability of inclusive education. What I have tried to relate in this chapter is how parents can become a valuable resource. The manner in which one approaches them is key. It should be non-hierarchical, non-authoritarian, essentially egalitarian with a large dose of compassion.

On reflection one can say it has been a long journey of three decades. Through the years our credibility and trust between ourselves were built up. How long-term this solution may be is open to question. Inclusive education in a country where there is systemic failure requires a bottom-up approach. It is also key to demonstrate the success of this approach and to show a paradigm shift from a specialist approach to a demystified approach. Finally inclusive education is not for affluent countries only. It can be carried out successfully in developing countries as well. Inclusive education is not only about funds. It needs a change of heart. It is about how one addresses diversity and differences. As Gandhi has said, 'you must be the change you seek.' As for me, being a parent and interacting with others has certainly added to my learning curve. I have learnt much more than I have given. As one of our leading Tamilian scholars, Thiruvallavur, has said:

> What I have learnt can only fill the palm of my hand; what I have yet to learn can fill an ocean.

Acknowledgement

I am grateful for the assistance and the help given by Mrs Varsha Hooja, Ms Janina Gomes, Ms Theresa Dacosta and Mr Manish Kapdoskar.

Notes

1 One of the most important messages from the *Bhagavad Gita*, a bible for the modern Hindus.
2 It seems right to say that I had a son while I was in England, Nikhil Chib, who has always taken a great interest in his family and stood by whatever we have done.

Bibliography

Alur, M. (1998) *Invisible Children: A Study of Policy Exclusion*. PhD thesis, University of London.
Alur, M. (2000) Inclusion for children with disabilities in India: a policy perspective. Paper presented at the Sixth International Congress on Inclusion of Children with Disabilities in the Community, Edmonton, Canada. Available at ADAPT (Formerly Spastics Society of India) Library, Mumbai.

Alur, M. (2003) Strengthening the community from within: a whole community approach to inclusive education in early childhood. Paper presented at The North South Dialogue II: From Rhetoric to Practice, Kerala, India.

Alur, M. (2004) Early intervention in inclusive education in Mumbai, India. Paper presented at the Twelfth World Congress of Education, Montpellier.

Alur, M. and Rioux, M. (2003) *'Included': An Exploration of Six Early Education Pilot Projects for Children with Disabilities in India*. Final report. Mumbai: SSI/ UNICEF Project.

Government of India (1994) *Integrated Child Development Services (ICDS)*. New Delhi: Ministry of Human Resources Development Department of Women and Child Development.

Chapter 6

Supporting parents and families in the development of inclusive practice

Garry Hornby (University of Canterbury, New Zealand)

This chapter begins with a rationale for the importance of parental involvement (PI) in terms of benefits to children with special educational needs (SEN), their families and the inclusive schools that they attend. A model for the effective organization of PI in inclusive schools is then presented which focuses on meeting parents' needs and utilizing their potential contributions. Emerging from the model is a list of key questions that schools can use to audit their provision for working with parents and families. Finally, findings from a survey of schools in New Zealand using the key questions are presented to highlight critical areas of parental involvement needing development in inclusive schools.

An important challenge for teachers in inclusive schools is working with parents of children with SEN. The role of PI in improving educational outcomes for all children has been recognised by governments in many countries around the world. PI is typically defined as 'parental participation in the educational processes and experiences of their children' (Jeynes 2007: 83). There is now considerable support for the importance of parental involvement in the education of their children across all age groups, abilities and disabilities, as well as the various cultures and communities in which children grow up. Most importantly, the effectiveness of parental involvement in facilitating children's academic achievement has been reported by recent reviews and meta-analyses of the now extensive international literature on this topic (Cox 2005; Desforges and Abouchaar 2003; Fan and Chen 2001; Henderson and Mapp 2002; Jeynes 2007; Pomerantz, Moorman and Litwack 2007).

There are other benefits of PI which emerge from these reviews that focus on teachers, children and parents. For teachers, effective PI is reported to improve parent–teacher relationships, teacher morale and school climate. For children, involvement of their parents is reported to lead to improvements in attitudes, behaviour and attendance at school, as well as in children's mental health. For parents, involvement in their children's education has been linked to increased parental confidence, satisfaction in parenting and interest in their own education.

However, in some traditional societies in which I have worked, such as in India and the West Indies, there is limited history or societal expectation of PI in education. Schools are seen as places where children are sent to be educated. Parents are not expected to be involved in schools or even in educating their children at home. Educating children is seen as the job of teachers and this is to occur in schools. Although these views are gradually changing they remain much more ingrained in traditional societies than in western countries, where there is now a commitment to PI. Teachers therefore have a more difficult job working with parents in countries with a traditional culture, as well as with parents living in western countries whose cultural background has led to a lack of appreciation of the importance of PI. Because of the increasingly multicultural nature of schools in many countries in recent years, working with parents from diverse cultural backgrounds is currently one of the biggest challenges for teachers (Hornby and Lafaele 2010).

The importance of addressing this challenge is reinforced by a classic study conducted twenty-five years ago. Clark (1983) carried out research on high-achieving students in an urban high school serving a poor black community where most of the students were failing. He found that what distinguished the parents of these high-achieving students from others at the school was that they believed that they should be involved in their children's education, by both supporting their learning at home and interacting constructively with schools. So these parents did such things as establishing routines for homework and bedtime; supervising their children's TV viewing; encouraging children's reading; talking with their children; and visiting schools in order to advocate for their children. Clark concluded that these simple activities were what made the difference between students at the high school succeeding or failing. This finding reinforces the need for all teachers to view their role as including a responsibility for working effectively with parents as well as for educating parents about the importance of their involvement in their children's education.

A model for parent involvement

In order to ensure optimal involvement of parents in the education of their children with and without SEN it is necessary for schools to have a model for PI and guidelines for its implementation, which is the major focus of this chapter. The theoretical model for PI that is described below was adapted from Hornby (2000) and is presented in Figure 6.1. The model consists of two pyramids joined at their bases, one representing a hierarchy of parents' needs, the other a hierarchy of parents' potential contributions. Both pyramids demonstrate visually the different levels of needs and contributions of parents. Thus, while all parents have some needs and some potential contributions which can be utilised, a smaller number have an intense need for

PARENTAL CONTRIBUTIONS

PARENT TIME   PARENT EXPERTISE

SOME   **POLICY**
                                     e.g. PTA members, school governors,
                                                    parent advocacy groups

MANY   **RESOURCE**
                                     e.g. classroom aides, fund-raising,
                                                       preparing materials

MOST   **COLLABORATION**
                                     e.g. home–school reading, maths
                                       and behaviour programmes

ALL   **INFORMATION**
                                     e.g. children's strengths, weaknesses,
                                           SEN, medical details

ALL   **COMMUNICATION**
                                     e.g. handbooks, newsletters, telephone
                                        contacts, homework diaries

MOST   **LIAISON**
                                     e.g. home visits, parent–teacher meetings

MANY   **EDUCATION**
                                     e.g. parent workshops

SOME   **SUPPORT**
                                     e.g. parent counselling and support groups

TEACHER TIME   TEACHER EXPERTISE
                                     PARENTAL NEEDS

Figure 6.1 Model for parent involvement.

guidance, or the capability of making an extensive contribution. The model also shows that, for parents' needs at a higher level, more time and expertise is required by teachers to meet these needs. Similarly, the parents who make a greater contribution require a higher level of expertise and time available (Hornby 2000).

Each of the components of the model will now be outlined and the knowledge and skills needed by teachers in inclusive schools for full participation in PI with parents of children with SEN will be identified.

Contributions by parents

Information

All parents can contribute valuable information about their children and will have ongoing contacts with professionals in order to assess and plan for meeting their children's needs. Information concerning children's SEN, strengths and weaknesses, along with any relevant medical details, can be gathered by teachers at parent–teacher meetings. Making full use of parents' knowledge of their children not only leads to more effective professional practice, it also makes parents feel that they have been listened to and that an active interest has been taken in their children. Therefore, teachers need to develop good listening, counselling and interviewing skills (Hornby, Hall and Hall 2003).

Collaboration

Most parents are willing and able to contribute more than just information. Most parents are able to collaborate with teachers by reinforcing classroom programmes at home, such as home–school reading programmes. However, some parents, at some times, are not able to carry out work at home with their children. This is typically because their resources are already fully committed in coping with their children at home, so they are not able to do anything extra. At a later time family circumstances may change and parents may then want to become more involved in their children's education. Teachers must respect parents' rights to make this decision in consideration of the wider needs of their families. So, although involvement in home–school programmes, or other requests for parents to carry out work with their children at home, should always be offered to all parents, including those who have not collaborated in the past, it should be expected that a small proportion of parents will not participate. Therefore, teachers need the skills of collaborating with parents in a flexible partnership in which parents' choices are respected.

Resource

Many parents have the time and ability to act as voluntary teacher aides, assisting in the classroom, or in the preparation of materials, or in fundraising. Others may have special skills which they can contribute such as helping prepare newsletters or craft activities, or curriculum areas in which they have a special talent. Some parents may have the time, skills and knowledge to provide support to other parents either informally or through participation in self-help or support groups. It is often the case that parents also benefit from acting as a resource. They may acquire knowledge which is helpful to their understanding of their own children. In addition, they often gain in confidence through helping at school and go on to further their own education. In order to enable as many parents as possible to act as a resource to the school teachers need practical management and communication skills.

Policy

Some parents are able to contribute their expertise through membership of parent or professional organisations. This includes being a school governor or member of the parent–teacher association (PTA), or being involved in a parent support or advocacy group. Others have the time and ability to provide in-service training by speaking at conferences or workshops, or by writing about their experiences. Teachers should continually be on the lookout for parents who can contribute in these ways so that their abilities can be used to the full.

Needs of parents

Communication

All parents need to have effective channels of communication with their children's teachers. They need information about the organisation and requirements of the school as it effects their children. They need to know when their children are having difficulties and what the school is going to do to address these. That is, parents need to know about their rights and responsibilities. This can be provided through handbooks or regular newsletters written especially for parents. Parents need to feel that they can contact the school at any time when they have a concern about their child. Some parents prefer to communicate by telephone, others would rather call in to see the teacher face to face, and still others find that contact through written notes or home–school diaries suits them best. Therefore, educators need to develop effective written and oral communication skills and ensure that a wide range of communication options are open to parents.

Liaison

Most parents want to know how their children are getting on at school. They want to find out what their children have achieved and whether they are having any difficulties. They regard teachers as the main source of information on their children's performance at school and therefore need to have a working partnership with them. Teachers can facilitate this by keeping in regular contact with parents through such means as telephone calls, home visits, home–school notebooks and weekly report cards and by meeting with parents at school. Therefore, teachers need to develop the skills of conducting formal and informal meetings with parents. In addition, they need to offer a range of options for liaison with parents so that those who do not feel comfortable coming to formal meetings with teachers have other forms of regular contact made available to them.

Education

Many parents are interested in participating in parent education (or parent training) programmes aimed at promoting their children's progress or managing their behaviour. Parent education can be conducted individually or in parent groups or workshops. Some parents will not want to take part in such programmes, for a variety of reasons. There will be those who, at a certain point in time, feel confident about the way they are parenting their children and do not see the need for parent education. Later, when their children reach a different developmental stage, they may think differently. For other parents, there will be practical difficulties such as arranging baby-sitters or transport. It seems that the most effective format for parent education is one which combines guidance about promoting children's development with opportunities for parents to discuss their concerns (Hornby and Murray 1983). This type of format enables parents to learn new skills and gain confidence through talking to other parents and teachers. To be involved in parent education, therefore, teachers need to have listening and counselling skills and the skills of group facilitation (Hornby 1994).

Support

Some parents, at some times, are in need of supportive counselling, even though they may not actually request it. This support can be provided either individually or in group counselling sessions. Although such support should be available to all parents, the majority of parents seldom need extensive counselling. The fact is that, if parents have good channels of communication and regular liaison with teachers, coupled with the opportunity to receive guidance about their children whenever they need it, only a few of them will need counselling at any particular time. Whereas most parents are reluctant to seek the help of professional counsellors, they will approach their children's teachers in search of guidance or counselling for the problems which concern them. Teachers should therefore have a level of basic counselling skills sufficient to be good listeners and to help parents solve everyday problems. They should also have the knowledge necessary to be able to refer parents on to professional counsellors when problems raised are beyond their level of competence.

Using the model to guide parent involvement practice

Using the model described above a comprehensive scheme of PI can be designed to suit each school. The model can be used to generate a checklist designed to ensure that procedures are in place to meet parents' needs and to make sure that parents' potential contributions are being fully utilised. The checklist which follows provides examples of the kinds of questions which teachers need to ask when reviewing their school's policy and practice regarding PI. Each level of the model for PI will now be considered in turn and questions posed for teachers to consider.

Policy

Does the school have a separate written policy on parent involvement? Does the policy clearly specify parents' rights and responsibilities and is it included in material distributed to all parents and teachers?

Have parents been involved in the formulation of this policy? For example, have the PTA or parent governors had input into the policy design process?

What monitoring procedures are in place to ensure that the policy is implemented? For example, how is feedback obtained from parents?

Is there an active parent–teacher association at the school? What can be done to encourage more parents to participate in PTA activities?

What involvement do parents have in discussions about the aims of the school, the curriculum and other issues such as parent–teacher relationships? For example, are parents views sought about the school's policy for meeting SEN?

Is there a room set aside for parents' use? Do parents use a spare classroom, or can the staffroom be used by parents during lesson times?

What means are there for encouraging parents to become school governors? Are all teachers on the lookout for parents who would be effective in this role?

Are parents involved in in-service training? For example, have parents of children with SEN been invited to talk about their experiences, expectations, needs and possible contributions?

Who is responsible for ensuring that parents with a particular talent for leadership are identified and encouraged to put their abilities to use? Who identifies parents who could contribute to the school in capacities such as becoming a member of the PTA or governing body?

Resource

In what kinds of activities does the school welcome help from parents? Are parents used to listen to children read or to assist in teaching or in preparing classroom materials?

How are parents informed about the ways in which they can help at the school? Is there a parents' handbook or a regular newsletter?

How is voluntary help from parents organised within the school? For example, is a particular member of staff assigned to coordinate the help or is it seen as the responsibility of each teacher?

Collaboration

How do parents contribute to the assessment of their children's needs? For example, by being asked for their observations or by completing checklists.

How are the results of school assessments communicated to parents? Are individual parent–teacher meetings scheduled?

What input do parents have in deciding the goals and teaching priorities for their children? For example, do parents discuss with teachers the emphasis which should be placed on developing basic academic skills or social skills, as part of the personal and social education curriculum?

How are parents encouraged to reinforce school programmes at home? For example, are they expected to participate in a paired reading scheme?

Are parents given a choice about the level of their involvement at home with their children? Is there discussion with parents beforehand so that they are not pressured into projects which they cannot afford the time or energy to carry out?

How are parents of children with SEN involved in developing their children's Individual Educational Plan (IEP)? For example, do they attend all the meetings and have a chance to discuss their child with any outside specialists involved, such as peripatetic teachers, educational psychologists or speech therapists?

How is parental involvement in reviews of their children's progress optimised? For example, by obtaining their observations beforehand and being an active participant in review meetings.

Information

How is information on children's special needs, medical conditions and relevant family circumstances gathered from parents? Are home visits used in addition to parent–teacher meetings at school?

How is relevant information from parents disseminated to all members of staff who work with their children? What systems are used to record, and communicate to teachers, information about such things as children's special needs and the medication they require?

What use is made of parents' insights on their children? For example, parents' knowledge of their children's strengths and weaknesses, likes and dislikes, or how they respond to different approaches.

Communication

What activities are used to ensure that all parents establish contact with the school? Are performances or exhibitions of work by the pupils, social occasions or talks by well-known invited speakers used to attract large numbers of parents into the school?

How does the school pass on information to parents about their rights and responsibilities and about school organisation? For example, is this information disseminated by means of newsletters and handbooks specifically aimed at parents or by holding meetings at which school policies are discussed?

Does the school have balanced procedures for contacting parents? That is, are parents contacted to inform them of their children's achievements as well as their difficulties or are they only contacted when there is a problem?

Does a member of staff visit families before pupils start to attend the school? Are home visits scheduled when children are changing schools, moving from primary to secondary school or being reintegrated following a period in a special school?

What guidelines are available for parents on visiting the school to talk over a concern with their children's teachers? For example, do they have to go through the head teacher, make an appointment directly with the teacher, or just come in whenever they can.

What channels of communication are there between parents and teachers? That is, can parents choose to telephone, write notes or call in to the school as and when necessary?

Liaison

What are the frequency and purpose of parent–teacher meetings? For example, are parents invited to attend termly or yearly meetings to review their children's progress?

Do parents regularly receive home visits? Are home visits made at least once a year, or only when there is a problem? Are visits made by class teachers or senior members of staff? Is there flexibility in the time of day used so that both parents can be present?

How are home–school diaries used? For example, are they used for all children or just for ones with SEN or for those with behavioural difficulties? Are diaries used daily or weekly?

What kinds of formal reports are sent home? Are reports sent termly or yearly? Are progress reports sent separately to records of achievement?

Education

Are parents invited into the school to observe teaching in progress? For example, are they invited to observe either their own child or other children in the school?

When are teachers available to provide guidance to parents? Do teachers make home visits in order to provide guidance to parents or does this only occur in parent–teacher meetings at school?

Are parent workshops organised by the school? For example, are there workshops for parents of children with reading difficulties or behaviour problems or for parents whose children are about to leave school?

Are parents informed about opportunities for parent education in the community? Is information about parenting courses provided in the community made available to parents?

Support

How are parents given opportunities to discuss their concerns on a one-to-one basis? For example, is this done on home visits or in specially scheduled parent–teacher meetings at school?

Are opportunities provided for parents to share their concerns with other parents? For example, are parents introduced to other parents who have children with similar difficulties? Are they given the opportunity of attending parent workshops?

Do teachers know where to refer parents for supportive counselling? Is there an awareness of services and groups within the local community that can provide supportive counselling such as social workers or self-help groups?

Are parents encouraged to participate in support groups and parent organisations for SEN?

Research on PI

Surveys have recently been conducted of parental involvement in schools in the Canterbury region of New Zealand. This research investigated policies and practices of PI at primary, middle and secondary school levels. Canterbury is a region of approximately 480,000 people living in urban and rural areas. School principals were interviewed using the key questions based on the model for PI presented above. Results of the surveys showed that there was a wide diversity of practice of parental involvement in the schools (Hornby and Witte 2010a).

Survey findings showed that there were very few aspects of PI which all schools used and few which none used. It seems that there are excellent examples of PI practice in schools, but these are not consistent across all schools. The overall impression from analysing the results is that parental involvement is not paid as much attention in secondary schools as it is in primary and middle schools; also, that urban schools were not as effective in their implementation of PI as rural schools because of closer links with their local communities.

Some innovative practices were reported. Examples included the use of school websites and email to provide information and a channel of communication for parents. Another was the inclusion of self-review in school reports in order to involve parents in the process. In addition, prize and award ceremonies were used to get parents into schools to celebrate their children's successes.

There were also some notable gaps in the PI being used by schools. First, there was the lack of written school policies on PI in most schools. However, a few schools had written PI policies, which shows that they saw the value in documenting their policies and having them available for teachers and parents to read. It is considered that all schools need to develop written policies for parental involvement. These should set out all the different ways in which parents can be involved in their children's education as well as the procedures through which schools and teachers can help parents to accomplish this.

Second, an important finding was that minimal parent education was typically organised by schools and that referral of parents to parent education sessions available in the community was patchy. When children move from primary to middle or secondary schools the way in which parents are involved in their education changes. Involvement at school becomes less important, while involvement at home, such as in supervising homework and advising on subject option choices, becomes more important. Without appropriate parent education, parents may not realise this and may fail to provide the kind of support at home that will optimise their children's academic achievements at this level and in their further education.

Third, the finding that there was minimal use of home visits by school staff indicates under-use of this aspect of PI. Many parents of children with SEN appreciate it when teachers make home visits, which can be very helpful for teachers in building rapport with parents and in gaining understanding of children's home circumstances. It is important for schools to attempt to overcome difficulties related to home visits such as time constraints, issues of personal safety and some teachers' diffidence in relating to parents, in order to make use of this aspect of involving parents when it is appropriate.

Fourth, another important finding was the lack of specific ideas to involve parents from ethnically diverse backgrounds. Schools in New Zealand, as in many other countries around the world, are becoming more ethnically diverse. Many of these parents have English as a second language and come from countries with traditional schooling systems in which PI is not emphasized and therefore find it difficult to get involved with their children's schools. It is essential for schools to reach out to such parents so that they realise the importance of their involvement in their children's education. Therefore, schools need to work hard to develop innovative ways to involve these parents.

Fifth, the diversity of practice among the schools highlighted important aspects of PI which were in place at some schools but missing at others. Overall organisation of PI in the schools appeared ad hoc and very much related to the views and experience of principals. As Epstein (2001) suggests, what is needed in schools is a comprehensive system of parental involvement which includes key aspects of PI, as discussed in this article. In order to achieve this it is suggested that schools need to have a PI coordinator who is an experienced teacher or member of the school's senior management team. The first job of the PI coordinator should be to conduct an audit of parental involvement at the school and prepare a report for the school's principal and governing body in order to facilitate the development of a comprehensive system for PI at the school.

Finally, the finding that there was a lack of training for teachers on working with parents, both pre-service and in-service, suggests that the success of initiatives in improving PI may be limited until this situation changes. Teacher education programmes need to include rigorous courses on working with parents and ongoing professional development must be provided for practising teachers. Training needs to be focused on enabling teachers to be comfortable using the wide range of aspects of PI that have been identified in this research, which are found to be useful by schools.

These findings support the overall argument presented in this chapter. However, the lack of effective training for teachers in working with parents is not because it cannot be done, as can be shown by research carried out in England and India some years ago. It was demonstrated that teachers can learn the knowledge, attitudes and skills needed to work effectively with parents and that these teachers considered modules on working with parents to be some of the most important ones on their SEN training courses (see Hornby 2000).

In conclusion, it is considered that effective education of children with SEN in inclusive schools requires schools to implement the wide range of PI practices described in this chapter. In order to achieve this, teachers need to develop the relevant skills, attitudes and knowledge which have been discussed.

Bibliography

Clark, R. (1983) *Family Life and School Achievement: Why Poor Black Children Succeed or Fail*. Chicago: University of Chicago Press.

Cox, D. D. (2005) Evidence-based interventions using home–school collaboration. *School Psychology Quarterly*, 20 (4): 473–497.

Desforges, C. and Abouchaar, A. (2003) *The Impact of Parental Involvement, Parental Support and Family Education on Pupil Achievement and Adjustment*. Research report 433. London: Department for Education and Skills.

Epstein, J. L. (2001) *School, Family and Community Partnerships*. Boulder, CO: Westview Press.

Fan, X. and Chen, M. (2001) Parent involvement and students' academic achievement: a meta-analysis. *Educational Psychology Review*, 13 (1): 1–22.

Henderson, A. T. and Mapp, K. L. (2002) *A New Wave of Evidence: The Impact of School, Family and Community Connections on Student Achievement*. Austin, TX: Southwest Educational Development Laboratory.

Hornby, G. (1994) *Counselling in Child Disability*. London: Chapman and Hall.

Hornby, G. (2000) *Improving Parental Involvement*. London: Cassell.

Hornby, G. and Murray, R. (1983) Group programmes for parents of children with various handicaps. *Child: Care, Health and Development*, 9 (3): 185–198.

Hornby, G. and Lafaele, R. (2010) Parental involvement in education: the gap between rhetoric and reality. *Educational Review*.

Hornby, G. and Witte, C. (2010a) A survey of parental involvement in secondary schools in New Zealand. *School Psychology International*, in press.

Hornby, G. and Witte, C. (2010b) A survey of parental involvement in middle schools in New Zealand. *Pastoral Care in Education*, 28 (1): 59–69.

Hornby, G. and Witte, C. (2010c) Parent involvement in inclusive primary schools in New Zealand: implications for improving practice and for teacher education. *International Journal of Whole Schooling*, 6: 59–69.

Hornby, G., Hall, E. and Hall, C. (Eds). (2003) *Counselling Pupils in Schools: Skills and Strategies for Teachers*. London: RoutledgeFalmer.

Jeynes, W. H. (2007) The relation between parental involvement and urban secondary school student academic achievement: a meta-analysis. *Urban Education*, 42 (1): 82–110.

Pomerantz, E. M., Moorman, E. A. and Litwack, S. D. (2007) The how, whom and why of parents' involvement in children's academic lives: more is not always better. *Review of Educational Research*, 77 (3): 373–410.

Chapter 7

The role of schools in establishing home–school partnerships

Rob Ashdown (St Luke's Primary School, Scunthorpe, UK)

The nature of partnerships

This chapter aims to outline how schools might develop equal 'home–school partnerships' mainly with reference to work with parents of pupils with special educational needs (SEN). Note that the phrase 'home–school partnership' is deliberately used instead of 'parent–school partnership' because a range of family members and other people, other than those with parental responsibility, may need to be included in any partnerships (Carpenter 2001; Dale 1996). Throughout the chapter what is said of 'parents' should also largely apply to any family members or other people who function as the primary 'caregivers' or 'carers'. For instance, one or both natural parents could be absent on account of illness, work, divorce, separation or death. It is not necessarily the mother who is the primary caregiver; this could be the father, a grandparent or other family member, including a sibling, and friends. Other significant people to be involved in partnerships could be residential child-care officers, foster carers and paid workers who provide regular short-term breaks. Thus, schools should not have preconceived notions about the form that partnerships must take. Home–school partnerships may also involve a range of professionals from other agencies and voluntary organisations depending upon the particular needs of the pupil and their parents. The ability of the parents to meet the welfare and other needs of their child depends upon how well their own support needs are met. So schools have to know about and have good contacts with a range of supporting professionals and organisations, locally and nationally, who have the capacity to provide the support that is needed at home.

The English context

Much of what is reported here relates to the UK government's programmes and legislation and to activities undertaken in England but the ideas will have resonance with readers from elsewhere. An overarching theme in the Labour government's Children's Plan (DCSF 2007a) and its SEN Strategy in

England (DfES 2004) at the time of writing is the importance for a child's education of an effective home–school partnership. It is worth remembering that most pupils spend only about one-quarter to one-fifth of their waking hours at school during a full year and most of the rest of the time is spent with their parents. Successive legislation has progressively strengthened parents' rights and entitlements to have their views taken into account when it comes to determining their child's needs, the most appropriate educational provision and the priorities for learning. A SEN Code of Practice (DfES 2001) affirms the rights of parents and, in setting out requirements on schools to provide information and consult with parents, emphasises the need for a close working relationship between parents and teachers.

Despite these positive developments, various writers have suggested that all is not well; when asked, sometimes parents reported that they did not get the information to which they were entitled, that they felt ignored or patronised and, despite official 'open door' policies, that they did not always feel welcome in school or the classroom. Carpenter (2001) argued that the phrase 'partnership with parents' had developed a 'hollow ring'. He doubted whether working with parents had been given sufficient attention in policy, planning and practice, as schools directed their main efforts at the implementation of the National Curriculum introduced in 1989 and meeting the requirements of a endless flow of legislation. Similarly, Mittler (2000) wrote that there is a need to rethink the whole basis of home–school relationships for all children. He queried whether home–school links were high enough on the priority list at any level in the education system – school, local authority or central government. He too felt that the changes that had been sweeping through schools in the previous decade had been directed mainly at raising standards of teaching and learning. There had been little room for innovations in developing home–school partnerships.

> Despite all the fine words about working with parents, there is still a velvet curtain between home and school. Teachers and parents may be friendly, helpful and polite to one another but there is an unavoidable underlying tension that arises from the imbalance of power between them.
>
> (Mittler 2000: 151)

Mittler argued that the education system as a whole had become distanced from the communities it is supposed to serve. Many individual schools had developed and enriched their links with parents and the local community, but many others had simply been overwhelmed with meeting externally imposed targets and constant exhortations to change.

On the other hand, both Mittler and Carpenter do recognise that successive governments have committed resources to tackle the exclusion of parents from discussion and decision making about the education of their children. The government's Children's Plan (DCSF 2007a) promises that families will be at the centre of reshaped, integrated services that put their needs first, regardless of traditional institutional and professional structures. Schools are expected to develop a new role as the centre of their communities and to work closely with other schools, the National Health Service and local authority children's services to engage parents and surmount the barriers to the learning and well-being of every child (DCSF 2008). *Every Parent Matters* (DCSF 2007b) outlines measures designed to help all parents shape the development of their children's provision. For instance, the school Self-evaluation Form, which schools are expected to update regularly as part of the school inspection process, asks schools to indicate how they gather the views of parents and to give examples of action taken as a result of their expressed opinions and those of other stakeholders. It is now almost commonplace for schools to routinely sample parental views about the school through anonymised questionnaires, structured interviews and focus groups. Moreover, parents can make up one-third of each school's governing body, and parent governors are encouraged in government literature and through its websites for governors and parents to both support and challenge the leadership of their child's school. By 2010 all schools are required, through links with local providers, agencies, and other schools, to provide access to a core offer of 'extended services', such as child care, parenting support and community use of facilities, including family learning. Schools are actively encouraged to seek with partners how to improve access to information, support and advice for parents, including parenting programmes, and address needs of parents facing specific challenges. The extended schools agenda is very challenging but could well give parents much-needed and valued support and, as a result, could result in improvements to home–school partnerships.

Models for home–school partnerships

A number of texts have discussed the needs of parents and ways of involving them in their child's education at home and at school (some particularly useful texts are Carpenter 1997; Dale 1996; Hornby 2000; Wall 2006). There is not the space here or the need to describe fully the various models for home–professional relationships. Historically, the balance has shifted from models that presented professionals, including teachers, as the sole experts on what needed doing, to a situation in which parents, as consumers, can exert a degree of control over the development and selection of services for their child. Increasingly, it was acknowledged that the home was a potentially important learning setting and, initially, professionals aimed to transplant their skills and expertise into parents, typically by organising workshops to train them to use professional techniques, particularly in relation to behaviour modification. Now, it is recognised that parents are 'children's first and most enduring educators' (DCSF 2007a: 11) and that the professionals have much to learn from them. Overall, the pervading message is that, when parents and teachers work together, the results have a positive impact on children's development and learning. Parents are seen as the expert on their child, whereas teachers, and other professionals, are the experts on the curriculum, personalised learning, resources and general approaches to teaching.

Carpenter (2001) suggests that the lessons that may be learned from these various models can be summarised in the following list of recommendations to all parties:

1   Be honest with each other.
2   Be willing to learn from each other.
3   Treat each other with respect and dignity.
4   Be willing to admit you make mistakes.
5   Work collaboratively and cooperatively.
6   Be yourself.

Carpenter writes both as a professional and as a parent of a child with SEN. However, it is very difficult for most professionals to truly appreciate how the birth of, and life with, a child with a disability impacts on family life. For the most part these are ordinary families who have to cope with extraordinary pressures because they happen to have a disabled child. They have to acquire knowledge, experience and skills on the job and rapidly. Hanrahan (2005) speculates what the job description would be for the parent of a child with a disability and makes plain how extremely demanding and stressful it can be to support one's child right across the life span. Parents have to be able to negotiate to gain support for this job; they need to be determined, assertive and proactive, accept that they are in a minority and accept that they and their child will be discriminated against throughout their lives. Tellingly, Mittler (2000: 170) quotes from Russell (1997) the following plea to professionals from a focus group of parents:

- Please accept and value our children (and ourselves as families) as we are
- Please celebrate difference
- Please try and accept our children as children first. Don't attach labels to them unless you mean to *do* something.
- Please recognise your power over our lives. We live with the consequences of your opinions and decisions.
- Please understand the stress that many families are under. The cancelled appointment, the waiting list no one gets to the top of, all the discussion about resources – it's *our* lives you're talking about.

- Don't put fashionable fads and treatments onto us unless you are going to be around to see them through. And don't forget families have many members, many responsibilities. Sometimes, we can't please everyone.
- Do recognise that sometimes we are right! Please believe us and listen to what we know that we and our child need.
- Sometimes we are sad, tired and depressed. Please value us as caring and committed families and try to go on working with us.

A particularly disadvantaged group of families are those from minority ethnic groups. Shah (1996) refers to the 'silent minority' of families with disabled children who experience the multiple prejudices of racism, poverty and misunderstanding about the wishes and feelings of families in the Asian community. She notes the barriers of inadequate information and lack of interpreters and the relatively poor housing and poverty which these families experience. Many cannot speak or write English, and they often have little knowledge of services that might support them. It may be argued that similar difficulties are experienced by the recent influx of families from countries in the extended European Union, notably those from Poland, and also refugees from other countries and war zones.

Some ways of involving parents

I. Policies

All schools are required to have a range of policies. For instance, the 'SEN policy' should include information about the school's provision for children with SEN, ways of providing access to the curriculum, arrangements for dealing with parental concerns and arrangements for eliciting and incorporating parents' views into formal assessments of SEN and subsequent reviews of any special arrangements for meeting these. Schools are required to have a 'Disability Equality Scheme' which is supposed to detail what is done to ensure equal treatment of its pupils, and any others involved in the school community, with any form of disability. Schools are further required to publish prospectuses and their procedures for dealing with parental complaints as well as informing parents about a range of policies that they must have (e.g. behaviour and discipline, admissions, dealing with common medical needs).

Of course, as Mittler (2000) points out, every policy has to go beyond fine words about principles and the true proof of a policy is how well it sets out how principles are to be translated into practice, how often it is reviewed and how much pupils, parents, governors and other members of the school community are involved in the initial formulation and review of the policy.

Ofsted, the office with responsibility for evaluating standards in education through the process of inspection, inquires into and reports on how
well each school works in partnership with others to promote learners' well-
being. Its inspectors will seek and comment on parents' views on the school.
It has been suggested that a home–school policy could be very worthwhile if
produced in consultation with parents and related to explicit planning and
actions (e.g. Mittler 2000; Farrell 2008). Carpenter (2001) explains how
Sunfield School, an independent residential special school, wrote a 'Family
Charter' which was developed and ratified by a consultation group of
families. The aim of this charter was to open two-way channels of communication and establish a partnership that was based on shared aims, principles
and aspirations. The charter opened with a clear statement of purpose and
articulated what families could expect of the school: respect, honesty and
integrity, confidentiality, regular communication, empathy, supportive listening, information, partnership, a safe environment. Importantly, these ideals
were backed up by concrete ways in which the school would fulfil these
goals: regular reports on pupils' progress, home–school diaries, systematic
telephone calls, provision of a parent information base, family fun days,
regular newsletters and so on.

2. Communication, listening and shared problem solving

If questionnaires are well constructed, the responses received from families
can be invaluable when evaluating current provision and planning future improvements. For instance, in the case of the special school where the author
works, surveys showed that parents valued the work of the school highly
but a significant proportion indicated that they would welcome more guidance on child development and the implications of particular disabilities.
Progressively, planning for 'parent training' has become better organised in
the school and consumes increasing staff time and effort necessitating careful
planning and budgeting for costs within the school development plan.

Teachers are expected to display genuineness, respect and empathy towards parents and active listening and negotiation are key to resolving any
differences and ensuring that all parties are in agreement about needs, targets and strategies. Both Dale (1996) and Hornby (2000) provide excellent
discussions of the knowledge and skills required for meaningful face-to-face
engagement. In the case of children with SEN, both individual statements of
SEN and Individual Education Plans required to address a child's learning
difficulties at school must be reviewed regularly as set out in the SEN Code
of Practice (DfES 2001). These represent a formal opportunity for eliciting
and listening to the views of parents about not only their child's progress
and needs, but also the family's needs. These meetings can be mismanaged
badly (Russell 2003; Wedell 2008) but can also be managed so that they are
'friendly' for parents and genuinely focus on their views and needs rather

than being a routine presentation of the reports of the various professionals. The professionals should be prepared to listen and show in their behaviour that they are listening – attitudes and skills which are seldom addressed during their initial teacher training. Active listening not only entails showing attentiveness and interest by body language but also demands that professionals should be skilled in seeking for the meaning behind parents' words, paraphrasing what they have said to check that they have got it right, drawing the parents out if other things need to be said and above all resisting the temptation to expound their own opinions or philosophy before they have heard properly the parents' story and learned what their views and needs truly are. Circumstances may often dictate, for instance, that the teacher's report for a review meeting be taken as read because the time available needs to be dedicated to fully discussing effective behaviour management strategies for home and school. Often, the time available may run out and another meeting may have to be set up to explore issues further. Sometimes issues are raised which indicate that the parents need support from a range of agencies and professionals so that they can meet the needs of their child and this may call for the school to initiate a common assessment using the national Common Assessment Framework (CWDC 2007) and organise follow-up meetings of all parties concerned to formulate plans. At all costs, it is important that parents are put at ease and feel able to discuss the issues that matter to them and their child and that the outcome is that action is taken to support them in addressing these.

3. Home visits

Home visiting by professionals is not favoured by all parents but many do welcome these and Mittler (2000, 2008) argues that they should happen before each child starts school and at least once per year thereafter if the gulf between home and school is to be bridged. Is there, he asks, any possibility of a return to the concept of home–school liaison teachers (see Wall 2006) that were touted in the 1960s but never took off nationally? Home visits make it possible to identify needs for support at home (e.g. information about child development, ideas for behaviour management or teaching personal self-care, improvements to the accommodation, putting up secure fencing, addressing moving and handling and other health issues). When a child is first due to start school, home visits provide a context for information gathering and a way of introducing the child to the professionals who will be their educators. They are also a means for giving parents the information that they need about the child's school: what they may reasonably expect of the teaching staff and what the school expects of them. A possible model for the conduct of home visits comes from the Portage home-visiting educational service for pre-school children with additional support needs and their families (www.portage.org.uk). Support offered through Portage aims to help parents to be confident in their key role of home educator whatever their child's needs may be. A Portage home visitor makes regular visits and works alongside parents to identify their child's strengths and goals for future learning, identify practical activities for implementation at home and help in recognising their child's progress. Significantly, the author's experience is that this positive input can be missed keenly by parents when their child starts school and Portage involvement ceases.

4. Sharing information about the child

There are many ways in which it is valuable for schools to work with parents to share information about their child and agree learning targets and teaching strategies. Three examples here will have to suffice. First, children who present challenging behaviours require consistent approaches to behaviour management across all settings enshrined in individual behaviour plans (IBPs). Parents will want to know that their child is treated appropriately and have much to contribute when it comes to identifying their child's strengths, needs, targets and strategies. They will have a great deal of knowledge about their child and will have a fund of information about the circumstances under which undesirable behaviours may occur and what may be sustainable as management strategies for IBPs. Second, they want to contribute to their child's education by continuing at home with work that is done in school. *Routes for Learning* is a set of assessment materials for children with profound and multiple learning difficulties produced for use by teachers in Wales (Qualifications and Curriculum Group 2006). The focus is on early communication, social interaction and cognitive skills that are crucial for all future learning. The materials offer ways of recording small-steps progress and target setting, and there is great potential for promoting discussion and consensus between teaching staff and parents about strategies for teaching. Finally, parents will want to be closely involved in the planning for transition at key stages in their child's school career: on entry to school, on transfer from the primary to the secondary phase and on leaving school to access further education in its various forms. There are very important considerations for schools and opportunities to cement home–school partnerships here (see Ashdown and Darlington 2007; Ashdown, Lee and Darlington 2008).

5. Media for home–school communication

Pupils with SEN often have communication difficulties and may not easily tell their parents what they have done in school or things they have experienced. So regular home–school communication is essential. The telephone is often the best way of having a useful exchange of information, particularly if parents have difficulties with writing. Commonly, schools will have a 'home–school book' (see Hornby 2000). This may be no more than a simple exercise book that travels to and from home in the pupil's bag but it could be a structured journal incorporating information about homework activities as well. The home–school book, in whatever form, should be there for both parents and staff to use. Frequency of communication can be an issue as busy teachers may not have the time or need to write daily and entries in the book are necessarily brief because the teacher may have to contribute to several books. The main value of a home–school book is to convey messages about positive happenings or things the child did. They are not the best place to raise sensitive issues or concerns (e.g. medical problems, challenging behaviour).

School and class newsletters seem to be much valued by many parents for the details they provide about activities experienced by the pupils, forthcoming events and activities, and general news and information of interest. The better school websites tend to have well-organised bulletin boards or accounts of events that are regularly updated.

6. Visiting arrangements

Visiting arrangements for parents can facilitate or frustrate attempts to form good home–school partnerships. In the case of many schools, parents may live well away from the school and it is to be hoped that these schools will want parents to feel able to visit during school hours for networking opportunities or to participate in activities or to meet their child's teacher. Of course, any visitors to a class may disrupt normal activities somewhat but teachers can prepare for this eventuality. Much depends upon how welcoming the teacher is and a school policy should stress the importance of these visits for parents and staff conduct. The need may arise for parents to discuss some aspect of their child's education at length or see a particular activity, and the school's willingness to engage in such meetings will be important to parents (Russell 2003).

7. Parent support programmes

There is a bewildering array of parenting support programmes available and there is no doubt that many can have positive outcomes (Rogers, Hallam and Shaw 2008). A real problem for schools is deciding which ones are most likely to be cost-effective and appropriate for identified needs. The UK government has recently established a National Academy for Parenting Practitioners (NAPP) to support the training of professionals who work with parents and act as a national centre providing advice on parenting and parenting support. NAPP has developed a web-based 'commissioning toolkit' (http://www.commissioningtoolkit.org) which provides comprehensive information about many parenting programmes. The searchable online database outlines for each programme its target audience, content, training requirements, aims and, most importantly, a measure of their quality and effectiveness. For example, it holds details about the 'Family Links Programme'. This is a universal programme designed for families of children aged 2–15 aimed at enhancing empathy between parent and child, leading to more effective and positive parenting. It is a ten-week group-based programme and the learning methods include parental handouts and role plays. There is a book called *The Parenting Puzzle* (Hunt and Mountford 2003) which gives a flavour of the programme and makes it available to everyone including people who cannot attend a group. The programme is based on social learning, behavioural and attachment theories and is built around core elements of self-awareness and self-esteem, appropriate expectations, positive discipline and empathy. It covers communication, effective discipline techniques and behaviour management. The programme is delivered at the author's school by teaching staff who attended an initial training course for accreditation and regular network meetings. Evaluations from parents who have gone through the course suggest they were very satisfied with it and felt that it had made or could make beneficial changes in their lives. Key factors appear to be the mutual support and feedback from other parents and the way the trainers put the parents at ease. NAPP notes that research shows that parents report an increased sense of empathy with their child and a better understanding of how to meet their child's emotional and behavioural development and manage any problems.

The author has found that the UK government's 'Early Support' programme provides good materials for working with parents of young children with disabilities. There is a website (www.earlysupport.org.uk) which provides downloadable materials for use with parents including information about particular categories of special needs such as cerebral palsy, multisensory impairment and autistic spectrum disorders (ASD). These materials could provide useful handouts for schools seeking to develop support packages for parents.

Some local authorities and schools have sought accreditation to use a comprehensive package for parents of children with ASD which is available through the National Autistic Society (NAS) (www.nas.org.uk). This is the 'Early Bird' programme, which is a three-month programme combining training sessions for groups of up to six sets of parents with individual home visits. Parents have to make significant commitments – to training sessions, home visits and ongoing work with their child at home. The aim of the programme is to reduce parental stress, modify their communication styles and develop more positive perceptions of their children. This programme is for parents of children under 5 years of age, but the NAS has developed a modified version, called 'Early Bird Plus', to meet the needs of families whose children are aged from 4 to 8 years. The programme provides a potential model for schools to develop their own intervention packages that match their particular physical, financial and human resources more precisely, perhaps using the increasing range of quality, accessible materials such as the Early Support materials cited above.

Many professionals have valuable skills and knowledge to share with parents. Again at the author's school, speech and language therapists have worked closely with the teaching staff to develop 'surgeries' and workshops for parents about various aspects of language teaching: language pro-grammes, use of pictorial communication folders and profiles of children that travel with the child and help people to understand their skills, abilities and needs.

Conclusions

Healthy home–school partnerships are crucial to the well-being of the pupil, and family support from schools can take many different forms. In the face of developments in knowledge about parenting support, including the value of new ICT-based technologies, and new accountabilities, schools cannot afford to be laggards in developing services that are responsive to parents' needs and views. There is a real expectation that they must continually and actively seek ways of strengthening home–school links and work towards empowering parents. Parents should be respected and their wishes, feelings, priorities and contributions to their child's education should be valued by teaching staff.

Ways of supporting pupils and their families demand careful considera-tion of the types of activity that are most likely to engage all family members. Partnerships cannot be taken for granted; they need to be established and carefully nurtured and their success or failure ultimately depends upon the attitudes and skills of the teaching staff and their willingness to foster equal-ity within the home–school partnerships.

Bibliography

Ashdown, R. and Darlington, C. (2007) Special school reorganisation by a local unitary authority: some lessons learned. *Support For Learning*, 22 (3): 137–144.

Ashdown, R., Lee, B. and Darlington, C. (2008) Transition planning in special schools. *PMLD–Link*, 20 (2): 5–7.

Carpenter, B. (Ed.) (1997) *Families in Context: Emerging Trends in Family Support and Early Intervention*. London: David Fulton.

Carpenter, B. (2001) Enabling partnership: families and schools. In B. Carpenter, R. Ashdown and K. Bovair (Eds) *Enabling Access: Effective Teaching and Learning for Pupils with Learning Difficulties*, 2nd edition. London: David Fulton.

CWDC. (2007) *Common Assessment Framework for Children and Young People: Practitioners' Guide: Integrated Working to Improve Outcomes for Children and Young People*. Leeds: Children's Workforce Development Council.

Dale, N. (1996) *Working with Families of Children with Special Needs: Partnership and Practice*. London: Routledge.

DCSF. (2007a) *The Children's Plan: Building Brighter Futures*. Cm 7280. London: The Stationery Office.

DCSF. (2007b) *Every Parent Matters*. Annesley, Nottingham: DCSF Publications.

DCSF. (2008) *The Children's Plan – One Year On: A Progress Report*. Annesley, Nottingham: DCSF Publications.

DfES. (2001) *Code of Practice on the Identification and Assessment of Special Educational Needs*, 2nd edition. London: HMSO.

DfES. (2004) *Removing Barriers to Achievement; The Government's Strategy for SEN*. Annesley, Nottingham: DfES Publications.

Farrell, M. (2008) *The Special School's Handbook: Key Issues for All*. Abingdon: Routledge.

Hanrahan, G. (2005) 'Parent of a disabled child' – would you apply for this job? *PMLD–Link*, 17 (2): 6–8.

Hornby, G. (2000) *Improving Parental Involvement*. London: Cassell.

Hunt, C. and Mountford, A. (2003) *The Parenting Puzzle: How to Get the Best out of Family Life*. Cowley, Oxford: Family Links.

Mittler, P. (2000) *Working towards Inclusive Education: Social Contexts*. London: David Fulton.

Mittler, P. (2008) Planning for the 2040s: everybody's business. *British Journal of Special Education*, 35 (1): 3–10.

Qualifications and Curriculum Group. (2006) *Routes For Learning: Assessment Materials for Learners with Profound Learning Difficulties and Additional Disabilities*. Cardiff: Department for Education, Lifelong Learning and Skills.

Rogers, L., Hallam, S. and Shaw, J. (2008) Do generalist parenting programmes improve children's behaviour and attendance at school. *British Journal of Special Education*, 35 (1): 16–25.

Russell, F. (2003) Expectations of parents of disabled children. *British Journal of Special Education*, 30 (3): 144–149.

Russell, P. (1997) Parents as partners: some early impressions of the Code of Practice. In S. Wolfendale (Ed.) *Working with Parents after the Code of Practice*. London: David Fulton.

Shah, R. (1996) *The Silent Minority: Children with Disabilities in Asian Families*, 2nd edition. London: National Children's Bureau.

Wall, K. (2006) *Special Needs and Early Years: A Practitioner's Guide*, 2nd edition. London: Paul Chapman Publishing.

Wedell, K. (2008) Seeing each other's points of view. *British Journal of Special Education*, 35 (1): 56–57.

Pupils as partners in inclusive education

Chapter 8

Valuing and learning from young people

Michael Shevlin (Trinity College Dublin, Ireland)

Many children and young people who have disabilities and/or special educational needs experience significant difficulties in developing autonomy in
learning and independence in their social lives within schools. This chapter will provide an overview of and an insight into the critical factors that
can constrain the academic and social development of these young people.
Drawing upon recent research the chapter will present the voices of these
young people as they reflect on and attempt to address these limiting factors
that inhibit their full participation within school life. The young people will
address a whole spectrum of access issues including physical, social and curricular that can have a profound effect on their capacity to participate. This
chapter will further consider how schools have and can develop structures
that promote awareness and positive expectations for these young people to
enable them to become active participants in their own learning.

Schools as a microcosm of society are experiencing the challenges
inherent in the inclusion agenda that seeks to promote and enhance the participation of marginalised groups in critical areas such as education, health
and the workplace. As a result, schools are key agents in addressing the
marginalisation experienced by children and young people with disabilities
and/or special educational needs among others. Children and young people
with disabilities and/or special educational needs have experienced marginalisation within schools; their participation has often been questioned and
their inclusion is heavily conditional. Within this context it is evident that
enabling young people with disabilities and/or special educational needs to
become active participants in school life will require proactive leadership
and a re-examination of traditional practices within schools. Implicit beliefs and practices about learning and notions of capability will inevitably
be challenged in this process. Teacher knowledge and understanding about
assessment, for example, will be confronted by alternative means of assessing learning and representing pupil knowledge and understanding (Hanafin,
Shevlin and Flynn 2002). The whole concept of assessment and validation of
learning contained within current assessment systems is stretched as government policies mandate equitable approaches and the creation of equitable

opportunities for marginalised groups to participate within the education system. The concept of 'reasonable accommodation' has been particularly contentious as critics believe that this type of accommodation lowers standards and confers unfair advantage. Teachers and schools face real difficulties in attempting to create inclusive learning environments as mandated in the Education for Special Educational Needs (EPSEN) Act (2004) within an Irish context. Teachers face real dilemmas in how to promote learning for pupils with disabilities and/or special educational needs. Lack of knowledge and insufficient experience in working with these children and young people is a contributory factor in the difficulties that teachers experience. Lack of knowledge about specific disabling conditions (and/or special educational needs) and the consequent implications for pupil learning adds greatly to teacher uncertainty and provides the context for some of the examples of less than inclusive practice cited within this chapter. There is little alternative to the inclusion process otherwise these children and young people of concern will become 'shadow' participants whose school lives will be characterised by dependence and a form of second-class belonging.

Facilitating active engagement for these pupils in school life will involve a concerted effort to seek out their voices and ensure that as a starting point they are involved in all the decision-making processes that affect their lives (Lewis and Porter 2007). Within this chapter young people with disabilities speak to critical issues that affect their participation in schools; the lack of knowledge and awareness; coping with how difference is construed and attributed; developing autonomy in school life and peer relationships; the representation of their views and concerns. From this informed perspective we can begin the process of developing a school environment that encourages and facilitates the participation of young people with disabilities and/or special educational needs on an equal basis alongside their non-disabled peers.

Background

The attitudinal issues and implicit expectations underlying educational provision for children and young people with disabilities and/or special educational needs are rarely critically examined and challenged. Priestley (2001) points out that there are numerous examples of negative portrayals of disability and that institutional discourses often focus on tragedy, medicalisation and otherness that result in the child being characterised as dependent and needy. The discursive categories employed in relation to these children are dominated by narratives of charity, intervention and treatment; as Priestley (2001) comments, this suggests non-reciprocal processes. This argument is reiterated by Gray (2002), who suggested that many established school policies and practices failed to acknowledge the influence of negative portrayals of disability and their practical consequences within school environments.

Although these issues have been initially raised in relation to disabled children it is fair to say that these insights have equal relevance for children with special educational needs. Lewis, Robertson and Parsons (2005) observed that despite good intentions all aspects of education can be affected by the implicit negative characterisation of these marginalised children. School policies and practices often fail to take account of how disability and/or special educational needs are conceptualised among teaching/support staff and peer group and how these underpinning belief systems could have negative consequences in practice for young people with disabilities and/or special educational needs (Gray 2002). Within this chapter the related themes of access, ambition and achievement will be examined as pupil voice will provide an insight into their experiences in relation to these critical issues within their school lives.

Access

The study by Kenny, Mc Neela, Shevlin and Daly (2000) illustrated many of the difficulties encountered by children and young people with disabilities as they attempted to negotiate their way through a complex, sometimes hostile environment. Personal needs often entered the public domain and, although teachers were supportive, this primary pupil had to access quite distinct toileting arrangements from his peers:

> It was a very old school and our parish priest got a ramp put in. If I wanted to go to the toilet, the cubicles were very small; I had to go to the teachers' room. They knew and I had someone outside the door just in case they'd come. It wasn't too bad.
>
> (p. 23)

Another pupil was extremely grateful for access arrangements and did not question the appropriateness of teacher involvement rather than the employment of a personal assistant:

> The primary school I went to was very good; the teachers were excellent to me. They put in a special wheelchair toilet for me you know? And some of them went so far as – taking me to the toilet. Which was very good of them.
>
> (p. 24)

Access to the built environment had a profound impact on curricular access and peer relationships. This speaker located her curricular access difficulty at the systemic level:

> I did Home Economics for my Junior and Leaving Cert. . . . . Myself and my teacher wanted a low accessible kitchen unit for me but they wouldn't give it. (Q: Who?) The architects and the government . . . the Principal.
>
> (p. 24)

The ability of pupils to gain physical access intersected, not only with access to academic options, but also with social interactions:

> If a class was downstairs, no problem. But stairs, there'd be a problem. Prefabs were a big problem, big steps into them, I had to be lifted. If my friends weren't around I wouldn't get there. I wouldn't go to the class.
>
> (p. 24)

Participants struggled to keep the system constantly reminded of what they needed – though often the reminders went unnoticed and essential pupil needs became invisible:

> There were glass fire doors, I couldn't open them. I went to the Principal, I went to everyone and they did nothing. . . . If I wanted to go to the bathroom during class, or if I was carrying something for art, it was a long way. There were really steep ramps and twice I fell. I'd have to wait for someone to help me. But you get used to it after a while.
>
> (p. 24)

> You had to fight. One girl had spina bifida. She couldn't handle the crowds; there were 1200 in the school. She left.
>
> (p. 24)

Lack of appropriate access supports for pupils had implications for peer relationships as in the following instance in which pupil safety was endangered:

> I had to go up four flights of stairs to get to my classroom and I had to come down before the rest. If I came down at the same time as them they'd just push; they basically knocked me down one flight of stairs.
>
> (p. 24)

'Asking for help' on a regular basis portrayed a vulnerable person who was overly dependent on peers for essential support:

> It was kind of difficult just to get around. And asking for help, I found that difficult. I didn't like asking the same person all the time . . . Some people would make a fuss over me and others wouldn't think – it was a mixture of reactions.
>
> (p. 25)

If I had a class upstairs I'd wait at the end of the stairs. They'd physically lift me, my friends. My friends were excellent.

(p. 25)

There has been evidence that schools are often well intentioned in relation to responding appropriately to the learning and social needs of children with disabilities and/or special educational needs (Lewis *et al.* 2005; Shevlin and Rose 2003). However, there can be problematic links between generalised kindness and pity as illustrated by a pupil comment in the Kenny *et al.* (2000) study:

People of authority like the Principal, would always ask me how I was . . . or if I needed a lift home or things like that but it was – like if a person with a disability came to the school 'oh look at that person' . . . It was horrible. Everyone was kind of saying 'oh the little girl she's deadly' – too much emphasis on her. There hadn't been enough people with disabilities integrating with people without disabilities.

(p. 23)

Lewis *et al.* (2005) highlighted the significant exclusion of children with disabilities from extra-curricular activities. Participation in certain activities was possible only with parental support and there were many examples of inadequate planning to take account of children's particular access requirements. Burgess (2003) cited instances of exclusion from school trips and extra-curricular activities. As Burgess pointed out, these types of activities often represent an opportunity to explore and develop peer relationships that is denied to these children and young people. Palmer (2006) reiterated the importance of enabling this type of participation and asserted that children with disabilities and/or special educational needs should not be denied 'everyday adventures' (p. 60).

Participation in extra-curricular activities was not guaranteed; the same wide variation in system responses pertained. Some schools were positively prepared as described in Kenny *et al.*'s (2000) study:

I went on a lot of trips. The other students had to make their own way; we got transport no problem from school.

(p. 32)

Even in schools with a positive disposition there were limits to participation:

Everybody had to do the school musical. I found I actually enjoyed it and it was one of the things I could be involved in. Then in transition year there were a lot of activities like swimming and trips, they wouldn't let me do for insurance reasons.

(p. 32)

One pupil speculated that his exclusion from extra-curricular activities was due to an 'over protective' attitude:

> I was excluded from my groups as far as going out with the class – I think they were nearly afraid I would hurt myself.
>
> (p. 32)

Some speakers felt they were left out simply because nobody thought of them:

> They didn't make an effort to think about it when it came to trips. Most times we couldn't go.
>
> (p. 32)

Another pupil felt his exclusion very keenly as the exclusion process extended to beyond the actual trip or outing:

> I would listen to them when they came back – 'you missed a great couple of days we'd great fun'. Even sitting beside them hearing them laughing, it was laughing at something you didn't understand. I didn't like that.
>
> (p. 32)

Ambition and achievement

Ambition for children and young people with disabilities and/or special educational needs is informed by a variety of intersecting factors including assumptions and expectations, the provision of appropriate supports and the recognition that the pupil concerned has a right to be fully involved in decisions affecting their education.

The attitudinal issues and expectations that inform provision need to be rigorously examined. There appears to be a tendency towards over-protectiveness as reported by a number of young people in research studies. In the Educable study (2000) (also reported in Horgan 2003), for example, young people with disabilities were trained to become researchers and investigate the school experiences of other young people with disabilities. As part of the project the Educable group of researchers reflected on their own experiences of education. One young woman commented that in the special school she attended:

> they couldn't let you do that [talk about having sex] because the cotton wool would be broken. The cotton wool that they wrap you up in the day you start. Then by the time you leave, the cotton wool has pretty much smothered you.
>
> (p. 17)

As a result these young people felt inadequately prepared for the adult world they subsequently entered. This well-intentioned adult world was evident in other settings, as participants in Wilson and Jade's (1999) study reported that teachers:

> treated them like 'Babies', giving them work which was too easy and not expecting enough of them. This was particularly true for students with speech and language difficulties, or who used wheelchairs.
>
> (p. 5)

These types of assumptions can become firmly embedded in school provision and practice. This can be particularly problematic where the school employs a streaming mechanism for class placement rather than mixed-ability groupings. Initial assumptions about ability will be a key determining factor in class placement. These children and young people can have their abilities seriously underestimated and as a result end up being placed in an unsuitable class setting where programmes are below their ability level, as reported in Kenny *et al.*'s (2000) study:

> I was in the second lowest class. I stuck that for three weeks and I said I'm not staying here, they were giving me real basic stuff . . . A lot of my class left [school]. They weren't interested basically.
>
> (p. 26)

In this particular situation the young person joined a seriously disaffected class grouping who had very negative views on schooling and she had to challenge the placement. There can also be a widespread perception that children and young people who have disabilities and/or special educational needs will not be able to meet the demands of the ordinary curriculum.

Within an Irish context students with certain disabilities (dyslexia/physical and/or sensory disability) are exempted from studying Irish and for two participants it was decided to exempt them without any discussion. This may have been motivated by kindness, a desire not to further burden these young people, though that is not how these young people viewed this decision. These young people perceived that this exemption separated them from others in the class as Irish is a compulsory subject and they felt deprived of this opportunity; as one participant stated, 'it was taken away from me'. This type of exemption had further consequences, some far-reaching, for their future educational career. For one, class placement was partially determined by proficiency in the Irish language:

> In the entrance exam they gave me everything except Irish. If they'd given me Irish I would have been in a higher class. I was supposed to have been in a higher class.
>
> (Kenny *et al.* 2000: 27)

Studying for examinations at the appropriate level is also a critical factor in order to access routes into higher education. This young person with a physical disability attributed the teacher decision to assign her to a less demanding course to lowered expectations and a belief that she would be unable to cope with the academic demands of a more challenging programme, as recounted in Kenny *et al.*'s (2000) study:

> [The teacher] told me I wasn't suitable for the higher class. But I got into it and I got a B1. She just assumed that because I had the disability I should be in the lower class.
>
> (p. 27)

This student was able to prove her capacity and later in the interview revealed how she had successfully challenged the initial teacher decision though this was not achieved without personal cost:

> This teacher told the rest I should go into lower pass. I went to the headmistress and said I wanted to go into the other class, and she said yes. Then the teacher I didn't want to go to gave out hell to me. She said I was opening a can of worms, and how dare I not want to go into her class.
>
> (p. 30)

Mac Arthur, Sharp, Kelly and Gaffney (2007) and Priestley (2001) maintain that these types of attitudes are often informed by a tragedy and charity discourse prevalent within society. As a result, these children are often characterised as passive, dependent, vulnerable and part of a homogeneous group whose learning needs are qualitatively different from their peers. From this perspective it appears reasonable that these children and young people should be protected and academic demands and challenges should be minimised. Participants in Kenny *et al.*'s (2000) study provide ample evidence that this perception can heavily influence teacher views of the capabilities of the pupils concerned. The following speaker, who had dyslexia, encountered this type of negative teacher expectation in her school:

> If you're dyslexic you won't be going anywhere so let's not bother, . . . So there was an attitude that if you have something wrong with you you don't have to reach the same standards others do.
>
> (p. 28)

The young person had to draw on her own resources to counter this negative assumption about her capacity to learn and have a worthwhile academic future:

I always set myself, my standards many times too high because I thought at least if you reach high you'll get somewhere.

(p. 28)

Poor examination results from a student with a physical disability elicited a sympathetic response, almost an acceptance that this was not unexpected, a reaction in direct contrast to similar performances from members of her class group:

If I got bad results in the exams it was try better next time as if . . . Whereas if anyone else got a bad result there was an in depth . . .

(p. 28)

In another school a student with a physical disability reported that teachers were finally convinced of her abilities when she performed well in the state examinations:

They did once I got my junior cert results to a certain degree because it went up by nearly two grades in a lot of subjects and some of the teachers were kind of a ok she's telling the truth.

(Kenny *et al.*, 2000, p.3 Unpublished transcript)

However, this student subsequently moved school to undertake senior cycle and encountered similar lowered expectations:

and then I moved school like I know I moved straight away and the whole thing started again really and it was all over again.

(Kenny *et al.*, 2000, p.3 Unpublished transcript)

Watson, Shakespeare, Cunningham-Burley, Barnes, Corker, Davis and Priestley (1999) observed that unwarranted differential treatment of children and young people with disabilities was quite common in their study, as these students were exempted from many normal requirements for punctuality and homework and this often caused resentment among their peer group and added to a sense of difference. This perception could be reinforced by separate seating arrangements and there was a propensity for schools to characterise these young people as qualitatively different from their peers through the discourse employed and the social organisation of the environment and support arrangements.

Generalised kindness can become pity and pedagogic decisions could be informed by this perspective where the student with a physical disability is not expected to complete the routine work expected from his/her peers, as illustrated by a participant in Kenny *et al.*'s (2000) study:

If I didn't do my homework they wouldn't really mind.

(p. 30)

Another participant was quite amused by his teacher's kindness, which had indicated that the student did not have to conform to ordinary classroom rules and routines:

Another teacher was nice. In class like he said to the boys one day, 'let him sleep away' like. I wasn't asleep at all ha ha!

(p. 30)

In the following extracts participants describe how some teachers appeared to have a serious difficulty engaging with them in classroom interactions:

I wanted to read. I didn't want to be left out, I wanted to be part of it but he went like 'you–you–you', and skipped me.

(p. 30)

This teacher practically said 'you won't go anywhere, you won't get a good job, you won't get anything cause you haven't good English'. That was some hell of a year with her. Practically all the time I put up my hand to answer questions, she never came to me.

(p. 28)

Other schools addressed the issue of accessing the curriculum and class placement in a notably different manner. One highly academic school that employed streaming had a highly flexible approach to including a student who had a physical disability that involved placing him in the most academically able class though he was taking the majority of his subjects at a lower level:

[I was placed in] the A class, though I studied pass maths and Irish. I only did History and Geography [exams] at pass level but I was studying at honours level, it was kind of honours/pass for me. For homework I didn't do as much detail as people doing honours.

(p. 26)

This student took programmes at his comprehension level whereas homework and examinations were taken at a lower level presumably because the assistive provision was unavailable or inappropriate for his needs. Kenny *et al.* (2000: 26) commented that: 'With more appropriate assistance, his performance might have matched his comprehension more closely'. The student in question believed that the school had offered him valuable opportunities to participate and he was satisfied with his academic and social experiences: 'I was happy out like, I didn't ask to be treated special and I wasn't' (p. 26).

Participants particularly valued the support of those teachers whose expectations were positive and empowering:

> One teacher kept driving me the whole way. Kind of 'put it in a context, fair enough you have a disability but – throw it away from you and continue on' like. From that day on I've never looked back. It was the best thing ever that, to stand up for ourselves.

> (p. 28)

Participants in the Educable (2000) study mentioned earlier had particular concerns around the low levels of teacher expectations for the academic learning of young people with disabilities within some special schools. Many of these young people had chosen specialist provision because of complex physical/medical needs that required specialist equipment and intervention programmes not readily available within mainstream schools. Participation in the research project represented an opportunity for participants to critically examine their own schooling experiences. Involvement in the research project had enabled the participants to develop confidence in their abilities and in a joint statement they expressed their views about intrinsic expectations within the schools they had attended:

> we are able to think things through and do work usually done by university graduates. Yet, of those of us who attended a special school, no one left school with more than three GCSEs at Grade C or above. That is why we decided to research the choices available in education for young people with disabilities.

> (p. 17)

It appeared that some special schools had limited subject availability because of their small size and limited expertise, which had a negative impact on the aspirations of the following speaker:

> For the course I want to do at University, I would need more specialised science subjects, but the school only does general science . . . I know I'm the only one in the school who wants to specialise in science and they can't put on a class just for me. But I wish there was a way around it.

> (p. 31)

Participants believed that even more dispiriting than the lack of subject choice was the generalised lowered expectations for academic success prevalent within the schools, especially when compared with the opportunities available in mainstream schools:

My sister is at grammar school now and I can see the choice she gets and I realise what a bad deal I got. We're forced to go on to further education really because the education we got at school wouldn't get us a job.

(p. 33)

It's not that I couldn't do them [exams], they just never gave me a chance to do them and I had seen other people doing exams and I thought why can't I do them. Every time I asked them, it was like 'because' all the time.

(pp. 33–34)

Subsequently this last speaker encountered a more empowering and facilitative approach in further education:

When I went to Pathfinders [support scheme in FE Colleges for disabled students] I put the emphasis on them that I want to do an exam in whatever and they said 'no problem go for it' and I left there with GCSEs, so.

(p. 34)

The following speaker provides a critical insight into the changes required to enable children and young people with disabilities to become full, active participants in the education system:

I find it very patronising to be told 'you shouldn't do that because it's not for you and wouldn't suit you'. And 'we're really thinking about you, you know'. And actually it's not us that has to change. It's the environment that has to change; it's the exam system that has to change; it's the schools and the teachers that will have to re-organise themselves to allow young people with disabilities get a decent education.

(p. 34)

Voicing concerns

Enabling children and young people who have disabilities and/or special educational needs to gain educational access and have educators who are ambitious for them to succeed academically will require a multifaceted response at systemic and local level (Rose and Shevlin 2010). Whatever combination of enabling policy, fostering increased school capacity and delivering appropriate supports is devised on an ongoing basis, the voice of the young people involved must be given meaningful recognition in policy and practice. There has been an increased recognition both internationally and at national level that children and young people with disabilities and/or special educational needs should be fully involved in decision making that affects their school careers.

Pupil consultation and participation underpin many policy initiatives and guidance for practice. The Scottish Curriculum for Excellence, for example, recommends that pupil consultation should infuse all aspects of school and classroom practice and not be limited to individual teachers and/or school committees (Deuchar 2009). The expanded Code of Practice (Department for Education and Skills 2001) recommends that:

> where possible, they [children and young people with special educational needs] should participate in all the decision-making processes that occur in education including the setting of learning targets and contributing to IEPs, discussion about choice of schools, contributing to the assessment of their needs and to the annual review and transition process.
>
> (p. 14, para. 3.2)

The Code of Practice acknowledges that this type of process is not straightforward and that schools, teachers and support staff face challenging dilemmas in implementing this policy in practice, though the following guidance in the Code does allow teachers to decide that active participation is not appropriate:

> there is a fine balance between giving the child a voice and encouraging them to make informed decisions and overburdening them with decision-making procedures where they have insufficient experience and knowledge to make appropriate judgements without additional support.
>
> (p. 14, para. 3.2)

Klein (2003) commenting on this guidance for practice asserts that:

> For the first time, children and young people with special needs are being actively encouraged by education policy to be involved in planning what services they receive at school and in communicating their views on how they should be delivered.
>
> (p. 42)

As Ravet (2007) points out, learner rights, in particular those of people with special educational needs, are an essential feature in the development of inclusive learning environments. Increasingly professionals in education, health and welfare are acknowledging the competence of children and young people with disabilities and/or special educational needs to be involved in a meaningful way in making critical choices in their lives (Woolfson, Bryce, Mooney, Harker, Lowe and Ferguson 2008).

Translating the principle of pupil consultation into practice is a challenging and multifaceted task for teachers, students and support personnel. However, as Rudduck and McIntyre (2007: 145) reported, the development of structured explicit pupil consultation as an ordinary feature of school life can have enormous benefits. This type of consultation can enable pupils to develop a greater sense of belonging to the school; a strengthened sense of self-respect; an enhanced belief in themselves as proficient learners; and a stronger sense of agency in making an impact on school policy and practice. When pupils with special educational needs are encouraged to actively participate in learning-focused dialogue, they have an opportunity to understand the learning processes at a deeper level and develop increased confidence in themselves as learners (Flutter and Rudduck 2004: 21). Failing to provide meaningful involvement for pupils in their individual education planning can result in the outcome described in Lovitt, Plavins and Cushing's (1999) study:

> Well I think it really is pretty stupid. I do my work and everything in school. I did everything that was on the list. But each year there is always an IEP. And each year the objectives are exactly the same . . . Just basically learning the same stuff over and over and over every year. And it's been like that since about 8th grade.
>
> (p. 71)

Higgins, Mac Arthur and Kelly (2009) argue very cogently that the key themes of agency, capability and transformative diversity need to be addressed in the development of inclusive learning environments. The authors maintain that schools need to provide opportunities for the children and young people of concern to demonstrate agency and capability by 'supporting the full social participation of disabled students in school activities and ensuring that the curriculum is accessible to disabled students' (p. 474). Teachers who support this position on inclusive practice would 'view disabled children as competent in the classroom and ensure that disabled children have opportunities to exercise their capability and agency' (p. 474). The concept of agency has emerged from newly developed sociological perceptions of childhood that have encouraged the view of children as active agents involved in building their own lives within families, schools and their local communities (James, Jenks and Prout 1998). This outlook challenges traditional perceptions of children as passive and dependent on adult support. Teachers and peers play a crucial role in facilitating or preventing the exercise of agency by disabled students within the school setting. Within Higgins *et al.*'s (2009) study a disabled student exercised her agency by actively engaging with her teachers to explain the nature of her disability and how this affected her ability to be always punctual. Although this initiative was not an unqualified success, as some teachers did not respond positively, it did however indicate that the student had been proactive in ensuring that her educational experiences could become more inclusive. In Shevlin and Rose's (2003) edited collection Thomas, a young boy who has Asperger's syndrome, was enabled through the support of his Learning Support Assistant (LSA) to inform teachers about how his special educational need affected his participation in classroom interactions:

> She [LSA] taught me how to understand the ways in which my Asperger's will affect me in my school life. We made a personal profile on 'PowerPoint' then she used it to train the teachers and it helped them to understand me. This has made things a lot better. We're going to do this every year so that I can reflect back on how I've changed.
>
> (p. 274)

It is evident that Thomas's school is receptive to his learning and social needs and have incorporated his perspective into school policy and practice. Demonstrating capability within the classroom can be difficult for disabled children, as illustrated in Mac Arthur *et al.*'s (2007) study in which Joanne had to actively challenge negative perceptions:

> Joanne: Just that 'cos some people think that like being disabled is the worst thing ever, but I just like proving people wrong like 'cos some people say 'Oh you can't do that' and then I show them that I can. And just showing people that I can do – I can try to do everything.
>
> (p. 10)

Developing appropriate supports for children and young people with disabilities and/or special educational needs can be problematic. Children and young people have reported their concerns about the appropriateness of special needs assistant support in a number of studies (Mc Conville 2007; Curtin and Clarke 2005; Higgins *et al.* 2009; Mc Arthur *et al.* 2007; Wilson and Jade 1999). Over-protective 'mothering' was a source of frustration for participants in Mc Conville's (2007) study, and a young boy resented the presence of a special needs assistant that marked him as different to his peers (Curtin and Clarke 2005). However, when a teacher in Mac Arthur *et al.*'s (2007) study recognised that a young boy was very uncomfortable with the constant focus of the assistant on him she restructured the role of the assistant to become a support to the whole class. Schools and teachers face the constant dilemma of how to structure support to enable student learning and social interaction without separating the child from his/her peers:

> There is a fine line between denying or minimising disabled children's learning, behaviour, communication or physical challenges on the one hand, and highlighting difference on the other.
>
> (MacArthur *et al.*, 2007: 16)

However, Lewis, Parsons and Robertson (2007) in their UK study of the educational experiences of children and young people with disabilities reported a contrasting view about support:

> There was little evidence that children and young people felt stigmatised or uncomfortable with the help received. This seemed to be an accepted normality for the pupils and the class.
>
> (p. 57)

Support needs to be offered in a sensitive, flexible manner that recognises the variation in individual need among the students. The need to foster autonomy was acknowledged by one participant who recognised the risk of over-reliance on support:

> Maybe I could like have less [support] so that I don't like depend on them because when I go to [the mainstream secondary] I might depend on them.
>
> (p. 42)

School Councils have often been advanced as a mechanism for ensuring that students with special educational needs can voice their concerns. Lewis *et al.* (2007) reported that the study participants concur with this view. In general, the study participants felt that they could express their viewpoint and get a hearing within schools. Their understanding of rights was extended and facilitated through their involvement in School Councils. However, the effectiveness of School Councils to deliver on a democratic agenda was dependent on a number of organisational factors and an empowering philosophy. Students required evidence that their participation made a difference and that change to an aspect of school practice could be facilitated through the School Council process. Over time this democratic approach can become firmly embedded in school life. Students with disabilities and/or special educational needs in Kenny *et al.*'s (2000) study were very sceptical about the effectiveness of School Councils/student representation in effecting change within the school environment:

> I don't think another student, I think a professional should be there. Somebody connected but detached a little. To know the facts, have the information to back up what you're saying, explain the situation.
>
> Five minutes after the student leaves it'd be back to normal. It definitely shouldn't be a student.
>
> (p. 44)

The need for effective representation of student views was very apparent from the following extract from the Educable (2000) study:

YP4:   The management in this school has their own ideas – like we have to wear uniforms but not all the time (laughs, because all are wearing football shirts) . . . how come she [Principal] is always able to give us big lectures like every Friday morning in Assembly but we can't put our point of view across?

YP7:   There's no respect. She just lectures us like children.

YP2:   Lecture, lecture, lecture, lecture, lecture.

YP3:   There used to be a regular meeting between teachers and student representatives and, okay, maybe it was mostly about silly things but she just done away with it.

YP4:   And she done away with . . .

YP3:   We used to have student representatives but she did away with them. She decided that we couldn't elect the Head Boy.

(p. 17)

Concluding comments

Developing inclusive learning environments requires the active participation of children and young people who have disabilities and/or special educational needs. Facilitating access involves re-examining assumptions and expectations regarding the capacity of these children and young people to be successful learners and social participants with their peer group. Within this chapter access issues have been examined from the experiential standpoint of these young people and the need to create an ambitious mindset in schools to facilitate their aspirations has been advocated. Meaningful consultation processes and the embedding of democratic practices within schools and classrooms remains a key task on the inclusion agenda. Children and young people have demonstrated their capacity to contribute to the development of inclusive learning environments and the contributions from the following speakers reiterate this point:

No one expects us to do well in exams and go on to have a career or even a decent job. Changing this means challenging a mindset that sees the disability, not the person, and that fails to recognise that while it might take a young person with a disability longer to achieve their goals, we can still do it . . . As a group of young people with disabilities, Educable has shown that we can do quite a lot. We have done something few non-disabled young people have: we've decided to do some research, planned it, learned how to do it, then did it and analysed the results. We think we came up with a lot of good recommendations . . .

[and] that our ideas would make school life better for all young people, not just those with a disability.

It would become normal, just everyday life and people would be able to understand it, 'ah sure we don't even know what that is, we just know it's a normal thing [he's] like everyone else'. When it comes like that we would get good jobs.

Bibliography

Burgess, E. (2003) *Are We Nearly There Yet? Do Teenage Wheelchair Users Think Integration Has Been Achieved in Secondary Schools in the UK?* Cardiff: Whizz Kids Millennium Award Report.

Curriculum Review Group. (2004) *A Curriculum for Excellence*. Edinburgh: Scottish Executive.

Curtin, M. and Clarke, G. (2005) Listening to young people with physical disabilities' experiences of education. *International Journal of Disability, Development and Education*, 52 (3): 195–214.

Department for Education and Skills. (2001) *Special Educational Needs Code of Practice*. Nottingham: DfES.

Deuchar, R. (2009) Seen and heard, and then not heard: Scottish pupils' experience of democratic educational practice during the transition from primary to secondary school. *Oxford Review of Education*, 35 (1): 23–40.

Educable. (2000) *No Choice: No Chance. The Educational Experiences of Young People with Disabilities*. Belfast: Save the Children/Disability Action.

Flutter, J. and Rudduck, J. (2004) *Consulting Pupils: What's in It for Schools?* Abingdon, UK: Routledge.

Government of Ireland. (2004) *Education for Persons with Special Educational Needs*. Dublin: Stationery Office.

Gray, P. (2002) *Disability Discrimination in Education: A Review of the Literature on Discrimination across the 0–19 Age Range*. London: Disability Rights Commission.

Hanafin, J., Shevlin, M. and Flynn, M. (2002) Responding to student diversity: lessons from the margin. *Pedagogy, Culture and Society*, 10 (3): 409–423.

Higgins, N., Mac Arthur, J. and Kelly, B. (2009) Including disabled children at school: is it really as simple as 'a, c, d'? *International Journal of Inclusive Education*, 13 (5): 471–487.

Horgan, G. (2003) Educable: disabled young people in Northern Ireland challenge the education system. In M. Shevlin and R. Rose (Eds) *Encouraging Voices: Respecting the Insights of Young People Who Have Been Marginalized*. Dublin: National Disability Authority.

James, A., Jenks, C. and Prout, A. (1998) *Theorising Childhood*. Cambridge: Polity.

Kenny, M., Mc Neela, E., Shevlin, M. and Daly, T. (2000) *Hidden Voices: Young People with Disabilities Speak about their Second Level Schooling*. Cork: South West Regional Authority.

Klein, R. (2003) *We Want Our Say: Children as Active Participants in Their Education*. Stoke on Trent, UK: Trentham Books.

Lewis, A. and Porter, J. (2007) Research and pupil voice. In L. Florian (Ed.) *The Sage Handbook of Special Education*. London: Sage

Lewis, A., Robertson, C. and Parsons, S. (2005) *Experiences of Disabled Students and Their Families*. Phase 1 Research Report to Disability Rights Commission, June 2005. Birmingham: University of Birmingham, School of Education.

Lewis, A., Parsons, S. and Robertson, C. (2007) *My School, My Family, My Life: Telling It Like It Is. A Study Detailing the Experiences of Disabled Children, Young People and Their Families in Great Britain in 2006*. Birmingham: University of Birmingham & Disability Rights Commission.

Lovitt, T., Plavins, M. and Cushing, S. (1999) What do pupils with disabilities have to say about their experience in high school? *Remedial and Special Education*, 20: 67–83.

Mac Arthur, J., Sharp, S., Kelly, B. and Gaffney, M. (2007) Disabled children negotiating school life: agency, difference and teaching practice. *International Journal of Children's Rights*, 15: 1–22.

Mc Conville, R. (2007) *Looking at Inclusion: Listening to the Voices of Young People*. London: Paul Chapman Publishing.

Palmer, D. Durability of changes in self-efficacy of pre-service primary teachers. *International Journal of Science Education*, 28 (6): 655–671.

Priestley, M. (2001) Introduction: the global context of disability. In M. Priestley (Ed.) *Disability and the Life Course: Global Perspectives*. Cambridge: Cambridge University Press.

Ravet, J. (2007) *Are We Listening? Making Sense of Classroom Behaviour with Pupils and Parents*. Stoke on Trent, UK: Trentham Books.

Rose, R, and Shevlin, M. (2010) *Count Me In: Ideas for Teachers to Engage Children in Active Classroom Learning*. London: Jessica Kingsley.

Rudduck, J. and McIntyre, M. (2007) *Improving Learning through Consulting Pupils*. London: Routledge.

Shevlin, M. and Rose, R. (Eds). (2003) *Encouraging Voices: Respecting the Insights of Young People Who Have Been Marginalized*. Dublin: National Disability Authority.

Shevlin, M. and Rose, R. (2008) Pupils as partners in education decision making: responding to the legislation in England and Ireland. *European Journal of Special Needs Education*, 23 (4): 423–430.

Watson, N., Shakespeare, T., Cunningham-Burley, S., Barnes, C., Corker, M., Davis, J. and Priestley, M. (1999) *Life as a Disabled Child: A Qualitative Study of Young People's Experiences and Perspectives*. Final Report. Swindon: Economic and Social Research Council (ESRC), Research Programme.

Wilson, C. and Jade, R. (1999) *Whose Voice is it Anyway? Talking to Disabled Young People at School*. London: Alliance for Inclusive Education.

Woolfson, R., Bryce, D., Mooney, L., Harker, M., Lowe, D. and Ferguson, E. (2008) Improving methods of consulting with young people: piloting a new model of consultation. *Educational Psychology in Practice*, 24 (1) 55–67.

Chapter 9

Engaging young children in research about an inclusion project

Phyllis Jones and Ann Gillies (both University of South Florida, USA)

Introduction

This chapter discusses a project designed to gather the views of twenty kindergarten children, including four children with labels of autistic spectrum disorders (ASD), about an inclusion project that they are currently involved in. A picture booklet, utilizing pictures of the inclusion classroom with prompts to support student responses, was adopted as a research tool. The chapter discusses the children's responses to the picture booklet as a research tool, and the discovery that, for some children, additional strategies and research processes were required to better hear their voices.

Listening to children

There is an old saying that goes "out of the mouths of babes," which recognizes the power of children to give a valuable and unique perspective on a situation. There are some fundamental principles underlying this statement that form the rationale for seeking children's perspectives on experiences of inclusion. First, it celebrates the fact that children "say it as it is" without worrying about the politics of a situation; what they see and think are expressed without the filtering adults tend to employ. Second, children are the primary consumers of school and therefore have something valuable to add to the discussion; they live the life day in and day out. They should be the focus of attention when considering how to provide the best educational programs for them. Last, children make up the culture of the classroom; they set the tone, they create the atmosphere, they build the community. The teacher can model, facilitate, and provide guidance, but the children themselves construct the connectedness and belonging of each class member within the whole. Even the youngest of children have ideals, values, and beliefs, and exhibit strong displays of emotion that come from their unique temperaments, personalities, and feelings about things (Liew, Eisenberg, and Reiser 2004). Children recognize and appreciate being treated fairly, having their chance to participate, contributing to successes of the group.

Children are strongly committed to the premise of equality of educational opportunity (Hodkinson 2007). Shapiro (1994) talks about how young children offer a fresh perspective on disability as "Young children have not yet learned society's myths, fears and stereotypes about disability" (p. 19). We should listen to children because through their voices we will hear their truth and gain some insight into how they make meaning of their classroom; if we as educators are to construct appropriate, effective programs for these children then we had better listen very carefully. However, for some children, the saying "out of the mouths of babes" is problematic; this group of children may be developing communicators or communicate in other ways than orally. These children also have a valuable perspective to offer, and it is a challenge to enable their meaningful participation in the process (Snelgrove 2005; Whitehurst 2006). In this situation, we need to be not only good listeners but good connectors to, observers, and interpreters of children and their behavior. This chapter explores the process of using a picture booklet to engage young children (5–7 years old) in conversations about a school experience of children with labels of ASD being included in a general education kindergarten classroom.

What are the ways children have been listened to in the past?

The gathering and understanding of children's perspectives is a growing body of work that is receiving much attention from a research process as well as a product perspective. Children demand that some of the more traditional approaches to collecting data be extended so that they can actively contribute their perspectives in a meaningful way. There are some interesting projects, which exemplify how researchers have engaged children with and without disabilities in the process of inquiry. Interviewing has been a popular tool to gather the views of children; indeed, interviewing is one of the most powerful ways we use to try and understand our fellow human beings (Fontana and Frey 1994). The challenge of researchers is to enable access to and participation in the interview by children, but also maintain a rigorous methodological process that supports the validity of emerging insights (Lewis 2004). Snelgrove (2005) sets the ethical and methodological foundation for seeking the views of students with intellectual disabilities. Her work on the process of developing a shared research process offers strong guidance on supporting meaningful participation through visual aids for a "Plain Language statement" (p. 315), attention to setting, and building up the children's skills as researchers. Meadan and Halle (2004) used a sociometric rating-scale technique to measure the acceptance of students with learning disabilities in an elementary inclusion classroom. Jones (2005) designed and administered a picture booklet for children aged 5–14 to complete with a familiar adult or independently to gather their views of inclusion. The use of pictures as a tool to engage children in the research process has proved to be highly effective (Swain, Cook, and French 2001). Lewis and Porter (2008) developed a set of guidelines for researchers' self-evaluation to guide the consideration of goals, ethics, sampling, research design, and communication in a researcher's work with children.

Clearly, to gather the views of children, adults need to choose from a wide variety of research tools, which may include direct observation of student behavior, listening to children's evaluations, or the administration of instruments (for example, The Adjective Checklist and The Shared Activities Questionnaire, Morton and Campbell 2007) that may or may not use forms with Likert scales (Schweinle, Turner, and Meyer 2008).

The school context

The elementary school where this project takes place is a public school in a mid-sized school district in the south-west of Florida, in the United States of America. The school serves 800 students in pre-kindergarten through fifth grade: students 3–12 years of age. In addition to services for the local catchment area, there are classes for students who are English language learners, students who have labels of gifted, students with varying exceptionalities, and students with ASD. The school is a district cluster program for students with labels of ASD. The ASD cluster program consists of seven self-contained classrooms; each classroom has one teacher and one or two assistants. Children in the ASD program receive weekly specialized services including speech and language therapy, occupational therapy, physical therapy, specialized physical education, and counseling as specified in each student's Individualized Education Program (IEP). The ASD program has an Exceptional Student Education liaison teacher who works with all seven classes. Inclusive practices at this school are encouraged by the administration, and individual teachers are supported to design and implement meaningful inclusion projects. For example, one teacher of students with ASD includes half of her class in the general education classroom for over 50 percent of the school day, and two other teachers of students with ASD mainstream several of their students for reading. Two other teachers invite general education students into their self-contained classrooms every day (reverse inclusion), and another teacher plans for her students to spend time with their typically developing peers during non-academic time including lunch and recess.

The classroom context

The kindergarten class at the center of this project has seventeen general education children including four about whom the teacher has current concerns. These four do not have any identified labels but they are the focus of the schoolwide CARE (Children At Risk in Education) team. One of the students has been retained in kindergarten for a second year. There are four students with labels of ASD who spend over half of the school day in the kindergarten class and have done so since the beginning of the school year 2008. The class is taught by one general education kindergarten teacher with three years' teaching experience and one special education teacher with ten years' teaching experience. This class serves children from families in low to upper middle-class socio-economic backgrounds who are African-American, Caucasian, and Hispanic. Children in this classroom have ability levels ranging from at-risk to gifted. Academic instruction is primarily delivered to the whole group and then students divide into small groups to complete individual and differentiated activities. Cooperative learning group methods are utilized, as are differentiated reading groups, independent work times, and one-on-one instruction with a teacher. The curriculum comprises objectives under the domains of Reading/Language Arts, Mathematics, Social Studies, and Science; these are the objectives adopted by the entire state of Florida. At the kindergarten level, curriculum objectives include mastering skills involving letters, letter sounds, sight word recognition, comprehension, numbers, shapes, citizenship, and problem solving.

The children with labels of ASD

In light of the work of Snelgrove (2005), the students are described by their abilities, preferences, and needs, whilst taking account of ascribed labels. This recognizes the positive individuality of each student. The four students with labels of ASD who are included in the kindergarten classroom each vary in their level of individualized support, learning preferences, strengths, and needs. All names are pseudonyms to maintain confidentiality.

Allan is 7 years old, and uses several spoken words but relies most on augmentative and alternative communication strategies. These include Picture Exchange Communication System and gestures. Allan shows a range of self-stimulatory behaviors including humming, jumping up and down, and flapping his hands, which are characteristics shared by many children labeled with ASD (Heflin and Alaimo 2007). Allan is able to visually discriminate, match, and sort objects and pictures. He is a very cooperative student who enjoys music, movement activities, and playing with favorite toys. Allan is most comfortable in a calm, structured, predictable environment with familiar people and routines, and responds well to most-to-least prompt hierarchies and positive reinforcement strategies.

Joey is 6 years old, and has good pragmatic and conversational verbal skills. He requires individualized support relating to behaviors characteristic of children with labels of high-functioning autism (Zager 2005). Types of support include multiple practice opportunities, positive behavior supports, and modeling. Academically, Joey functions at grade level with more support needed in handwriting. He enjoys playing with his favorite toys and watching his favorite cartoons, and will create imaginative stories centered on his interests. Joey is most comfortable in an environment with consistency in the daily schedule, work expectations, and consequences of behavior. Positive behavior supports are programmed throughout his day.

Brian is 5 years old, and is a highly verbal student; he uses more sophisticated vocabulary than his peers in the kindergarten class. He is reading at a second-grade level. Brian requires individualized support with socialization skills including conversational turn taking, social awareness of other students, and listening to others. These characteristics are shared by children with the label of Asperger's syndrome (Gutstein 2000). He masters new concepts in reading and math very quickly. Brian is a very active boy with many ideas he wishes to creatively express at all times. He enjoys the company of adults and is cooperative in efforts to get him to engage in conversations with peers. Brian benefits from teacher modeling, multiple practice opportunities, redirection, and the use of Social Stories.

James is 5 years old, and is also a student with above-average intelligence who requires individualized support with communication and socialization similar to Brian. His reading and math skills are at least two years above grade level and he picks up new skills through observation of others. James loves school and is passionate about letters, numbers, song titles, and elevators and wishes to share these passions with others. Effective instructional strategies with James include modeling, positive reinforcement, repeated practice, written directions, and Social Stories (Gray 2004).

The inclusion program

Allan, Joey, Brian, and James arrive in the kindergarten class when the morning bell rings to begin the school day. They eat breakfast with their general education peers and then begin their morning work at four different tables with peers within the classroom. Each of the students sits at a different table with at least three general education peers with whom they work on small group assignments. Each child in the inclusion class is assigned a designated spot on the rug for large group activities. Each student has their picture on a cabinet with their name and weekly class job, and each student has their own bear, which displays stars earned for appropriate behavior as per the classroom behavior management system. The two teachers co-teach, teach small groups simultaneously, and provide support as necessary in every activity with all students. Supports include positive reinforcement strategies, prompt hierarchies, visuals, modeling, redirection, individual behavior plans, contracts, and proximity. Indeed, through their joint practices it is clear the teachers consider all students their shared responsibility and attend to each student every day.

The picture booklet

A picture booklet was designed to support all children in the kindergarten inclusion project in offering their opinions about key concepts of inclusion identified as Having Fun, Joining In, and Learning Together. The booklet was based upon a design previously used with success in the UK (Jones 2005). However, the design of the current picture booklet was developed to increase participation of the young children in this particular setting by including photographs of the actual children in the classroom where the inclusion project took place (Whitehurst and Howell 2006). Each of the photographs included a child with the label of ASD. The picture booklet was administered by a familiar adult (one of the teachers, Mrs. Brown) who was able to respond proactively to individual communication strengths, preferences, and needs of all of the children. The three photographs were followed by prompt questions that engaged the children in discussion about the photograph and then progressed to engaging the children in conversations about Having Fun, Joining In, and Learning Together. Having Fun is an essential element of belonging and participation for a young child and offered a warmup activity for the interaction between the adult and the child. Joining In and Learning Together were accepted as relevant to successful inclusion experiences of belonging and participation (Ryndak, Jackson, and Billingsley 2000). Marsh, Bradley, Love, Alexander, and Norham (2007) discuss belonging as "central to our understanding of how people give meaning to their lives. Our sense of identity is founded on social interactions that show our belonging to particular communities through shared beliefs, values, or practices." (p. 7). The foci of Joining In and Learning Together are natural elements of belonging, but perhaps more concrete to see, to try to understand, and to engage in conversation about. Inclusion has been defined by Allen and Schwartz (2001) as about belonging to a community; having a group of friends, a school community, or a neighborhood. Participation is a more concrete context in itself and is more observable. One of the major research foci of researchers of inclusion has been the barriers to active participation and the difference between placement and participation (Ainscow 1999). The opportunities a child has to join in and learn together with their peers can be a good reflection of the opportunities they have for active participation in an inclusion scenario. In this way, the exploration of children's views of Joining In and Learning Together offers a perspective to the study of children's experiences and views of inclusion from a belonging and participation viewpoint. The current project wanted to explore how young children responded to conversations about inclusion using a familiar picture booklet as a research strategy.

The pictures were enlarged to cover the whole page of the booklet and positioned so that children could see the picture throughout the whole conversation about that section. An example for the Learning Together section can be seen in Figure 9.1.

Discussion:

Look at the picture. These children are at school
What are the children doing?

What kinds of things can the children do to help
themselves to learn better together?

What could the teacher/adult do to help?

Your Turn:
*Do you learn better on your own or with other
people?*
I learn better...

*In what ways do other people stop you
learning together?*
Other people stop me learning with others
when they...

*What can you do to help yourself learn
better with others?*
I can do these things...

*What can adults do to help you to learn
together?*
Adults can help me by doing these things...

Figure 9.1 Illustration of Learning Together section of picture booklet.

The children are shown a picture of a group of the children sitting in the classroom working on individual projects, including one of the children who has a label of ASD. The picture booklet has prompts, some related specifically to the picture and some related to the child's views of their personal experience. Inviting the children to talk about the picture in descriptive terms is intended to serve as an orientation to the subsequent Your Turn section. For example, in the Learning Together section, after the children talk about the picture of children working together around the table, they are prompted to share their views about what helps and what stops their learning together, and how adults and the children themselves can help facilitate learning with others.

Sharing the booklet

As mentioned, a familiar adult, Mrs. Brown, shared the booklet with each of the children on an individual basis. This allowed for individual scaffolding and support of each child's engagement in the sharing of the booklet. For example, Mrs. Brown responded to children by including additional support strategies (gestural prompting to the pictures). This was noted in the booklet. This familiarity also ensured the adult was sensitive and responsive to how the children were responding to the activity. During the sharing of the picture booklet, Mrs. Brown made notes about the children's responses directly into the booklet. These notes included information about what the children were saying as well as notes about the process of sharing the booklet itself.

Ethical considerations

When including children in research it is of paramount importance to follow strong ethical guidelines to ensure the children are safeguarded and can actively make a choice about being part of the research (Lewis 2004; Snelgrove 2005). For this project, Institutional Ethical Reviews were carried out at the university and school district level. Here, the protocol for the research was evaluated prior to permission being given for the project to commence. Parents of each of the children were sent a letter telling them about the project and a copy of the booklet and were asked to talk to their children about an invitation they would get from Mrs. Brown to share the picture booklet with her in school. Parents were told about the aims of the project and specifically how their child would participate and add value to the project. Twenty-one letters of invitation were sent out to all children in the kindergarten classroom and the four children with labels of ASD. Twenty parents responded that they wanted their children to be invited to participate in the project including all four of the children with labels of ASD. The children were invited to join Mrs. Brown using the following script:

> Would you like to share a picture booklet with me? (Showing booklet) We are going to have a conversation about some pictures of our classroom and I am going to ask you some things about the pictures. I'm going to write down what you say.

A couple of the children asked why and Mrs. Brown responded:

> I'm going to school and working on a project and want to get your ideas about our classroom and all the kids in it.

The process of sharing the booklet

There were twenty children who accepted the invitation to share the booklet; sixteen general education kindergarten students and the four children with labels of ASD. The first three conversations with kindergarten children were held outside the classroom on a picnic bench; Mrs. Brown sat across the table from the children. Mrs. Brown noted that the children were quieter than usual, and their body language indicated they were uncomfortable, which is different from their behavior in classroom interactions. Indeed she noted they were responding as they would in a testing situation; their facial expressions indicated some anxiety and they were asking for reassurance from Mrs. Brown. Mrs. Brown decided to change the venue; the following conversations were held inside the classroom in a "toy area" where children usually go to play in self-directed activities. The children were invited to sit on the floor with Mrs. Brown with both of them sitting cross-legged and knee to knee. Mrs. Brown observed that the children appeared more comfortable; their body posture was relaxed, they were smiling and laughing with Mrs. Brown, and several children requested to "do the booklet" again. This affirms the work of Snelgrove (2005), who highlights the importance of setting when researching the views of children.

The booklet itself

From the experience of sharing the booklet with the children, several issues emerged about the picture booklet itself, including the use of familiar pictures, the use of gestural prompting by Mrs. Brown, some students' interpretations of the pictures, and also the role of observation as a research tool.

The use of familiar pictures

Mrs. Brown observed that the children's responses to the familiar pictures were very positive, which suggests this research tool can potentially play an important role in engaging young children in conversations about their classroom. When shown the three pictures in the booklet, children showed interest, talked about the pictures, and also asked or commented about where they were in reference to the pictures.

The children's interpretations of the pictures

In the section of the booklet Joining In, the picture depicted a group of children on the carpet and one child sitting on the side. When talking about the picture, eight of the twenty children made comments about the child sitting on the side as being naughty, for example, "He's in trouble" and "He's bad." This suggests that 40 percent of the children made an assumption that is generally negative about the child on the outside of the group. This affirms the findings of Jones (2005), in which children responding to a picture of a child with Down syndrome sharing an activity with a general education peer assumed that the child with a disability was being "helped" by his peer. This raises a question related to the claims of Shapiro (1994), who suggests children do not have society's myths about disability: at what age do children begin to make assumptions about other children in their classroom? And, more importantly, why?

The use of additional prompting

Continual visual referencing to the pictures was used as a supplementary prompt by Mrs. Brown to support more elaborate interaction by the children. For example, in the Joining In section, seventeen out of twenty students made no response to the first prompt of "what are the children doing in the picture?". However, after Mrs. Brown employed finger referencing to focus attention to a particular part of the picture, all of the children responded. The range of number of words in the children's responses ranged from one word to seven words and the choice of words chosen were appropriate and applicable to the picture.

The role of observation

It became clear to Mrs. Brown that her observations of the children, both in the sharing activity and in the classroom more generally, were yielding important information related to the children's responses to the inclusion project. Joey responded verbally to prompts and showed interest in the pictures by sustaining his gaze, smiling, having a relaxed posture, and initiating comments about the pictures, including "Hey, that's Ella!", and "That is my red table." Joey appeared to respond better to prompts about the pictures rather than prompts about himself. For example, in the Learning Together section, Joey's response to the prompt "What kinds of things can the children do to help themselves learn better together?" was "help raise hand and have a quiet hand," whereas his response to the prompt "What can you do to help yourself learn better with others?" was "work and stuff." Brian appeared very engaged with the pictures; he was very talkative and initiated discussion about who was in the pictures and what the children were doing. His responses were relevant; for example, in the Having Fun section he responded, "There's me, can I play with them?" (pointing to the other children). Indeed, Brian's responses illustrated that he liked being in the class with the kindergarten children; for example, in Learning Together when given the prompt, "In what ways do other people stop you learning together?" his response was "I want to be with all my friends, yes I learn with my friends." James appeared to enjoy sharing the booklet and looking at the pictures; Mrs. Brown noted that he was focused and attentive to them, naming all the children and smiling and laughing throughout. When Allan was invited to engage in the booklet, a visual aid was utilized and the conversation was conducted in a highly structured work area within the self-contained classroom where Allan always responds well. The visual picture-and-word response card that was used was a familiar tool Allan uses around the classroom to identify feelings of happy, sad, angry, and scared as illustrated in Figure 9.2.

The picture booklet activity was included in his daily schedule because he becomes agitated with activities not included on his schedule. Allan was very responsive to the activity, he responded positively to the pictures with smiles and focused attention, and he stayed seated and engaged throughout the activity. When asked "How does she feel?" in the Having Fun section of the booklet, he responded well by visually scanning his picture-and-word

Figure 9.2 Visual picture-and-word response card.

response card, and eye-pointed to the symbol for happy. Figure 9.3 shows Allan using his visual aid in the interview with Mrs. Brown.

In the picture for the Joining In section of the booklet, Allan made an independent verbal response of "sit" when asked what the children were doing. This is a major response for him; he also verbally copied the names of the children in the pictures. Although Allan's verbal responses were limited, Mrs. Brown was able to observe changes in his behavior that appeared to represent his responses to the different classroom environments. Research notes by Mrs. Brown illustrate this:

> I have been Allan's teacher for 2½ years and have developed a strong, connected relationship with him. We can read each other's body language, facial expressions, tones of voice, requests, verbalizations, and gestures. I feel confident that I am able to interpret Allan's feelings and thoughts well through observations of his body, facial expressions, reactions to stimuli, engagement, and responses. We share an unspoken language that is consistent, predictable, communicative, strong, and stable. In the Kindergarten class, children interact verbally with Allan but do not invade his personal space. Allan sits next to peers, smiles, relaxes, makes happy sounds, and is even beginning to initiate touch with others. He completes activities in a calm and comfortable state. In the self-contained classroom, which Allan shares with eight other children who have complex ASD, it is often noisy with unpredictable responses by his peers. Allan reacts negatively to this level of noise by throwing himself on the ground, hitting his head, and biting his wrist. Allan often asks for the "bathroom," and it is believed he does this to

Figure 9.3 Allan using the visual aid.

remove himself from the self-contained classroom. Allan does not ask for the bathroom unnecessarily when he is in the Kindergarten class.

Clearly, Allan's behavior reflects a powerful message about his response to the two classroom contexts, far beyond his responses to the picture booklet itself. For Allan, and other children who may share his level of communication and understanding, the booklet could be developed to simplify the concepts and provide a more elaborate visual response system. For example, pictures of both classroom contexts can be included in the booklet and the concepts could be initially simplified to "happy/sad" using a visual aid.

Conclusion

The project discussed in this chapter began with an intention to gather the views of the children about the inclusion project in the school. However, it became much more of a discussion of the process of researching the views of young children including children with labels of ASD. The work of Snelgrove (2005) offers a view of research as an ongoing process that builds on relationships and meaningful communication between children and the researcher. This was affirmed in the current project where some children responded effusively to the picture booklet while others needed additional visual support strategies; for other children, the picture booklet needs further development, to be simplified and include additional meaningful pictures. This project supports an idea of research as a process that is centered upon a strong relationship between the researcher and the young children; particularly those with labels of disabilities. This will support the meaningful involvement of students with disability in the inclusion debate through the adoption of a sensitive and responsive research process that is constructed with different research tools including picture booklets, visual aids to support conversations, and observations, but has a strong relationship between the researcher and children as a foundation. These tools, together, construct a collage approach to researching children's views: a collage made up of data gathered through different data-gathering processes. Thus, the chapter invites researchers to be creative and responsive in the range of research tools adopted in order to gather meaningful information about the views of young children about inclusive school experiences.

Bibliography

Ainscow, M. (1999) *Understanding the Development of Inclusive Schools*. London: Falmer Press.

Allen, K. and Schwartz, S. (2001) *The Exceptional Child: Inclusion in Early Childhood Education*. Albany, NY: Delmar.

Fontana, A. and Frey, J. (1994) Interviewing. In N. Denzin and Y. Lincoln (Eds) *Handbook of Qualitative Research*. Thousand Oaks, CA: Sage.

Gray, C. (2004) Social Stories 10.0: the new defining criteria & guidelines. *Jennison Autism Journal*, 15 (4): 2–21.

Gutstein, S. (2000) *Autism Aspergers: Solving the Relationship Puzzle*. Arlington, TX: Future Horizons.

Heflin, L. and Alaimo, D. (2007) *Students with Autism Spectrum Disorders*. Upper Saddle River, NJ: Pearson Education.

Hodkinson, A. (2007) Inclusive education and the cultural representation of disability and disabled people: recipe for disaster or catalyst of change? An examination of non-disabled primary school children's attitudes to children with disabilities. *Research in Education*, 77: 56–76.

Jones, P. (2005) Inclusion: lessons from the children. *British Journal of Special Education*, 32 (2): 60–66.

Lewis, A. (2004) 'And when did you last see your father?' Exploring the views of children with learning disabilities. *British Journal of Special Education*, 31 (4): 3–9.

Lewis, A. and Porter, J. (2008) Interviewing children and young people with learning disabilities: guidelines for researchers and multi-professional practice. *British Journal of Learning Disabilities*, 32 (4): 191–197.

Liew, J., Eisenberg, N., and Reiser, M. (2004) Preschoolers' effortful control and negative emotionality, immediate reactions to disappointment, and quality of social functioning. *Journal of Experimental Child Psychology*, 89 (4): 298–319.

Marsh, P., Bradley, S., Love, C., Alexander, P., and Norham, R. (2007) *Belonging*. Social Issues Research Centre. Accessed 10 March 2009 at http://www.sirc.org/publik/belonging.pdf.

Meadan, H. and Halle, J. (2004) Social perceptions of students with learning disabilities who differ in social status. *Learning Disabilities Research & Practice*, 19 (2): 71–82.

Morton, J. and Campbell, J. (2007) Information source affects peers' initial attitudes toward autism. *Research in Developmental Disabilities*, 29: 189–201.

Ryndak, D., Jackson, L., and Billingsley, F. (2000) Defining school inclusion for students with moderate to severe learning disabilities: what do experts say? *Exceptionality*, 8 (2): 101–116.

Schweinle, A., Turner, J., and Meyer, D. (2008) Understanding young adolescents' optimal experiences in academic settings. *Journal of Experimental Education*, 77 (2): 125–143.

Shapiro, Joseph P. (1994) *No Pity*. New York: Random House.

Snelgrove, S. (2005) Bad, mad and sad: developing a methodology for inclusion and a pedagogy for researching students with intellectual disabilities. *International Journal of Inclusive Education*, 9 (3): 313–329.

Swain, J., Cook, T., and French, S. (2001) Voices from segregated schooling: towards an inclusive education system. *Disability in Society*, 16 (2): 293–311.

Whitehurst, T. (2006) Liberating silent voices: perspectives of children with profound and complex learning needs on inclusion. *British Journal of Learning Disabilities*, 35 (1): 55–62.

Whitehurst, T. and Howell, A. (2006) When something is different people fear it: children's perceptions of an arts-based inclusion project. *Support for Learning*, 21 (1): 40–44.

Zager, D. (2005) *Autism Spectrum Disorders Identification, Education, and Treatment*, 3rd edition. Mahwah, NJ: Lawrence Erlbaum Associates.

Chapter 10

Beyond tokenism?

Participation and 'voice' for pupils with significant learning difficulties

Hazel Lawson (University of Exeter, UK)

Introduction

In an era when human and children's rights are emphasised, participation of, and consultation with, children and young people in many areas of educational decision making and practice is now commonplace and there is increasing professional and statutory commitment to this. This chapter explores the concept and practice of participation for pupils with significant learning difficulties. How are participation and 'voice' for pupils with significant learning difficulties conceptualised? How can this be meaningfully enacted in practice? This chapter draws upon research and practice in England to examine issues in this area.

Significant learning difficulties

The focus in this chapter is on children and young people with significant learning difficulties. In England, these children may be defined as having 'severe learning difficulties' or 'profound and multiple learning difficulties' (DfES 2003). 'Severe learning difficulties' is a term used to describe children and young people who have significant intellectual or cognitive impairments and experience significant difficulties in learning. They represent 0.36 per cent of school-aged children in England (DCSF 2008a). They may be variously labelled in different parts of the world as 'mentally retarded', 'mentally handicapped' or having 'severe intellectual disabilities'. 'Profound and multiple learning difficulties' is a term used in England to describe children and young people who have complex learning needs. In addition to very severe intellectual and cognitive impairments, pupils have other significant difficulties, such as physical disabilities, sensory impairments or medical conditions. This group of children require a high level of adult support, both for their learning needs and also for their personal care (DfES 2003). They represent 0.11 per cent of school-aged children in England (DCSF 2008a).

Children experiencing such significant learning difficulties in the UK were considered 'ineducable' until the early 1970s. They often communicate through non-traditional means and generally need high levels of adult support to access the school curriculum. The majority of these children are educated in special schools or units (DCSF 2008a).

Children's participation and voice

Emphasis on the participation and voice of children and young people is now seemingly ubiquitous in many areas of public life. This builds upon the United Nations Convention on the Rights of the Child (UNCRC) (United Nations 1989), particularly Articles 12 and 13, that children's opinions must be listened to seriously in all matters that affect their lives and that children have the right to express themselves freely and to access information, subject to prevailing laws. In the UK recent related policy drivers, alongside the children's rights agenda, include the Every Child Matters agenda relating to education and social care (DfES 2004a), citizenship education (DCSF 2007; Lawson 2009) and a personalised learning agenda (DfES 2006). Since the Education Act 2002 all schools are required to consult with pupils. The schools' self-evaluation form specifically asks 'What are the views of learners, parents/carers and other stakeholders and how do you know?' and the schools inspectorate reports on the degree to which schools seek and act upon the views of pupils (Ofsted 2005). There is thus a 'corporate requirement' (Fielding 2006: 306), almost a 'commandment' (Bluebond-Langner and Korbin 2007: 243), to seek the views of children.

Hargreaves (2004: 7) defines pupil participation and voice as:

> how students come to play a more active role in their education and schooling as a direct result of teachers becoming more attentive, in sustained or routine ways, to what students say about their experience of learning and of school life.

Pupil participation and voice activities in education include choice and involvement in decision making within the classroom, pupil consultations, peer support arrangements (for example, buddying systems, peer tutoring, peer teaching, circle time), formal systems-related participation (for example, individual education plan processes, school councils, students on governing bodies, students on appointment panels for new staff) and some activities that encourage 'overt student leadership' (for example, students as lead-learners and student-led learning walks) (Fielding 2004). The notion of participation is used in different ways which imply different levels of participation and engagement – from being informed, taking part and being consulted, to collaborating as reciprocal partners (May 2004; Hart 1992; Rudd, Colligan and Naik 2006; Shier 2001). A further interpretation regards pupil participation as pupils influencing decision-making processes and decisions about their lives which lead to change (Davies, Williams and

Yamashita 2006; Treseder 1997). Participation is, in this view, about making a difference and having a clear sense of agency; it is much more than 'consultation', 'hearing children's views' or 'listening to children's voices'.

Limitations: the professional arena

However, the concepts of pupil participation and voice, far from being emancipatory, have arguably become co-modified as part of an increasing audit culture (Arnot and Reay 2007). Much current activity in this area is critiqued for being instrumental, for its 'naiveté' and 'technicist engagement' (Fielding 2006: 310), as being 'delineated' by professionals (May 2004: 69) and serving adult purposes. Attempts to seek children's views through formal consultation exercises have been critiqued for being 'symbolic gestures' (Allan 2008) and 'empty exercises' (Neale 2004) which rarely lead to changes in practice and thus may be viewed as tokenistic. Lundy (2007: 931) suggests that involvement of pupils in decision making should be seen not as 'an option which is in the gift of adults' but as 'a legal imperative which is the right of the child.'

A number of commentators have cautioned against the wholesale assumption of authenticity in pupil participation. Connolly (1997: 163), for example, contends that children have a 'multiplicity of authentic voices' depending on what they are asked, how they are asked and who asks them. In turn, the audience rearticulates the children's voices through its own interpretations. Bluebond-Langner and Korbin (2007: 243) also argue that we need to pay attention to how what children say is played out in relation to the 'social and cultural constraints' in operation and Roche (1999) warns that we need to be more critical of the circumstances in which children are asked to participate in decision making. Participation for, often compliant, institutional purposes such as Ofsted pupil surveys and consultation about improvement in the appearance of the school is of a different nature, for example, from participation encouraged and practised for the improvement of learning (Lodge 2005). Aspis (2002) makes a similar distinction in discussing self-advocacy in adult learning disability settings, where boundaries are often set which determine what people can advocate for and results are frequently superficial.

Limitations: whose voices?

Much UK government guidance to schools (for example, CYPU 2001; DfES 2004a,b; DCSF 2008b) reflects a commitment to increase children's and young people's participation. It is also noted that pupils with special educational needs may require particular support to participate in pupil voice approaches (Whitty and Wisby 2007). However, even with the possibility of adaptations to processes, limits to participation are evident within the guidance.

In the Education Act 2002 children's views are to be considered 'in the light of [their] age and understanding' (p. 105). In the special educational needs (SEN) Code of Practice (DfES 2001), although it is recognised that support is required to enable some children to participate, it still states that children should 'where possible' (p. 14) participate, and that children 'who are capable of forming views' (p. 14) have participation rights. The Code thus empowers professionals to decide whether participation is appropriate for pupils and whether their views should be taken seriously and, in so doing, 'legitimises a very limited version of participation' (Quicke 2003: 51): conditional participation – if you are old enough, mature enough, understand enough (May 2004). Norwich and Kelly (2006) note a possible tension between participation and protectiveness, that a child protection principle sometimes comes into opposition with the participation principle. This is particularly interesting as these are two of the three underlying UNCRC principles of protection, provision and participation.

Lundy (2007), examining UNCRC Article 12 in depth, draws attention to the two parts of the article. The first part gives 'the child who is capable of forming his or her own views the right to express those views freely in all matters affecting the child'; the second part continues, 'the views of the child being given due weight in accordance with the age and maturity of the child'. Thus, 'children's right to express their views is not dependent upon their capacity to express a mature view; it is dependent only on their ability to form a view, mature or not' (Lundy 2007: 935). Are children and young people with significant learning difficulties able to form a view? And, if so, how can we access this? There is a widespread assumption that 'language acquisition, "being able to talk", is a significant marker of competency in forming and expressing perspectives' (Lancaster 2006: 3) and a further assumption that 'inability to use language equals inability to communicate' (ibk 2004: 7). Some pupils with significant learning difficulties do not use speech or language but their communication may include use of symbols, signs, gesture, eye contact, vocalisation, facial expression and changes in behaviour (Goldbart 1994). For some children, then, *listening* to their 'voice' may involve *looking* (Lancaster and Broadbent 2003), observing, actively 'doing' and building a relationship together. Understanding and interpreting a pupil's communication in this way enables others, perhaps, to have some appreciation of the pupil's perspective and then to act as advocates, formally or informally (ibk 2004) representing the pupil. There are probably more examples of formal advocacy approaches with adults (Gray and Jackson 2001), but there is a growing commitment to such advocacy for children and young people with learning difficulties in schools through, for example, person-centred thinking (Murray and Sanderson 2007).

The following examples illustrate pupil participation practices with children and young people with significant learning difficulties. Following the examples, issues relating to personalisation of approaches and authenticity are considered. Names of pupils have been changed.

Example from practice 1: involving pupils in the target-setting process (drawn from South West Regional Partnership 2007)

Sam is a teacher in a school for pupils with severe and profound and multiple learning difficulties. She wanted to improve pupil participation in target setting for their individual education plans. 'The target setting process', she suggested, 'felt like something that the pupils had no involvement in at all and certainly held little if any meaning for them.' Her aim was for the pupils to have a real feeling of ownership of their targets, which in turn, she hoped, would lead to an improvement in their understanding of their own abilities. Although Sam held a leadership position in the school she decided to start this work with her own class of pupils, aged 14–16 years, with a project lasting one school term. She explained, 'I would experience all the benefits and pitfalls myself before trying to convince other teachers across the school that it was a, hopefully, worthwhile process.'

Sam chose to work with the pupils on their behaviour targets and devoted specific time to developing pupils' understanding of these targets and the words and concepts used in the target-setting process (for example, easy, hard, achieved, change, more work), using symbols (Widgit software 2000) and the idea of an arrow hitting a target. With their consent, each pupil's behaviour target (for example, 'to do work on my own') was revisited at the beginning and end of each day with the whole class, using an interactive whiteboard to display the target. Sam reported that the pupils became very proficient at being able to give examples of when they had done something that day towards meeting their target. They were also very supportive of each other.

After six weeks the pupils were asked to review whether they had met their targets (see Figure 10.1). Sam said

> This experience showed me that we needed to change the symbol used for 'achieved' as some pupils thought that it meant 'good'. On the next form I use I am also going to change the word 'hard' to 'difficult' as some pupils had circled this saying they had 'worked hard'. I was surprised by how many of the pupils were able to realistically assess whether they had met their targets.

Sam continued displaying the new targets morning and afternoon during the next half term and pupils also set the adults some targets.

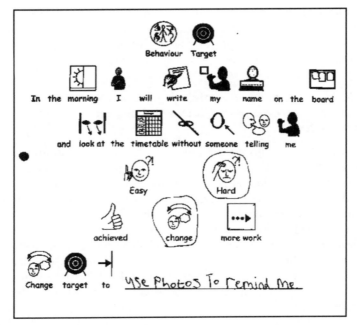

Figure 10.1 Review of behaviour target.

Sam reflected:

> The effects of this project went far beyond my aims. The whole experi-
> ence really made me feel that we were all working together as a class,
> not just as the pupils and the adults and that we were all engaged in
> learning together. Some of the pupils were far more insightful about
> their own capabilities than I had previously believed. By the end of the
> project pupils were suggesting ways in which they could meet their tar-
> gets – for example, Liam couldn't remember to bring a magazine in but
> remembered that a visual prompt had helped him remember his morning
> routine and suggested the same could help him this time. Ultimately all
> pupils are far more involved in and responsible for their own learning.

Example from practice 2: involvement in annual review processes

Drew is 16 years old and attends a school for children and young people with
severe and profound learning difficulties. He has cerebral palsy, significant
medical conditions and profound cognitive difficulties. Drew communicates
through eye pointing, using a yes/no eye communication board, and loud
vocalising, for example laughing, screaming with apparent delight and

crying with apparent pain. He is beginning to show consistent recognition of personalised objects of reference (Ockleford 2002), for example his own swimming towel as a cue for going to the school hydrotherapy pool.

In England statements of special educational need are reviewed annually. In Drew's school, pupils are closely involved in the annual review processes and time is spent preparing for the annual review meetings. The members of Drew's class take it in turns to be in the 'hot seat' while other pupils and staff brainstorm what they like about that pupil. These comments are made into a poster for the meeting. Photographs taken over the year, illustrating activities Drew has participated in, things he seems to like and those he does not seem to like, are gathered and five are selected for a slide show which will be switch-activated by Drew. One of the photographs shows Drew working in physiotherapy, where his facial expression appears to indicate dislike (a view supported by the teaching assistant who is Drew's key worker in school). Another shows Drew in the school hydropool. This is an activity Drew appears to enjoy; he kicks, splashes and laughs in the pool and cries when he has to leave the pool at the end of the session. Drew is supported in selecting music to play at the beginning of the meeting. Three pieces of music which staff have previously recorded as Drew's preferences are played and Drew's responses to these are interpreted to decide upon one choice: 'Mamma Mia!'

On the day of the meeting, Drew is told who will be at the meeting, including his mum. Staff are not sure that he understands this information but always inform pupils what is going to happen. The meeting is based upon the person-centred model developed by Sanderson, Jones, Mathieson, Ali and Hibbs (n.d.). Drew's music is playing as the facilitator (a facilitator-trained teaching assistant) welcomes the attendees of the meeting with Drew: Drew's mum and dad, his teacher, his key worker teaching assistant, the headteacher, Drew's social worker, his physiotherapist, a school nurse, his respite carers and his Connexions personal adviser (a careers and personal development service providing information and advice for young people). The meeting commences with each person stating what they like and admire about Drew; the class poster is shared. Large pieces of paper are on the wall for the attendees to complete about what is currently working and what is not working for Drew and about what Drew needs to keep safe and healthy. It is difficult for Drew to participate in this part of the meeting but all conversation is directed to Drew. Drinks and snacks are served during this time. Drew then shares his photograph slide show and an action plan is compiled, drawing upon the range of points, comments and issues raised in the meeting. For Drew this included the instigation of a timetable in school involving an increasing proportion of sensory elements, for example music, music therapy, sensory stories, rebound (using the trampoline) and massage in addition to hydropool. These were activities he seemed to enjoy the most and during which he appeared to be making most communicative progress.

Example from practice 3: pupil consultation about the school playground and outside area

Selina is the inclusion coordinator at a school for children with severe learning difficulties and profound and multiple learning difficulties, with 120 pupils aged 3–19 years. She led a consultation project with the children and young people focusing on the school playground and outdoor area. This sloped area included grassy areas and tarmac, some climbing equipment and a slide, a gazebo, some trees and a tarmac path.

Several pupils were selected from each age group and from the school council – thirteen pupils in total. Selina worked with these pupils in pairs or small groups using different participatory methods to explore the pupils' own views and to enable them to advocate on behalf of their peers with more profound and complex needs.

For consultations with the younger children, Selina introduced them to Colin, a metre-long blue-green iridescent beanbag toy lizard. Colin brought with him his own bag containing items which were of importance to him in his life. This included three small beanbag toy friends, toy motor cars and a small ball (some of his favourite play activities), and symbols representing his family and his home (see Figure 10.2). Selina talked with the children about Colin and what he liked and this supported the children in sharing what activities they liked to do at playtime, and what they liked and did not like about their school playground. They told Colin what they would do to the playground if they could do anything they wanted, big or small. Selina asked children to 'take Colin out to play' and to show him what they do at playtime, then observed the children on the playground – they swung him on the swing, they slid him and his toy cars down the slide, they buried him in leaves, they ran around with him and some chewed his tail. This was thought to indicate what areas and aspects of the playground and activities they liked.

Some pupils physically explored the playground with a friend who had more profound and complex needs and with Selina. Nick noticed that his friend, Barney, a wheelchair user, would not be able to use the sand pit as he could not get close to it with his wheelchair, and also noted that there was a step to enter the gazebo. Other pupils used photographs and discussion. Mark, who had attended the school for twelve years, observed that the playground area had been made smaller as the school itself had grown larger. Some children spoke about their ideas: 'The sand pit's too small and there is no sand in it'; 'The grass gets muddy and it's bumpy. Children fall over.' Another child commented that, when it rained, children needed extra help from staff so they did not slip in the mud. Richard asked for high fences to stop balls going over. Emma requested more space and a race track painted on the tarmac pitch so she could go faster in her electric wheelchair. Younger pupils found it difficult to comment on what they did not like, but some

Figure 10.2 Colin the lizard with his bag and contents.

older pupils mentioned the problem of the slope and the unevenness of the ground.

Daniel, who experiences severe autism and 'challenging behaviour', worked with his own teacher to explore some of these issues. Daniel expressed his liking for the 'tapping bell'. There was no bell in the playground and to start with it was assumed he meant that he would like there to be a bell to ring. However, after careful observation by his teacher, it transpired that the 'tapping bell' was a part of the climbing frame which Daniel tapped with a stick for it to make a ringing sound.

Selina organised all of the children's views into categories and displayed these on the school hall wall, using a tree (with green leaves on the tree for 'what's working?' and brown leaves on the ground for 'what's not working?') with an overarching rainbow covered with 'in my dreams'. In a training session the school staff then looked at the pupils' views and added their own comments on a second tree and on the rainbow. Many of these were similar to the pupils, for example, 'it gets very muddy in winter, which means half the playground can't be used'. Dreams included: 'a safe slope', 'windows in the gazebo so it is sheltered', 'a playground maintenance person'.

Following the consultation the school has decided initially to flatten the playground. This is, of course, a major structural and expensive action and will take time to instigate, one drawback as the children cannot see immediate results. The consultation process continues and is now focusing on questions about play in different weathers and whom the children play with.

Some issues around participation and voice for pupils with significant learning difficulties will next be examined drawing upon the above three examples.

Personalised approaches

Macbeath, Demetriou, Ruddock and Myers (2003) suggest three types of approaches for pupil participation: directed, prompted and mediated approaches. *Directed approaches* are those whereby pupils are asked directly for their views through writing, talking or other forms of communication. This may include, for example, questionnaires; individual, group or class conversations, interviews or discussions; or posting views in a box. Many different modes can be used to respond to questions; for example, written, verbal, drawing, communication devices, use of cameras, smiley faces, symbols or moving to different corners of the room according to one's view. In the playground consultation example above, a directed interview/conversation approach was taken with some pupils and verbal responses made. *Prompted approaches* are those whereby a stimulus is used to 'prompt' pupils to express their views, for example through videoing or taking photographs and then discussing these. Selina used this approach in the playground consultation example, using Colin the lizard, symbols and photographs as prompts with some children. In the target-setting example, Sam uses pictorial and symbolic prompts, for example the arrow and target. *Mediated approaches* are those whereby pupils express their views through other media or mediated activities, including drawing, taking photographs, making videos, writing stories, being observed and advocacy approaches. Selina uses a number of different mediated participatory methods; for example, observation of children using the playground, observation of children with Colin the lizard and peer advocacy. In the second example, Drew's likes and dislikes are interpreted over time and advocated by those working closely with him.

The examples in this chapter demonstrate the need for 'person-centred approaches to student voice' (Fielding 2006: 310), for participatory approaches which are flexible and personalised, and for time to be taken, according to the requirements and preferences of each pupil. Lewis, Robertson and Parsons (2005) used a range of methods in their research study on the educational experiences of disabled students and their families: one-to-one interviews, small group interviews, diamond ranking activity, cue card prompted interviews, a photographic trail using photos taken by the child/young person, drawings, mapping, puppets and self-reports to video. They note:

> Most importantly, no single approach was deemed to be the 'right one' to use. Rather, researcher flexibility was considered to be crucial. This involves working with a portfolio of approaches, responding to the preferences of research participants and where appropriate, co-constructing and using research tools.
>
> (p. 59)

For some children, it may be important to use more than one approach to build up a complete picture of their views. Bishton (2007) used three different types of media in her small-scale study eliciting the views of children with severe learning difficulties (interviews with puppets and symbol cue cards, a diamond ranking exercise of likes/dislikes and photographs taken by the children) and found that only 42 per cent of responses were mentioned by the children in more than one medium.

Authenticity

Ruddock (2003) reminds us of the importance of 'hearing the quiet voice and avoiding the creation of a pupil voice elite' (p. 7). Some children with significant learning difficulties are more articulate or strident than others though most children with significant learning difficulties communicate in non-traditional ways. How can the expression of the voice of all children be ensured? In the playground project, Selina attempted to find ways to access a wide range of pupils' views. In the annual review example, all of the pupils at Drew's school are closely involved in annual review processes, although pupils with profound learning difficulties such as Drew may be those whose voices are most complex to ascertain. For children with significant learning difficulties an extensive amount of intensive observation and interaction may be necessary.

However, Ware (2004) highlights the importance of maintaining criticality and honesty about the limitations of participation for children and young people with significant learning difficulties. It is easy to assume pupils' understanding, as illustrated in the different understandings of the symbol for 'achieve' and the word 'hard' in the target-setting example. Ware argues that, although children and young people with profound learning difficulties may express like or dislike, this does not amount to 'expressing a view'. It is often inferred from positive responses and photographs showing children enjoying an activity that they therefore want to participate in that activity; similarly, negative reactions are assumed to indicate a wish not to participate. Selina in the playground consultation example and Bishton (2007) both note that it is more difficult for children to express negative views. Furthermore, we all have a range of voices, multiple perspectives and changing points of view. This polyphony (Sidorkin 1999, cited in Fielding 2006) is important to recognise and encourage, using multiple activities, approaches and situations in which to ascertain children's views (Lewis 2002). We should also consider that 'some children may genuinely and freely prefer silence to voicing their views' (Lewis and Porter 2007: 224). Facilitators and advocates need to maintain ethical awareness of their interpretative role (Connolly 1997), being cognisant of whose agenda is being served and of the selective and uncritical use of pupils' voices (Bluebond-Langner and Korbin 2007). Additionally, listening to learner voice alone is not sufficient; what happens next is of great importance (Robinson and Taylor 2007). Pupils need to know what is happening as a result of their participation.

In all three examples, pupils are supported in expressing their views (or, at least, their likes/dislikes), they are consulted and their views are seriously taken into account in decision making. In this way, these examples have moved beyond Hart's (1992) tokenistic level of (non-)participation. However, further involvement in decision-making processes, greater staff–pupil collaboration and pupil-initiated and directed participation would be required to move to higher levels of participation (Shier 2001; Rudd *et al.* 2006). Are the examples, then, portrayals of limited forms of participation?

Conclusion

This chapter has explored some of the issues around pupil participation and voice with specific reference to pupils with significant learning difficulties, for whom participation may frequently be dismissed, limited or tokenistic. Examples of participation activities have illustrated some attempts to move beyond tokenism and concerns have been raised about levels of participation and authenticity.

Shevlin and Rose (2008: 429) state that 'our appraisal of capability [must] be rigorously pursued in order to ensure that *all* pupils gain a right of *full* participation' (added emphasis). Current limitation clauses in legislation and guidance with reference to capability and 'wherever possible' (DfES 2001: 14) do not support this right. Lundy (2007) argues that the full obligation of Article 12 has been lost in abbreviations such as 'pupil voice' and proposes a stronger interpretation composed of four elements: *space*, children being given the opportunity to express a view; *voice*, children being facilitated to express their views; *audience*, their views being listened to; and *influence*, their views acted upon, as appropriate. Even then, Article 12 does not take the participation of children beyond the expression of a view and having 'due weight' given to it. It does not include fuller child participation in initiation, decision making and action.

Returning to Hargreaves's (2004: 7) definition –

> how students come to play a more active role in their education and schooling as a direct result of teachers becoming more attentive, in sustained or routine ways, to what students say about their experience of learning and of school life

– the responsibility is given to teachers (and other staff) to be attentive. The examples from practice in this chapter illustrate that the participation of children and young people with significant learning difficulties, in particular, '*depends* on the approach of staff and the atmosphere and ethos of the classroom and the school' (Lawson 2003: 31, added emphasis). The 'voices' of children and young people with significant learning difficulties are 'not immediately accessible and apparent' (James 2007: 262); we therefore need to consider the way voices are represented, how and by whom.

Acknowledgments

Sam Keegan, Mayfield School, Torquay, UK
Selina Lingley and Pam Long, Ellen Tinkham School, Exeter, UK

Bibliography

Allan, J. (2008) *Rethinking Inclusive Education: The Philosophers of Difference in Practice*. Dordrecht, The Netherlands: Springer.

Arnot, M. and Reay, D. (2007) A sociology of pedagogic voice: power, inequality and pupil consultation. *Discourse: Studies in the Cultural Politics of Education*, 28 (3): 311–325.

Aspis, S. (2002) Self-advocacy: vested interests and misunderstandings. *British Journal of Learning Disabilities*, 30: 3–7.

Bishton, H. (2007) *Children's Voice, Children's Rights: What Children with Special Needs Have to Say about Their Variously Inclusive Schools*. Nottingham: NCSL.

Bluebond-Langner, M. and Korbin, J. (2007) Challenges and opportunities in the anthropology of childhoods: an introduction to 'children, childhoods and childhood studies'. *American Anthropologist*, 109 (2): 241–246.

Connolly, P. (1997) In search of authenticity: researching young children's perspectives. In A. Pollard, D. Thiessen and A. Filer (Eds) *Children and Their Curriculum*. London: Falmer Press.

CYPU (Children's and Young People's Unit). (2001) *Learning to Listen: Core Principles for the Involvement of Children and Young People*. London: DfES.

Davies, L., Williams, C. and Yamashita, H. (2006) *Inspiring Schools: A Literature Review*. London: Carnegie Young People Initiative/Esmee Fairbairn Foundation. Accessed 4 March 2010 at www.cypi.carnegieuktrust.org.uk

DCSF (Department for Children, Schools and Families). (2007) The Children's Plan. Nottingham: DCSF.

DCSF. (2008a) *Special Educational Needs in England: January 2008*. Accessed 4 March 2010 at http://www.dcsf.gov.uk/rsgateway/DB/SFR/s000794/SFR15_2008_Final.pdf

DCSF. (2008b) *Working Together: Listening to the Voices of Children and Young People*. Accessed 4 March 2010 at www.teachernet.gov.uk/wholeschool/behaviour/participationguidance/

DfES (Department for Education and Skills). (2001) *Special Educational Needs Code of Practice*. Nottingham: DfES.

DfES. (2003) *Data Collection by Type of Special Educational Need*. Nottingham: DfES.

DfES. (2004a) *Every Child Matters: Change for Children*. Nottingham: DfES.

DfES. (2004b) *Working Together: Giving Children and Young People a Say*. Nottingham: DfES.

DfES. (2006) *2020 Vision: Report of the Teaching and Learning in 2020 Review Group*. (Gilbert report). Nottingham: DfES.

DfES. (2007) *Curriculum Review: Diversity and Citizenship*. (Ajegbo review). Nottingham: DfES.

Education Act 2002. London: TSO.

Fielding, M. (2004) 'New wave' student voice and the renewal of civic society. *London Review of Education*, 2 (3): 197–217.

Fielding, M. (2006) Leadership, radical student engagement and the necessity of person-centred education. *International Journal of Leadership in Education*, 9 (4): 299–313.

Goldbart, J. (1994) Opening the communication curriculum to students with PMLD. In J. Ware (Ed.) *Educating Children with Profound and Multiple Learning Difficulties*. London: Fulton.

Gray, B. and Jackson, R. (Eds). (2001) *Advocacy and Learning Disability*. London: Jessica Kingsley.

Hargreaves, D. (2004) *Personalised Learning: Student Voice and Assessment for Learning*. London: Specialist Schools Academies Trust. Accessed 4 March 2010 at http://www.ssat-inet.net/resources/publications/publicationdescriptions/personal-isinglearningseries1.aspx

Hart, R. A. (1992) *Children's Participation, from Tokenism to Citizenship*. UNICEF: Florence.

ibk initiatives. (2004) *An Advocacy Service for Disabled Children in Sheffield*. Sheffield: ibk initiatives.

James, A. (2007) Giving voice to children's voices: practices and problems, pitfalls and potentials. *American Anthropologist*, 109 (2): 261–272.

Lancaster, Y. P. (2006) *RAMPS: A Framework for Listening to Children*. London: Daycare Trust.

Lancaster, Y. P. and Broadbent, V. (2003) *Listening to Young Children*. Maidenhead: Open University Press.

Lawson, H. (2003) Pupil participation: questioning the extent? *SLD Experience*, 36: 31–35.

Lawson, H. (2009) Promoting access to community and participation: What role can citizenship education play? In J. Seale and M. Nind (Eds) *Understanding and Promoting Access for People with Learning Difficulties*. London: Routledge.

Lewis, A. (2002) Accessing, through research interviews, the views of children with difficulties in learning. *Support for Learning*, 17: 109–115.

Lewis, A. and Porter, J. (2007) Research and pupil voice. In L. Florian (Ed.) *The Sage Handbook of Special Education*. London: Sage.

Lewis, A., Robertson, C. and Parsons, S. (2005) *Experiences of Disabled Students and Their Families – Phase One*. London: Disability Rights Commission.

Lodge, C. (2005) From hearing voices to engaging in dialogue: problematising student participation in school improvement. *Journal of Educational Change*, 6 (2): 125–146.

Lundy, L. (2007) 'Voice' is not enough: conceptualising Article 12 of the United Nations Convention on the Rights of the Child. *British Educational Research Journal*, 33 (6): 927–942.

Macbeath, J., Demetriou, H., Ruddock, J. and Myers, K. (2003) *Consulting Pupils: A Toolkit for Teachers*. Cambridge: Pearson.

May, H. (2004) Interpreting pupil participation into practice: contributions of the SEN Code of Practice (2001). *Journal of Research in Special Educational Needs*, 4 (2): 67–73.

Murray, P. and Sanderson, H. (2007) *Developing Person Centred Approaches in Schools*. Stockport: HSA Press.

Neale, B. (2004) Introduction: young children's citizenship. In B. Neale (Ed.) *Young Children's Citizenship: Ideas into Practice*. York: Joseph Rowntree.

Norwich, B. and Kelly, N. and Educational Psychologists in Training. (2006) Evaluating children's participation in SEN procedures: lessons for educational psychologists. *Educational Psychology in Practice*, 22 (3): 255–271.

Ockleford, A. (2002) *Objects of Reference*. London: RNIB.

Ofsted (Office for Standards in Education). (2005) *Pupils' Satisfaction with Their School*. HMI 2494. London: Ofsted.

Quicke, J. (2003) Educating the pupil voice. *Support for Learning*, 18 (2): 51–57.

Robinson, C. and Taylor, C. (2007) Theorising student voice: values and perspectives. *Improving Schools*, 10 (1): 5–17.

Roche, J. (1999) Children: rights, participation and citizenship. *Childhood*, 6 (4): 475–493.

Rudd, T., Colligan, F. and Naik, R. (2006) *Learner Voice*. Bristol: Futurelab. Accessed 4 March 2010 at http://www.futurelab.org.uk/resources/publications-reports-articles/handbooks/Handbook132/

Ruddock, J. (2003) *Research Briefing: Consulting Pupils about Teaching and Learning*. Cambridge: TLRP (Teaching and Learning Research Programme).

Sanderson, H., Jones, S., Mathieson, R., Ali, A. and Hibbs, W. (n.d.) *Person Centred '14' plus Reviews*. Accessed 4 March 2010 at http://www.helensandersonassociates.co.uk/PDFs/Person%20Centred%20Transition%20-%2014%20reviews%20_Hull%20final%20version_.pdf

Shevlin, M. and Rose, R. (2008) Pupils as partners in education decision-making: responding to the legislation in England and Ireland. *European Journal of Special Needs Education*, 23 (4): 423–430.

Shier, H. (2001) Pathways to participation: openings, opportunities and obligations. *Children and Society*, 15: 107–117.

South West Regional Partnership. (2007) *Pupil Participation: Beyond Tokenism*. Accessed 4 March 2010 at http://www.sw-special.co.uk/documents/students/docs/PupilParticipationBooklet.pdf

Treseder, P. (1997) *Empowering Children and Young People*. London: Save the Children.

United Nations. (1989) *Convention on the Rights of the Child*. New York: UN.

Ware, J. (2004) Ascertaining the views of people with profound and multiple learning disabilities. *British Journal of Learning Disabilities*, 32 (4): 175–179.

Whitty, G. and Wisby, E. (2007) *Real Decision Making: School Councils in Action*. Research Report DCSF-RR001. Nottingham: DCSF.

Widgit Software. (2000) *Writing with Symbols*. Accessed 4 March 2010 at www.widgit.com/products/wws2000/index.htm

Section 4

Professional development for inclusion

Chapter 11

Teacher education for inclusion

Chris Forlin (Hong Kong Institute of Education, China)

Introduction

The inclusion of all learners regardless of specific educational need into regular schools continues to be promoted as the best option for ensuring equitable educational opportunities for all. (NB: The term 'learner' is used throughout to denote children and young people as applied in the Professional Standards for Teachers in England). Preparation of teachers during their initial training programs should, therefore, be providing a suitable foundation to enable them to support this aim. At least at a minimal level newly graduated teachers should have the understanding that their role will require them to differentiate the curriculum and their pedagogy to ensure that all learners within their classes will be able to access an appropriate education.

In this case, why is it that after four years of training almost all new teachers continue to claim that they are unprepared for the reality and challenges of regular classrooms; particularly in respect to catering for the special education needs of an increasing number of their learners? Granted that for some teachers, especially those who aim to work in secondary schools, their training in education is less rigorous and usually only one to two years as an add-on degree; however, they should still have a more reasonable expectation of their responsibility as a regular class teacher. Why do newly qualified teachers, therefore, appear to have a misconception about their role and rather negative attitudes about the inclusion of learners with diverse needs? This chapter will evaluate a range of current initial training programs by deconstructing them in order to identify the potential underpinnings of this negativity in relation to the perceptions of newly graduated teachers.

The inclusion of all learners

During the past three decades there has been a significant change in the way learners with disabilities are educated. In the 1950s and 1960s there was a plethora of special schools opened to enable the education of learners with specific disabilities alongside similar peers in segregated categorically based schools. The movement toward a more inclusive educational system that encourages and supports the education of all learners within the same general schools began with the normalization principle in the early 1970s (Loreman, Deppeler, and Harvey 2005). This was supported by the strength of international declarations that resulted in important assertions such as the key Salamanca Statement (UNESCO 1994), which promoted inclusion as being the most effective means of educating the majority of children while combating discriminatory practices.

The guiding principle underpinning inclusion is that regular schools should accommodate all learners regardless of their physical, intellectual, sensory, emotional, or other special needs (Forlin 2008). Inclusion in an educational context means that every child should be a valued member of the school community and none should be marginalized, alienated, humiliated, teased, rejected, or excluded. Thus, the implication follows that all teachers should have the appropriate skills to be able to provide suitable programs for the diversity of learner need to be found in their classrooms.

Whereas the initial focus of inclusion was on catering for learners with disabilities, it has become much broader in its interpretation. There is now a stronger emphasis on the need for the restructuring of schools to accommodate learners with a broader range of diverse learning needs, including those from different ethnic and racial backgrounds and those with alternative languages, cultural differences, learning difficulties, and any other potentially marginalizing difficulty. The needs of learners are not only confined to those at the lower end of the IQ range but also include high-achieving students who are not achieving to potential. In many instances school systems are addressing this by taking a whole-schooling approach to inclusion.

With this change in education for learners with special needs has been concomitantly a change in the role of the teacher in supporting inclusion. Clearly, if the classroom structure is to change from a homogeneous grouping of learners to a heterogeneous one, then curriculum and pedagogy must also change to enable the teacher to accommodate all learners' needs. To facilitate this change it follows quite simply that teacher preparation programs must also transform to ensure that newly qualified teachers (NQTs) are prepared to teach in diverse classrooms and have the necessary skills to adapt the curricula and their pedagogy to meet the needs of all learners. This is not an easy task to accomplish when according to Milner, Tenore, and Laughter (2008):

> Never before have public school teachers in the United States been faced with the challenge of meeting the needs of so many culturally diverse learners. The teaching force in the U.S. is increasingly white, monolingual, middle class, and female, whereas the student population is increasingly diverse.
>
> (p. 18)

Such comments are not confined to the US as similar issues are arising in many jurisdictions that have increasing diversity in their populations but an under-representation of teachers from minority groups.

Changes in initial teacher training for inclusion

Teacher training institutions have been to some extent slow in many regions to make the necessary adjustments to their courses in order to prepare teachers for inclusion (Forlin 2008; Loreman *et al.* 2005). An analysis of current programs indicates three most common methods for addressing inclusion during initial teacher training (ITT). These relate to (1) conforming to a set of government standards to enable teacher registration; (2) conforming to state requirements for including specific programs within ITT courses; and (3) independent decision making by the training institution.

Teacher registration is fast becoming the norm in many regions and this is having a positive impact on improving the rate of change to ITT. Where registration is mandatory, governments have greater control over the content of ITT programs, being able to demand that courses meet specified standards in relation to inclusion (Forlin, Loreman, Sharma, and Earle 2007). In some states, where specific standards for registration are not yet in place, local governments have stipulated minimum hours of study about inclusion in order for ITT courses to be registered. In situations where teacher registration does not specify the training curriculum, and local government does not stipulate minimum study in the area, the emphasis on preparing teachers for inclusion continues to rely upon individual universities or colleges to determine their own courses and consequently varies enormously between them.

The Qualifications and Curriculum Authority (QCA) in England monitors ITT and provides an International Review of Curriculum and Assessment (INCA), which includes a description of government policy on education in various jurisdictions. Table 11.1 outlines the organizing bodies responsible for ITT.

Where teacher registration is compulsory, for example in the USA, Canada, England, and many other countries, this has resulted in institutions being obliged to ensure that all students have certain knowledge, skills, and attributes that, consequently, need to be included in their courses. In addition to preparing teachers for inclusion, though, many institutions are faced with continually needing to revise their courses to address other school reforms and incessantly changing outcomes that governments want included in the school syllabus, which all impact on curriculum and pedagogy and place high demands on ITT institutions.

The foremost aspect of education reform in the past decade across almost all regions, nonetheless, has without doubt been the expectation for teacher training courses to better prepare teachers for inclusion. This has been led by various government initiatives that have raised the requirements for NQTs

Table 11.1 Organizing bodies responsible for initial teacher training

Responsibilities of organizing bodies

	Standards for teaching qualification	Teacher training curriculum guidance/standards	Registration agency
England	National ministry	Non-departmental public body	Statutory body
Ireland[a]	National ministry/statutory body	Statutory body/individual universities	Statutory body
Northern Ireland	National ministry	National ministry	Statutory body
Scotland	National ministry	National ministry	Statutory body
Wales	Non-departmental public body	Non-departmental public body	Statutory body
France	National ministry	National ministry	Local authority
Germany	Federal ministry	Federal ministry	Federal ministry
Hungary	National ministry	National ministry/individual universities	n/a
Italy	National ministry	National ministry	Local authority
Netherlands	National ministry	National ministry/individual universities	n/a
Spain	National ministry	National ministry	Local authority
Sweden	National ministry	National ministry/individual universities	n/a
Switzerland	National ministry	National ministry	National ministry

Australia[b]	National ministry or statutory body and federal ministry	Federal ministry or statutory body	Statutory body
Canada	Federal ministry or statutory body	Federal ministry or statutory body	Federal ministry or statutory body
Japan	National ministry	National ministry	Local authority
Korea	National ministry	Teacher training institutions	Local authority
New Zealand	Statutory body	Statutory body	Statutory body
Singapore	National ministry	National ministry	National ministry
USA[c]	Federal ministry	Federal ministry	Federal ministry

Source: INCA (2008: 49).

Notes

National ministry: The Ministry of Education in each country, which determines and funds broad policies dealing with the "national interest."

Federal ministry: State Ministry of Education, responsible for education in the specific state/province.

Statutory body: Body independent from government that was established by legislation.

Non-departmental public body: Body set up, sometimes under statute, to carry out specific functions on behalf of government; however, although non-departmental public bodies are government funded, they are not government departments or part of government departments.

Local authority: Regional education headquarters; the local arm of the Ministry of Education.

a   The Ministry is responsible for the standards for obtaining a teaching qualification for primary education, whereas a statutory body (the Registration Council for Secondary Teachers) is responsible for the standards for secondary education. Individual universities are responsible for the content of the teacher training curriculum for primary education, whereas a statutory body (the Registration Council for Secondary Teachers) has overall responsibility for the secondary teacher training curriculum. In 2006, a Teaching Council was established in Ireland. Its role includes promoting teaching as a profession, the continuing professional development (CPD) of teachers and the regulation of standards in the profession.

b   Although the States and Territories retain control of their own education systems, a national education and training framework is emerging through the Ministerial Council on Education, Employment, Training and Youth Affairs (MCEETYA), including the 2003 National Framework for Professional Standards for Teaching.

c   Although most responsibility lies with the federal ministries in the individual states, to qualify for certain funding strands, states must meet certain national requirements.

by specifying minimum standards and monitoring their achievement in an attempt to improve teacher quality. Some major leaders in this area have been the USA and the UK, but many government systems have to some degree commenced a review of ITT programs to consider how they are best meeting the needs of teachers in the twenty-first century (see Table 11.2).

In the USA a highly qualified teacher is now defined as "a teacher who meets the standards of the definition in the No Child Left Behind (NCLB) legislation" (USA Funds Education Access 2005). To ensure that all teachers are highly qualified on completion of their training, states have had to make certain that NQTs are competent in the core academic subjects that they will teach. To be deemed highly qualified, teachers must:

1   have a bachelor's degree;
2   hold full state certification or licensure; and
3   prove that they know each subject they teach.

In an attempt to acknowledge that some NQTs may be required to teach subjects for which they were not originally trained, especially if working in rural communities, a three-year grace has been introduced to allow them to become qualified in these additional core areas.

In England the Training and Development Agency for Schools (TDA 2008) has similarly set standards for qualified teacher status (QTS) that denote the required knowledge and skills for new teachers. One section focuses specifically on achievement and diversity (see Table 11.2). The TDA has also introduced a range of new routes into teaching so that QTS can now be obtained through alternative avenues. Such options include school-based ITT for postgraduates; an assessment only option for teachers with substantial experience; and employment-centered opportunities such as the Graduate and Registered Teacher Programmes (TDA 2006).

A review of the factors that support high-quality ITT in England found that there was little variation between the success rates of NQTs from the 127 different institutions investigated, regardless of the institute's level of research or quality as determined by the Office for Standards in Education inspections (Smith and Gorard 2007). Based on data from 1998 to 2001, Smith and Gorard also reported that female NQTs were more successful on average than male peers in obtaining QTS, as were younger rather than older trainees and whites as apposed to all other ethnic groups; although there were no differences subsequently in obtaining teaching positions.

Agencies supporting initial teacher training for inclusion

In order to respond to the concerns raised over the quality of some ITT programs various safeguards have been implemented recently to ensure that training institutions are producing high-quality and competent teachers

(Smith and Gorard 2007). In some jurisdictions governments have initiated specific agencies to oversee the ITT and ongoing professional development of teachers to ensure they are able to meet the diverse needs of learners. For example, in England the Teacher Training Agency (TTA) took on a new role in 2005 as the TDA to ensure that all schools were able to access high-quality relevant training and development for their staff to keep their knowledge and skills current. The three major roles of the TDA are to (1) attract able and committed people into teaching; (2) provide schools and staff with good information on training, development and workforce remodeling; and (3) create a training and development environment that enables the whole school workforce to develop its effectiveness (TDA 2009). The TDA also works with ITT institutes to ensure a high quality of training to prepare teachers to join school teams.

To ensure that trainee teachers are required to achieve QTS before teaching, the regulations were changed in England in 2007 to remove the previous five-year grace period. This has meant that NQTs who wish to work in a state-maintained school must now pass the appropriate skills test and meet all professional standards before they can be employed and begin their induction. The newly finalized standards apply to all programs in England commencing after 1 September 2007. The standards are organized under three categories – professional attributes; knowledge and understanding; and skills – and "formally set out what a trainee teacher is expected to know, understand and be able to do in order to be awarded QTS and succeed as an effective teacher" (TDA 2009).

Are newly qualified teachers ready for inclusion?

As teaching has become progressively more multifaceted and the role of a teacher in a regular classroom has dramatically changed, research has clearly shown that many regular class teachers continue to feel unprepared for inclusion and are not overly eager to participate in full inclusion (Yeun, Westwood and Wong 2004).

Early research by Cains and Brown (1998) found that both primary and secondary NQTs in England and Wales felt poorly prepared to deal with special needs issues and children with learning difficulties. In particular, primary school teachers found general classroom issues significantly more demanding than did their secondary counterparts. Cains and Brown proposed that their demands were greater because of a number of features unique to primary schools:

- having to work with, and therefore continually adapt teaching approaches for, the same special needs children throughout the school day, five days per week;
- having associated contact with these children's parents;

Table 11.2 Teacher training requirements in relation to special educational needs (SEN)

Region	Teacher training in relation to SEN/diversity
Australia	Content in the *National Framework for Professional Standards for Teaching* related to diversity or SEN: "teachers have to be both knowledgeable in their content areas and extremely skilful in a wide range of teaching approaches to cater for the diverse learning needs of every student" (p. 3). "[Effective teachers] know and understand and take account of the diverse social, cultural and special learning-needs background of their students and the influences these have on teaching and learning" (p. 11). "[Teachers] uphold high professional ethics with regard to their own conduct and that of others and respect their students and value their diversity" (p. 11).[a]
Hong Kong	According to the White Paper *Equal Opportunities and Full Participation: A Better Tomorrow for All*, "Special education is the responsibility of all teachers in the school system. To enhance teachers' understanding and acceptance of children with special educational needs, there is an element in the initial teacher training for ordinary school teachers on the education of children with special educational needs" (p. 52).[b]
New Zealand	Points of Graduating Teacher Standards related to diverse learners: Know how to develop metacognitive strategies of diverse learners Demonstrate high expectations of all learners, focus on learning and recognize and value diversity Promote a learning culture which engages diverse learners effectively.[c]
Singapore	According to *Singapore Education Milestone 2004–2005: Time & Space*, "Training in special needs will also be provided for selected mainstream teachers to raise general awareness of the different types of learning difficulties, and help them identify and manage children with mild learning difficulties" (p. 35).[d] The Ministry of Education "aims to train 10% of teaching staff in all schools over the next five years so that they are better at recognizing students with special needs and helping them."[e]

England   The minimum standard of competence by the TDA in SEN includes being able to:

"Q 18   Understand how children and young people develop and that the progress and well-being of learners are affected by a range of developmental, social, religious, ethnic, cultural and linguistic influences.

"Q 19   Know how to make effective personalised provision for those they teach, including those for whom English is an additional language or who have special educational needs or disabilities, and how to take practical account of diversity and promote equality and inclusion in their teaching.

"Q 20   Know and understand the roles of colleagues with specific responsibilities, including those with responsibility for learners with special educational needs and disabilities and other individual learning needs."[f]

USA   In the USA a highly qualified teacher is now defined as "a teacher who meets the standards of the definition in the No Child Left Behind (NCLB) legislation."

a   Ministerial Council on Education, Employment Training and Youth Affairs (http://www.mceetya.edu.au/verve/_resources/national_framework_file.pdf).
b   Hong Kong government (http://www.fhb.gov.hk/download/press_and_publications/otherinfo/WP95ENG.DOC).
c   New Zealand Teachers Council (http://www.teacherscouncil.govt.nz/education/gts/gts-poster.pdf).
d   Ministry of Education, Singapore (http://www.moe.gov.sg/about/yearbooks/2005/pdf/time-and-space.pdf).
e   Ministry of Education, Singapore (http://www.moe.gov.sg/media/speeches/2005/sp20051110a.htm).
f   Training & Development Agency (2008: 8).

- having to meet the teaching needs of these children across most or all of the curriculum;
- having to deal continually with associated emotional aspects;
- having to produce frequent reports and keep ongoing records of pupil performance and development;
- having continually to plan, evaluate, and modify teaching approaches often in conjunction with external agencies;
- needing a sound understanding of formal special needs procedures and policies (p. 350).

For the past decade there are limited data on a broad enough scale to make valid judgments on the appropriateness of all ITT courses. For example in England, even though the TDA routinely surveys all NQTs on their training programs, according to Barber and Turner (2007, p. 33):

> While the widely published key points from the 2004 survey indicate a general improvement in NQT ratings of their ITT, there is no specific mention of their level of satisfaction regarding working with children with special educational needs.

Similarly, concern about the quality of ITT has been raised in most recent Australian reviews, suggesting that training institutions are out of touch with reality (O'Keefe 2009). Of major concern is that NQTs continue to report that they are dissatisfied with their pre-service education and that they do not have what they deem essential competencies to solve the challenges they are confronted with in the classroom. The general view has been that NQTs are not prepared in the art and craft of teaching and that there is too much focus on theory rather than practice.

Whereas in general inclusion is not perceived as overly stressful by regular class teachers, there are certain aspects that do cause teachers considerable concerns (Forlin, Keen, and Barrett 2007). Teachers who are including children with an intellectual disability full-time in their classes, for example, are most concerned about classroom issues related to challenging behaviors and a lack of support, and they also feel a perceived threat toward their own personal competency (Forlin et al. 2007). Teachers are also more supportive of including students with mild disabilities rather than those with more challenging needs. For all the criticisms about the poor quality of various ITT programs, there is increasing evidence, nevertheless, that teacher education does matter for teacher effectiveness (Darling-Hammond 2006).

Teacher attitudes toward inclusive education

One of the most difficult challenges in preparing teachers to work in diverse classrooms is that of ensuring that they have a positive attitude toward learners with different backgrounds and special educational needs (SEN) and that they are willing participants in the inclusion movement. Acceptance into teacher training regrettably tends to pay slight attention to the conviction of pre-service teachers toward their anticipated role, giving more weight to the need to fill places to guarantee the preservation of university courses (Forlin 2008). As a teacher's behavior in class is likely to be influenced by their own efficacy expectations and their belief that what they do will be effective (Palmer 2006), it is important to ensure that NQTs, although not necessarily commencing their course with a positive attitude toward inclusion, at least leave their course with one. This is even more challenging in systems where NQTs are frequently from different cultural backgrounds from the students they will teach (Milner *et al.* 2008) and a teacher's own prior notions of need may be quite different from the reality within the local community.

In many school systems additional support can be provided to learners by means of participation in out-of-class activities or remediation programs. Such support is usually accessed by referral from the class teacher. Referral processes have a tendency to be complex and require the teacher to make judgments based on their own beliefs. To ensure that the needs of all learners are addressed equally, teachers must be prepared to consider untraditional cohorts of students for referral and to look beyond traditional expectations for recommendation. This is especially pertinent when considering high-achieving learners, as "Deficit thoughts and beliefs may cause teachers to lower their expectations for culturally diverse male students because teachers have preconceived notions about students' potential and ability" (Milner *et al.* 2008: 20).

The initial attitudes of NQTs are, therefore, critical to the success of inclusion (Forlin 2006). Consequently, ITT plays pivotal roles in ensuring teachers have appropriate attitudes and skills to enable inclusion to be successful (Sharma, Forlin, and Loreman 2008). Closer contact with people with disabilities and involvement in teaching students with diverse needs during ITT has been found to have a significant effect on improving attitudes toward inclusion (Ellins and Porter 2005; Forlin *et al.* 2007) and making NQTs more receptive to inclusion. In addition, it has been found that a significant and positive difference in attitudes and instructional competences can be obtained from undertaking just one course in preparation for inclusive education (Chong, Forlin, and Au 2007; Forlin *et al.* 2007).

Newly qualified teacher induction

Once they have completed their ITT a key time for NQTs in preparing them to cater for the diverse needs of learners would seem to be during their induction period. In some systems (e.g. England and the USA) a formalized statutory induction period is provided. This period of time has been found to be critical for raising NQTs' confidence and competence in working with learners with SEN. It also allows for connections between theory and practice to be made explicit as considerations are given to real cases within their new schools. Two key factors identified that contribute to increased confidence of NQTs during their induction period in the area of special educational needs include day-to-day experiences and support and advice from experienced colleagues. According to Barber and Turner (2007) success of induction in relation to inclusion relies on many factors, however, including:

- variations between schools with regard to how well they identify and meet the needs of pupils with special educational needs;
- variations in SENCo [SEN coordinator] knowledge, skill and experience;
- access to in-service training (INSET);
- quality of INSET provision;
- access to other agencies, including psychology services;
- quality and extent of existing school and SENCo links with other agencies;
- collaborative versus co-operative cultures in schools; and
- their own age and prior experience.

(p. 24)

The way forward for ITT programs for inclusion

A major challenge in the past decade for ITT institutions has been the rapid increase in breadth of curricula that has to be covered, in most instances with no reciprocal increase in the length of teacher education courses. Preparing teachers for inclusion has been one of the most dramatic changes needed in ITT programs but how successful have they been in addressing this? Why is it that NQTs continue to report that they feel unprepared for inclusion and have somewhat mediocre attitudes toward it? It would seem that there are several key issues that have emerged which underpin the success of ITT programs in preparing NQTs for inclusion.

The foremost issue would have to be the extreme differences to be found among ITT courses between and within different regions. Whereas some countries have implemented specified standards and formal requirements for teacher registration, others have made no such move and training programs rely on each institution to make its own judgment on course content. Even in systems where registration is mandated success in achieving the required standards is assessed by individual training institutions without cross-institutional moderation and the awarding of QTS is considered to be an "unstandardised qualification given by institutions to very high number of trainees that simply fails to differentiate between more and less competent professionals" (Smith and Gorard 2007: 481). Without any system of moderation in England, for example, the quality of ITT institutions relies on Ofsted inspections, which continue to report that they "vary considerably in quality, most significantly in their ability to recognize good teaching, but the institutions' outputs do not reflect this variability" (Smith and Gorard 2007: 481). Greater standardization and rigor in the certification of teachers across ITT institutions is needed in order to improve the quality of teaching.

Another key issue is the lack of sufficient authentic experiences for teachers during their training. Creating more opportunities for interaction and learning with and about people with disabilities and other diverse learning needs has been found to have a positive impact on attitudes toward inclusion and perceived confidence in inclusion, yet few ITT courses have embraced this. Newly qualified teachers continue to raise concerns about their training being too theoretical and lacking in practice, and this is not just related to preparing to work with learners with SEN. Increasing genuine opportunities for engagement with learners with diverse needs during training would assist in developing more realistic and, one hopes, more positive perceptions about inclusion. This is particularly pertinent where inclusion is a new approach and NQTs have, thus, not experienced inclusive practices in their own schooling.

A further concern that emerges particularly in the Asia-Pacific region, and in many educational systems where long-established pedagogical approaches are very firmly entrenched, is the inflexibility of existing practices and the incongruence with changes in ITT. Even when ITT courses have restructured to provide NQTs with the knowledge, skills, and appropriate sentiments to support inclusion, in many instances the movement toward inclusion in schools is being held back by systems that remain inflexible and unprepared to allow them to change the existing status quo in their classrooms. In the Asia-Pacific region, for example, this is particularly pertinent (Forlin 2008). The dissonance experienced by teachers across this region, in providing a developmental learning approach that is required for an inclusive philosophy while still being expected to meet examinations and standards using a didactic traditionalist approach, provides an almost impenetrable challenge for NQTs trying to implement an inclusive philosophy. Clearly there is a need for greater collaboration between ITT institutions and schools to ensure a better alignment in their pedagogies and practices.

Although it is clear that ITT courses "cannot be expected to equip NQT's with all the skills they will need to maximise effectiveness" (Cains and Brown 1998: 351), they must at least provide sufficient knowledge to enable NQTs to commence teaching with a rudimentary understanding of inclusion and how to support learners with a broad range of diverse needs. Ongoing professional development, nevertheless, is still required to improve and enhance early competency.

New models of ITT

The new area of teacher preparation for inclusion, which is gradually permeating training institutions, results in some ITT institutions being required to offer compulsory courses to meet registration or department requirements and others being able to recommend inclusion as an elective area of study. If inclusion is to be embraced by all NQTs then there is a pressing need to ensure that all ITT programs address diversity by incorporating opportunities for reflection about authentic practices that consider how current philosophies, ideas, and strategies can be best employed for the benefit of all learners. Teachers need to have not only the theoretical and practical knowledge but also the capacity to bring about optimal levels of learning for all students. This requires a self-critical outlook involving constant reflection and introspection (Forlin 2008).

A number of new models of ITT have consequently emerged in recent years to better prepare teachers for catering for diverse classrooms by encouraging reflective practice while providing opportunities to engage in authentic experiences. Good ITT practices include a range of options that comprise a variety of different approaches to provide teachers in training with the basic knowledge and skills about inclusion and to help them develop appropriate attitudes. Such programs include a range of the following:

- Provide access to readings that can serve as counterpart to a teacher's own beliefs (Milner *et al.* 2008).
- Combine formal lessons with direct contact with people with disabilities (Chong *et al.* 2007).
- Embed issues of diversity in methods and content-area courses as well as in dedicated modules (Milner *et al.* 2008).
- Embody a wide range of literacy texts by diverse individuals.
- Initiate guided field experiences so as not to reinforce existing stereotypes regarding diversity.
- Provide a range of intercultural experiences.
- Operate Teaching Clinics that deliver content and pedagogy in real-time school classrooms that bridge the theory–practice divide (O'Keefe 2009).

(See also Forlin 2010 for a further range of innovative practices for ITT.)

Conclusion

Teacher training in preparation for inclusion is without doubt a critical aspect of supporting the inclusive paradigm being promoted in schools and in ensuring its continuation. By the end of a teacher's initial training they must have a strong belief in their role as an inclusion teacher, having acquired a sophisticated range of knowledge, dispositions, values, and performances required to succeed (Turner 2003).

Effective inclusive teaching involves a high level of ethics and morals; an appreciation that a teacher's responsibility is not only to inform and facilitate learning but also to act as a role model for guiding the development of their students; and a commitment to facilitate inclusion. Without at least a minimal understanding of diversity and most importantly a positive attitude toward and belief in inclusion, newly qualified teachers cannot be expected to embrace such a philosophy. The onus is unmistakably on all ITT institutions to ensure that they provide quality training that prepares teachers for diversity, regardless of whether this is mandated or not. At least NQTs will then be starting their teaching career from a positive foundation, which can be built upon by good induction and ongoing professional development.

Bibliography

Barber, N. and Turner, M. (2007) Even while they teach, newly-qualified teachers learn. *British Journal of Special Education*, 34 (1): 22–29.

Cains, R. A. and Brown, C. R. (1998) Newly qualified teachers: a comparison of perceptions held by primary and secondary teachers of their training routes and of their early experiences in post. *Educational Psychology*, 18 (3): 341–382.

Chong, S., Forlin, C., and Au, M. L. (2007) The influence of an inclusive education course on attitude change of preservice secondary teachers in Hong Kong. *Asia Pacific Journal of Teacher Education*, 35 (2): 161–179.

Darling–Hammond, L. (2006) *Powerful Teacher Education: Lessons from Exemplary Programs*. Berkeley, CA: Jossey–Bass.

Ellins, J. and Porter, J. (2005) Departmental differences in attitudes to special educational needs in the secondary school. *British Journal of Special Education*, 32 (4): 188–195.

Forlin, C. (2006). Inclusive education in Australia ten years after Salamanca. *European Journal of Psychology of Education*, 21 (3): 265–277.

Forlin, C. (2007) A collaborative, collegial and more cohesive approach to supporting educational reform for inclusion in Hong Kong. *Asia-Pacific Education Review*, 8 (2): 1–11.

Forlin, C. (2008) Education reform for inclusion in Asia: what about teacher education? In C. Forlin and M.-G. J. Lian (Eds) *Reform, Inclusion & Teacher Education: Towards a New Era of Special Education in the Asia-Pacific Region*. Abingdon: Routledge.

Forlin, C. (Ed.). (2010) *Teacher Education for Inclusion: Changing Paradigms and Innovative Approaches*. Abingdon: Routledge.

Forlin, C., Loreman, T., Sharma, U., and Earle, C. (2007) Demographic differences in changing pre-service teachers' attitudes, sentiments and concerns about inclusive education. *International Journal of Inclusive Education*, 22 (2): 150–159.

Forlin, C., Keen, M., and Barrett, E. (2008) The concerns of mainstream teachers: coping with inclusivity in an Australian context. *International Journal of Disability Development & Education*, 55 (3): 251–264.

INCA. (2008) *Comparative Tables, July*. Accessed 19 March 2009 at http://www.inca.org.uk

Loreman, T., Deppeler, J. M., and Harvey, D. H. P. (2005) *Inclusive Education: A Practical Guide to Supporting Diversity in the Classroom*. Sydney: Allen and Unwin.

Messiou, K. (2008) Encouraging children to think in more inclusive ways. *British Journal of Special Education*, 35 (1): 26–31.

Milner, H. R., Tenore, F. B., and Laughter, J. (2008) What can teacher education programs do to prepare teachers to teach high-achieving culturally diverse male students. *Gifted Child Today*, 31 (1): 18–23.

O'Keefe, D. O. (2009) Learning at the chalkface. *Education Review*, (February) 10–11.

Palmer, D. (2006) Durability of changes in self-efficacy of preservice primary teachers. *International Journal of Science Education*, 28 (6): 655–671.

Sharma, U., Forlin, C., and Loreman, T. (2008) Impact of training on pre-service teachers' attitudes and concerns about inclusive education and sentiments about persons with disabilities. *Disability & Society*, 23 (7): 773–785.

Smith, E. and Gorard, S. (2007) Who succeeds in teacher training. *Research Papers in Education*, 22 (4): 465–482.

Training & Development Agency (TDA). (2006) *The Training Process*. Accessed 5 March 2009 at http://www.tda.gov.uk

TDA. (2008) *Qualified Teacher Status and Requirements for Initial Teacher Training*. (Revised 2008). Accessed 10 March 2009 at http://www.tda.gov.uk/partners/itt-standards.aspx

TDA. (2009) *Making a Difference to Every Child's Life: The Teacher Training Agency's Extended Remit*. Accessed 4 March 2009 at http://www.tda.gov.uk/

TDA (n.d.) *QTS Standards*. Accessed 5 March 2009 at http://www.tda.gov.uk

Turner, N. D. (2003) Preparing preservice teachers for inclusion in secondary classrooms. *Education*, 123 (3): 491–495.

UNESCO (United Nations Education, Scientific and Cultural Organization). (1994) *The Salamanca Statement and Framework for Action on Special Needs Education*. Spain: Author.

USA Funds Education Access. (2005) *Highly Qualified-Teacher Definition Revised for Teacher Loan-Forgiveness Program*. Accessed 4 March 2009 at http://www.usafunds.org/news/06sep2005/ob090605b.htm

Yeun, M., Westwood P., and Wong, G. (2004) Meeting the needs of students with specific learning difficulties in the mainstream education system: data from primary school teachers in Hong Kong. *International Journal of Special Education*, 20 (1): 67–76.

Chapter 12

Promoting teacher development for diversity

Leena Kaikkonen (Jyväskylä University of Applied Sciences, Finland)

It has been suggested that teacher attitudes are one of the key factors in pro-moting – or main obstacles in hindering – the development of more inclusive education. Several researchers have reported that the situation in respect of equipping a teacher workforce to address the challenges of inclusion has changed only slowly in recent years (Tilstone 2003). Teacher attitudes towards inclusion have been investigated extensively since the 1980s. It is generally reported that teachers are positively disposed towards inclusion. However, many teachers still feel that they lack the knowledge and the re-sources needed to implement inclusive practices in their classrooms. Though studies raise a number of paradoxical issues, it may be said that much of the research indicates that teacher attitudes are more affected by traits of students, for example the degree or nature of their needs, than by issues related to teachers themselves such as gender, age or years of teaching expe-rience. When asked about confidence in relation to working with students with special educational needs (SEN), teachers who express confidence in their professional competence and who have had positive experiences of in-cluding students with special educational needs understandably demonstrate more positive attitudes to inclusion. The implications are that successful development of inclusive education requires good planning of the process, diverse forms of support for teachers and the development of a positive working environment, and most importantly effective teacher development (Avramidis and Norwich 2002; Avramidis and Kalyva 2007; Ferguson 2008; Keefe, Rossi, De Valanzuela and Howarth 2000; Marshall and Palmer 2002; Moberg and Savolainen 2003; Rose, Kaikkonen and Kõiv 2007; Scruggs and Mastorpieri 1996; Seppälä-Pänkäläinen).

When considering teacher development, questions have been raised about the efficacy of teacher education programmes with some concerns that they have not been able to prepare teachers for implementing those processes required for greater inclusion. However, it may be perceived that it remains unclear what the necessary teacher skills, competencies or competences are for meeting diversity, how these may best be developed and what the devel-opment of these skills demands from teacher education. Furthermore, a lack of clarity with regards to the format or structure of teacher development courses has added to the confusion for those involved in the training of teachers. Perhaps the only point that has been clearly made is that, if we want to respond to the diverse needs of all learners, there needs to be a change in teacher education. Accordingly, this raises the question, if attitudes are so important, what can be done to ensure that teacher training elicits a positive response from teachers?

In this chapter I reflect upon these questions by drawing on my own work as a teacher trainer during the last twenty years for post-compulsory level teachers in Finland as well as within European in-service training collaborations, especially in the new EU member states and access countries. In my reflections I use my own experiences and some of my previous writings and research studies related to the theme. In this text I also use the word 'we' frequently, referring to the most important source of my experiences and my own competences, which is the development undertaken collaboratively with colleagues for teacher education at my university. Developments that are undertaken for the entire teacher education programme (JAMK 2009) are described here, however not focusing on the structure of courses but on the basic elements. The programme described here in some detail is organised with an intention to promote inclusive practice through enabling individuality in learning for teacher students within a teacher education course.

Starting from learning

From a constructivist view of education, the starting point in learning is to help the learner combine new knowledge with his/her existing structures. Accordingly, an important issue in teacher education is to consider how issues related to special needs and inclusive education might be matched with student teachers' previous understanding of these matters. A simple method quite often used is to start with recollections of a person's own experiences about difficulties in learning. However, in many cases student teachers have themselves been 'good students' who have encountered few obstacles to learning and have achieved high levels of success in education. This being the case, one might encourage such students to recall someone close to themselves or present them with case stories to reflect upon the difficulties experienced by others. These recollections can then be accompanied by reflections upon how in these situations the learner was heard or treated, and how they were affected by these negative learning experiences. This approach may be followed by considerations such as: If you had been the teacher here what would you have done differently? Why, how and what might have been the impact of your actions for the individual (yourself) or for the rest of the group, and so forth? The idea in these kinds of exercises is to learn to see a clearer overall picture from the point of view of the learner and the teacher, and to reflect upon the impact of actions upon the whole class.

However, based on my own experiences it seems to me that even this method might be jumping too quickly into issues of special needs, which may result in resistance on the part of some students. In many cases, teacher students show their opposition to, or at least uncertainty about, addressing learning difficulties and the individuality of their students, with comments such as 'I have 300 students in my auditorium, how do you expect me to focus on them individually?' or 'there is so much included in the curricula for me to go through with my students, I cannot devote time to working with one individual'. There are of course exceptions, but in many cases for teachers with minimal teaching experience issues of SEN seldom seem to be a major focus of interest.

Practising what we preach

Reluctance such as that demonstrated in the comments above seems often to have a basis in an interpretation of the teacher's work as being focused upon transferring knowledge, delivering subject content. Additionally, the current demands on teachers to achieve higher academic outcomes, which come with greater accountability of schools, increase the pressure upon teachers in a way which may negate any commitment towards students with special educational needs. For many there appears to be a conflict between how they may address increasing demands set in national and local curricula priorities whilst maintaining a focus upon student individuality. For many prospective teachers the questions related to meeting the diverse needs of individual students seem to come lower down the list of priorities than those which they perceive to be subject to national and local scrutiny. Their first interests are more likely to be focused on questions such as: How do I manage in class? Am I competent and up to date with my professional/subject knowledge? Am I aware of the demands of working life? To support teacher students to widen their views of their work and responsibilities, the start of the process must be sensitive and build in small steps upon their personal experiences. One route to start with might be the phrase 'inclusive (or special) education is nothing but good education'. This saying, however, seems to raise quite emotional comments both for and against. However, I believe that starting from the idea of constructing 'good teaching' (without introducing ideas about special needs) might encourage student teachers to widen their understanding of the teacher's work in respect of developing one system for all. This as opposed to constructing two separate systems, general and special, as their starting point, and in the worst case leading to thinking that special education has nothing to do with their own personal work.

To facilitate a more positive approach towards inclusive education one might start with focusing on 'only' learning itself and its relationship with personal experience, starting with an expression of the individual student's point of view and emphasising how we all differ as learners. Most students can articulate concepts such as what the best way is for me to learn, what my preferences in learning situations are, and so forth. When these are expressed through personal experiences students often highlight differences in preferred learning approaches and this gives a basis to start discussions in relation to their expectations in terms of their own studies, and how they themselves could facilitate these needs and expectations as teachers. In most cases, these discussions also bring into question the diversity of learning needs related to their cultural, linguistic and religious backgrounds in addition to their social and educational needs. It has been my experience that these small exercises and discussions seem to emphasise personal experiences that encourage student teachers later on within their studies to widen their views, finding ways of enabling individual approaches to learning for their own students.

At times teacher education has been blamed for not being able to prepare teachers for the implementation of inclusive teaching practices, whereby students' individual learning needs are heard and paid attention to. Consequently, the questions that should be raised are: Do we practise what we preach in teacher education? How do we organise teacher training so that student teachers themselves get experiences of being heard and treated individually? How do methods used in teacher education simulate the approaches that they will exercise in their future practice? In our teacher training, this is organised so that each student teacher's learning process is based on a common curricular framework but implemented through an individual focus supported by a personal learning plan. A very important part in enabling individual and flexible routes for student teachers is the use of open-ended learning assignments. These give student teachers an opportunity to use their previous experiences and know-how, focus according to their own needs and interests, and combine issues to be learned with their own organisations' development.

Through the approach adopted, the first two steps towards inclusive understanding are experiential and contextual learning, that is to start with the individual knowledge and experiences of each student and combine them with an opportunity to proceed through their own process, from their own angles, in their own context. These are of course accompanied with some more theoretical viewpoints as knowledge is a critical factor in determining teachers' attitudes towards students with special needs. However, knowledge itself is not enough. Although knowledge is needed, a more crucial issue is centred on how it is transferred to the everyday practice of the teachers and schools, and how it would change existing approaches for the better. If we want our student teachers to understand this as a basis for their own work in schools we also need to act differently in teacher education. For this reason assignments that enable experiential and contextual learning are kept in focus throughout the teacher education programme.

The underlying idea of teacher education is to teach student teachers to develop pedagogy for all. The starting point is to train teachers to work with learners with diverse learning difficulties, yet it is not considered to be simply providing them with training on special educational needs. The focus is not on acquiring knowledge from books and replicating it in exams; in fact, we have not had any exams in our teacher education college since the 1990s. Instead, the focus is on real-life situations, actual students in their classes, observing their students' learning, and additionally their own actions, then combining knowledge and theories with these real-life matters. In sum, they are gaining a way of acting by means of problem solving and also learning to understand problems as part of a bigger picture. In order to achieve this, demands are set on the assignments used, but also on the development of wider structures defining teacher education, for example through the formulation of curricula, assessment, learning methods and cooperation, replicating the actions which we have seen in the development of inclusive schools.

Matching general and special – heading towards education for all

The promotion of inclusive education starts from the notions that, first, everybody can learn and, second, teachers believe this, as well as developing a knowledge how this might be achieved. However, and maybe slightly surprisingly, though the heart of the action in schools is to support the *learning* of *all* learners, discussions surrounding development of inclusive education do not often include considerations of learning as such.

Traditionally learning has been understood as remembering facts and accumulating knowledge. However, much of the current literature describes a more modern understanding of learning (see Table 12.1), which starts from considering the construction of knowledge as an individual process and regarding learners as dynamic actors. In such an approach ideas such as individuality, active participation and learner-centredness are emphasised. A learner is considered able to set targets for his/her learning and assess his/her learning processes and the outcomes that emanate from these. Accordingly, the teacher's role is more closely related to that of a facilitator who can enable learning through constructing diverse learning environments – not only physical but psychological, virtual, collaborative, cooperative and attitudinal. The role of a teacher has to become more like a promoter of learning instead of focusing simply on the transfer of knowledge.

Current approaches to learning also demand the amendment of our focus, and the understanding of assessment (see Table 12.2). Such an approach is challenging teachers to move towards a different understanding of the evaluative processes and their meaning. Accordingly, teachers need to establish different ideas of evaluation methods and have the skills to use a variety of them during the different phases of learning.

For schools and teachers this change in comprehending learning also sets a demand to move from transferring information to learning–teaching

Table 12.1 Two ways of understanding and managing learning

Transferring information	Constructing knowledge
'Traditional'	'Modern'
Teacher's activities/actions important	Student's activities/actions important
Memorising (details of) information	Constructing, renewing knowledge
Knowing by heart	Comprehending/understanding knowledge so that it can be used in problem solving in real situations
Learner not involved in planning and learning process	Learning process is planned and implemented in cooperation between learner and teacher
Assessment/evaluation (of memorising facts) conducted by the teacher	Assessment/evaluation focused on real-life situations and managed in collaboration with the student

Table 12.2 Two ways of understanding assessment

Traditional assessment	Assessment based on constructivist ideas of learning
Mainly quantitative	Mainly qualitative
Emphasis on repeating what is learned 'by heart'	Emphasis on understanding knowledge and capability to reconstruct knowledge
Artificial test situations	As natural (authentic) assessment situations as possible
Separated from learning process	A part of the whole learning process
Teacher assesses	Teacher, student and peers assess, self-evaluation important
Focus on final result/product	Focus on learning process, change/development
Past-oriented, retrospective; assessment *of* learning	Future-oriented, developmentally oriented; assessment *for* learning

Source: Stenström and Laine (2006).

processes that produce understanding. In moving forward in this approach 'assessment and evaluation' seem to be the critical points for consideration. The change in understanding learning demands a change in understanding assessment as a tool for looking forward (assessment for learning) and not only backwards (assessment of learning). Also, a shift to move from individual to collaborative approaches in learning is set for both teachers and their learners, especially emphasising collaboration for teachers instead of working alone. It requires the understanding of teachers' own expertise not (only) as a matter of content or substance but seeing teachers' proficiency as more diversified, including an emphasis on such skills as problem solving, interaction and communication, as well as continuous learning skills. This demands that teachers develop the ability to cooperate, network and construct learning environments.

This kind of wider development of teachers' skills requires the promotion of a reflective approach towards both theory and practice. In today's world, teachers working in any level of educational establishments must, if they wish to meet the challenges entailed by their job, constantly interpret both their own role as a teacher and the purposes, contents and objectives of their teaching. There is no returning to instruction in which identical contents are repeated time and time again, and where the emphasis is on knowledge transfer. As teachers develop their own work, they must try to link their pedagogical decisions with the complex processes of change taking place in both individuals and society. In doing such work, teachers need more than ever courage, flexibility and an ability to endure many forms of uncertainty and conflict. They must construct a reflective attitude towards their work in order to be able to appropriately respond to the challenges of the present time, and to meet the individual needs of each of their diverse students.

As can be seen from Table 12.3, which describes traditional and inclusionary approaches in education, many of the ideas found in the literature related to modern learning (see Tables 12.1 and 12.2) are quite parallel to an inclusive approach and its development. This approach should be emphasised more. Otherwise, discussions might easily lead to the development of 'special' procedures for learners described as having special educational needs, instead of developing pedagogy for all and schools as inclusive organisations. It could be said that schools following current and modern ideas of learning in the development of their provision might also be on track for following the ideas of inclusive education.

As the underlying idea in developing inclusive education is to develop pedagogy for all, this development presents a demand that we rethink provision of all education. Instead of focusing on students' disabilities and how to cope with them, there is a need to focus on how to build learning based on their abilities and strengths. Even more, it is necessary to focus thinking about the disabilities of the educational system, and the changes needed within these provisions in order to respond to the needs of all learners (see Clark *et al.* 1995; Skidmore 2004). The importance of providing an opportunity for every learner to participate in the decision-making process of their own learning requires educational staff to have a positive attitude about the learning abilities of all learners, those with and without special educational needs.

Table 12.3 Comparison of traditional and inclusionary approaches

Traditional approach	Inclusionary approach
Focus on individual student	Focus on group/classroom/entire school organisation and wider work and life surroundings
Assessment of student (disabilities) by specialists	Examination/assessment of teaching and learning factors, school's learning culture and student abilities
Diagnostic/prescriptive outcomes	Collaborative problem solving, focusing on future development
Separate student programme, separate methods	Strategies for teachers to respond to learner's needs and school development with focus on learning for all
Student placement in appropriate programme	Adaptive and supportive regular classroom and other learning environments

Sources: Porter (1995); amended Kaikkonen (2008).

An approach is demanded which will equip every teacher with an understanding of more holistic questions of learning and teaching in their current and future practice, as opposed to a concentration upon teaching approaches specifically aimed only at special needs. This is based on the idea of training reflective teachers who would be able to promote the development of pedagogical actions which take full account of their learners' needs, social backgrounds and context, as well as the wider working life and societal contexts influencing educational settings and provisions. Developing curricula and pedagogy also demands directly addressing underlying attitudes, beliefs and value systems.

Towards inclusive culture

On the way towards inclusive education there is still one major factor that needs to be mentioned, which is important in fostering teachers' positive attitudes towards students with special needs. This concerns the ideological commitment to the principle of inclusion which forms the ground of facilitating the learning of students with special needs.

Booth and Ainscow (2002) regard this creation of inclusive culture as being at the heart of school improvement, and crucial for further development of inclusive policies and practices on the path towards inclusion within a school. Commitment to including all students within the mainstream school settings comes first, although there is a need to increase special educational knowledge as well. However, fostering inclusive beliefs is essential. Skidmore (2004) calls this a process of moving from the discourse of deviance to the discourse of inclusion, and claims that the development of more inclusive provision raises several dimensions that should be discussed among teachers, and keenly integrated with the idea of developing pedagogical procedures for all students. Teachers need to form their own practical theory. Important elements of this are teachers' own educational philosophies and their understanding of the concepts of humanity, of knowledge and of learning. The understanding of these concepts has an impact on teachers' attitudes, beliefs and understanding of learners. In addition the way in which teachers construct these concepts can be regarded as crucial for the development of more inclusive practices.

A final issue demands our consideration. This relates to the challenge for teachers to listen to the voices of their students. We have described elsewhere (Kaikkonen, Maunonen-Eskelinen and Aidukiene 2006; Kaikkonen 2010) student experiences of their involvement in the learning of their teachers, which positively influenced changes in teacher attitudes. In order to illuminate the importance and meaning of including wider perspectives in teacher education concerning teachers' work and development of more inclusive education I provide here a further example.

Some years ago I was involved in an experiment to train teachers to work with adults with severe learning difficulties (an issue which at that time had been afforded little attention). The pedagogical training of these teachers was organised through an analysis of their own work (see Kaikkonen 2001, 2003 for more details). In most cases their previous work was related not to education, but to nursing in different types of institutions for adults with severe learning difficulties. The intention was that the development of teachers and education for adults with severe learning difficulties would happen through modifying the actions of these institutions to become more pedagogically oriented. This experiment was undertaken mostly with persons working in segregated settings. However, within this example I hoped to show that if the focus in a teacher education programme is on the wider perspectives and contexts of a teacher's work it might give a basis for understanding which may promote inclusive learning cultures, values and positive attitudes towards students with special needs, the development of educational organisations, collaboration and teacher development.

The essence of the programme described was to concentrate on adult education itself, not on special education for adults with special needs. For the teachers this meant a demand to focus on the issue of adulthood. This philosophical–ethical question set up a demand to consider how to be able to listen to the voice of another adult person and, based on this, to set meaningful goals for enabling learning. Adulthood was not seen as a highlighted peak in a life career but, instead, adulthood like the other phases of human life was also seen as being affected by a postmodern world's fragmentation and obligation for individualisation. However, concerning adults with severe learning difficulties, it may appear as if their life is arranged according to a different more traditional lifestyle where life phases follow each other in a linear line; from day care to school, from school to further training, followed by work or some day activities. However, even this might not be the case for some adults with severe learning difficulties. In their human relations they are strongly dependent on their family members, or on some institutional staff as substitutes for them. Participation in life's networks does not materialise easily and spontaneously. Finding adulthood in all its various forms is out of their reach.

Thus, teacher students noticed that the learning of adults with severe learning difficulties is challenged not only by supporting interaction and encouraging the voices of these adults themselves, but also by the diversity of a late modern world. How could the individualised processes of adult life be illuminated in various late modern ways for adults with severe learning difficulties as well? Where they are concerned, the continuous need to analyse and interpret one's life choices time and again is placed in somebody else's hands, often a teacher's. How are you able to do this as a teacher without making clones of your own life choices? Or, even more typically, without repeating solutions once found for someone else with a similar type of difficulty, or leaving your students to play with obvious routine-like choices?

The question of 'who is an adult with severe learning difficulties', which was a big issue at the start of the teacher education process, changed into a question about adulthood in general. What does it mean to be an adult in the late modern world, what is it for each of us? As a life phase it does not seem to be so obvious any more as people can do and must do different things while being the same age, and the same things while at a different age, and there are no good fundaments to argue that there exist life phases which are totally separated from each other. Consequently, questions to reflect upon were: How would diverse adulthoods be possible? How could I, as a teacher, interpret my own personal adult life values and emphasis in order to enable diverse adult lives?

This metacultural awareness was considered as an important part of teachers' professional skills. Educational staff should have skills to understand diverse cultures of families in educating and rehabilitating young persons. Through this approach a worker can encourage the person, or the family, in the route they have chosen. So, the challenge is not only to hear the voices of all adult learners, but also to enable diverse life paths and adult everyday cultures. When adopting this challenge, teachers consider it to be vital to hear the needs and wishes of their students, that is to understand 'how these adults would build their life if they could and what would be the story they would tell if allowed' (Greenleaf, Hull and Reilly 1994: 530).

Adulthood is most often connected with the idea of independence. The contradiction that the staff working with adults with severe learning difficulties confronted was that these adults quite often are very dependent on others. Teachers needed to consider how to give space for their students' own decision making but, on the other hand, not to leave them neglected in their needs. Additionally, teachers started to consider their students, as well as themselves, as life-long learners. When describing the diverse interpretations of adulthood as a basis for adult education, the need for continuous learning might be the most essential feature in the present conceptualisation of adulthood. In a learning society, it is at the same time a possibility and an obligation which also includes informal and participatory learning communities. It is worth emphasising that, when the teachers in our experiment reconceptualised their understanding of adulthood, it also strengthened their belief in their students' learning abilities. The starting point for their pedagogical development was based on the willingness to look for possibilities for diverse and separated life paths. This led teachers to reflect on their own actions as teachers and their own teacher development but also the development of their organisations.

Accordingly, assessment of their old working methods and reconstructing their foundations for their own teaching made them consider the present institutional structures within which they worked. Among other things, this allowed them to focus on interaction and communication at the institutional level. Through this approach they understood that the administrative-level renewals that had taken place in recent years within their institutions (as a part of national and local developments) would not, in themselves, change anything. This was particularly true if the working procedures of these renewed institutions had not been questioned as a whole and put under conscious criticism.

All in all, succeeding in evolving towards inclusive education demands that teaching staff critically assess their own actions and develop the entire school's activities to meet the needs of all students, not just develop special solutions for students with learning difficulties. Concerning adult students, this quite often demands collaboration and networking in wider contexts. Development of inclusive education for inclusive life is a collaborative process. No teacher can do it alone but each teacher needs to be involved. This can also be formulated by saying: the greater the student's learning difficulties, the greater the demands on the teacher to have wider perspectives on circumstances affecting education. Besides respecting all students and encouraging their voices to be heard within educational settings, a teacher's own self-esteem is important in building tomorrow's society.

Bibliography

Avramidis, E. and Norwich, B. (2002) Teachers' attitudes towards integration/inclusion: a review of the literature. *European Journal of Special Needs Education*, 17 (2): 129–147.

Avramidis, E. and Kalyva, E. (2007) The influence of teaching experience and professional development of Greek teachers' attitudes towards inclusion. *European Journal of Special Needs Education*, 22 (4): 367–389.

Booth, T. and Ainscow, M. (2002) *Index for Inclusion: Developing Learning and Participation in Schools*. Bristol: Centre for Studies on Inclusive Education.

Clark, C., Dyson, A., Millward, A. and Skidmore, D. (1995) Dialectical analysis, special needs and schools as organisations. In C. Clark, A. Dyson and A. Millward (Eds) *Towards Inclusive Schools?* London: David Fulton.

Ferguson, D. (2008) International trends in inclusive education: the continuing challenge to teach each one and everyone. *European Journal of Special Needs Education*, 23 (2): 109–120.

Greenleaf, C., Hull, G. and Reilly, B. (1994) Learning from our diverse students: helping teachers rethink problematic teaching and learning situations. *Teaching and Teacher Education*, 10 (5): 521–541.

JAMK. (2009) *Your Study Guide*. Accessed 26 October 2009 at http://aokk.jamk.fi/

Kaikkonen, L. (2001) Studying the development of 'teacherhood' of trainee teachers for the education of adults with severe learning difficulties. In R. Rose and I. Grosvenor (Eds) *Doing Research in Special Education: Ideas into Practice*. London: David Fulton.

Kaikkonen, L. (2003) *Opettajuutta kehittämässä: vaikeimmin kehitysvammaisten aikuisten (VaKA-) opettajaksi kehittyminen opettajankoulutuksen aikana ja viisi vuotta koulutuksen jälkeen.* [Developing teacherhood: development of teachers for adults with severe learning difficulties during their teacher education programme and five years after.] Doctoral dissertation. Reports of Jyväskylä University of Applied Sciences 23.

Kaikkonen, L. (2008) Growth of more inclusive education as a challenge for school and teacher development. *International Magazine for Educational Sciences and Practice*. Issue 2, June: 13–21.

Kaikkonen, L. (2009) Changing practice? Results of national study on changing role of Special Education Teachers in Finnish vocational education. Paper presented at European Conference on Educational Research, 29 September, Vienna, Austria.

Kaikkonen, L. (2010) Including students with special education needs in professional learning for teachers. In C. Forlin (Ed.) *Teacher Education for Inclusion: Changing Paradigms and Innovative Approaches*. London: Routledge.

Kaikkonen, L., Maunonen-Eskelinen, I. and Aidukiene, T. (2006) Supporting teachers' competencies towards development of more inclusive school – listening to the voices of students with special educational needs in educational transitions. Paper presented at ATEE Spring Conference, 3 June, Riga, Latvia.

Keefe, E. B., Rossi, P. J., De Valanzuela, J. S. and Howarth, S. (2000) Reconceptualizing teacher preparation for inclusive classrooms: a description of the dual license programme at the University of New Mexico. *Journal of the Association for Persons with Severe Handicaps*, 25 (2): 72–82.

Marshall, R. S. and Palmer, S. (2002) 'I wasn't trained to work with them': mainstream teachers' attitudes to children with speech and language difficulties. *International Journal of Inclusive Education*, 6 (3): 199–215.

Moberg, S. and Savolainen, H. (2003) Struggling for inclusive education in the North and the South: educators' perceptions on inclusive education in Finland and Zambia. *International Journal of Rehabilitation Research*, 26 (1): 21–31.

Porter, G. (1995) Organization of schooling: achieving access and quality through inclusion. *Prospects*, 25 (2): 299–309.

Rose, R., Kaikkonen, L. and Kõiv, K. (2007) Estonian vocational teachers' attitudes towards inclusive education for students with special educational needs. *International Journal of Special Education*, 22 (3): 97–109.

Scruggs, T. E. and Mastorpieri, M. A. (1996) Teacher perceptions of mainstreaming/inclusion, 1958–1995: a research synthesis. *Exceptional Children*, 63 (1): 59–74.

Seppälä-Pänkäläinen, T. (2009) Oppijoiden moninaisuuden kohtaaminen suomalaisessa lähikoulussa. [Confronting the diversity of learners in a Finnish neighbourhood school. An ethnographic study of the challenges and opportunities of adults learning together in a school community.] Jyväskylä Studies in Education, Psychology and Social Research 364. Doctoral dissertation. Available at: http://urn.fi/URN:ISBN:978-951-39-3660-0.

Skidmore, D. (2004) *Inclusion: The Dynamic of School Development*. Buckingham: Open University Press.

Stenström, M.-L. and Laine, K. (Eds). (2006) *Quality and Practice in Assessment: New Approaches in Working-Related Learning*. Jyväskylä: University of Jyväskylä, Institute for Educational Research.

Thomas, G. and Vaughan, M. (2004). *Inclusive Education: Readings and Reflections*. Buckingham: Open University Press.

Tilstone, C. (2003) Professional development of staff: steps towards developing policies. In C. Tilstone and R. Rose (Eds) *Strategies to Promote Inclusive Practice*. London: Routledge.

Chapter 13

Teachers' professional learning and inclusive practice

Lani Florian and Martyn Rouse (both University of Aberdeen, UK)

Although there is widespread support for inclusion at a philosophical and ideological level, there are concerns in many countries that the policy of inclusion is difficult to implement. In part, this is because it is believed that teachers are not sufficiently well prepared and supported to work in inclusive ways. Inclusion requires teachers to accept the responsibility for creating schools in which all children can learn and feel they belong. In this task, teachers are crucial because of the central role they play in promoting participation and reducing exclusion, particularly of children who are perceived as having difficulties in learning. And yet too many teachers do not see this as part of their professional responsibility.

This chapter considers the ways in which the roles, responsibilities and identities of teachers are crucial in the development of greater inclusion. It draws on Shulman's (2007) conceptualisation of professional learning as apprenticeships of the head (knowledge), hand (skill, or 'doing') and heart (attitudes and beliefs) to provide a framework for thinking about the content and structure of teacher professional development so that there is a balance between the skills, knowledge, attitudes and beliefs necessary to promote inclusive practice. The chapter explores two examples of how these 'elements' might be integrated in teacher professional learning.

Introduction

Recent developments in Scotland are attempting to develop inclusive education within the broader global context of the 'Education for All' (EFA) agenda (UNESCO 2008). These developments focus on the preparation of teachers because teachers' professional development is recognised as crucial to the process of achieving the aspirations and goals of EFA. This chapter provides a framework for thinking about initial teacher education and the professional learning of teachers to ensure that there is a balance between the skills and actions, knowledge, attitudes and beliefs that are required if inclusive education is to fulfil its promise as a strategy for achieving EFA (Peters 2007). A series of key questions are addressed:

- What is the current international policy context for inclusion?
- What do teachers need to know and be able to do in order to develop inclusion?
- How might teacher education contribute to the development of teachers who can engage with inclusive practices?
- What are the essential features of a framework for professional learning that is designed to support inclusion?

The current international context for inclusion

The EFA Global Monitoring Report (GMR) has warned that the 'deep and persistent disparities based on wealth, gender, location, ethnicity and other markers of disadvantage are acting as a major barrier to progress in education' (UNESCO 2008: 3). It argues that future progress in achieving EFA requires a focus on equity in policy, funding and governance reforms if all children, youth and adults are to have an equal chance for learning. A key finding of the report, which provides a comprehensive analysis of the state of education in the world today, is that:

> progress towards the EFA goals is being undermined by the failure of governments to tackle inequality based on income, gender, location, ethnicity, language, disability and other markers of disadvantage. Unless governments act to reduce disparities through effective policy reforms, the EFA promise will be broken.
>
> (p. 4).

In many countries significant numbers of children do not have opportunities to attend school. There are many reasons for this, including a shortage of accessible school places and insufficient numbers of teachers. Many of these problems and concerns are being addressed through recent global initiatives such as the Millennium Development Goals and EFA, which are designed to achieve universal access to primary education for all children by 2015. Whereas many people see these initiatives as being aimed at the least economically developed countries, they are relevant elsewhere because even in the 'well-schooled' nations (OECD 2007), where there may be fewer problems with access and a shortage of teachers, there are problems in achieving meaningful participation in learning for some children and young people.

It is known that poverty, social disadvantage, disability and poor educational achievement are inextricably linked and attempts to tackle the causes and consequences of these inequalities have been largely unsuccessful because they usually focus on only one aspect of the problem and ignore the broader cultural, social and economic context (Ainscow, Dyson, Goldrick, Kerr and Miles 2008). Disparities in education systems and outcomes are partially explained by disparities in resource allocation (including teachers), which are associated with wealth or the lack of it. As a group, students living in poverty are more likely to be disabled or described as having special educational needs, are less likely to do well in school and are less likely to attend well-equipped and well-staffed schools, in both rich and poor countries. As the GMR (UNESCO 2008) notes, although students in developing countries have higher proportions of low achievement and access to fewer resources, the disparities between rich and poor also exist within all countries. Although the GMR argues that student performance depends on an adequate supply of well-prepared teachers and reasonable pupil/teacher ratios, it also finds that with regard to the teaching workforce:

> Governments will have to recruit and train teachers on a vast scale to meet EFA goals. Globally, an estimated 18 million more primary teachers are required by 2015, with the most pressing need for additional teachers (1.6 million) in Sub-Saharan Africa.
>
> (UNESCO 2008: 22)

> There are large national and regional disparities in pupil/teacher ratios, with marked teacher shortages in South and West Asia, and sub-Saharan Africa. But it is *within countries* that the greatest disparities exist, with teachers unevenly distributed across regions.
>
> (UNESCO 2008: 6, emphasis added)

Arguably, teachers are the most important element in the development of education systems. They are the one resource schools cannot do without. Yet very little attention has been paid to issues of teacher preparation and development as part of the EFA agenda, other than to note the important disparities in teacher supply, quality, qualifications and deployment (UNESCO 2008). Even in countries that are described as 'well-schooled', such as Scotland (OECD 2007), there is concern that some children are not well served by current arrangements for schooling because not all children participate and learn in meaningful ways and their levels of achievement are seen as unacceptably low. Although there is widespread support for inclusion at a philosophical and ideological level in many countries, there are concerns that the policy of inclusion is difficult to implement. In part, this is because the principles of inclusion may be seen as conflicting with other education policies, such as the increased demand for higher standards (Rouse and Florian 1997), because separate systems of schooling give clear messages about who should receive their education in mainstream settings and who should be responsible for educating children who have difficulties in learning.

In recent years, many countries have enacted educational policies designed to encourage greater inclusion of children considered to have disabilities or difficulties. Many of these policies have been focused on the relocation of (special needs) children from separate special to mainstream settings. In some countries, a broader conceptualisation of inclusion is apparent; for example, in Scotland, the Education (Additional Support for Learning) (Scotland) Act 2004 points out that a child may require additional support for a variety of reasons, not only relating to special educational needs. Yet, despite positive pro-inclusion policy frameworks in many countries, achieving successful inclusion is difficult, because, as previously mentioned, barriers to inclusion arise from inflexible or irrelevant curricula, didactic teaching methods, inappropriate systems of assessment and inadequate preparation of, and support for, teachers. Inclusion policies have implications not only for the structure and organisation of school systems, but also for the roles and responsibilities of teachers as well as professionals working in health, social work and other agencies. The crucial task of preparing and supporting professionals to work in inclusive schools is a challenge faced in many parts of the world.

This challenge was acknowledged by the 2008 International Conference on Education, 'Inclusive Education: The Way of the Future' (UNESCO 2008), attended by representatives of 153 nations, which called 'upon Member States to adopt an inclusive education approach in the design, implementation, monitoring and assessment of educational policies as a way to further accelerate the attainment of Education for All (EFA) goals as well as to contribute to building more inclusive societies' (http://www.ibe.unesco. org/en/ice/48th-session-2008/conclusions-and-recommendations.html). One strand of the Conference concluded with six recommendations specific to teacher education and development:

1   Reinforce the role of teachers by working to improve their status and their working conditions, and develop mechanisms for recruiting suitable candidates, and retain qualified teachers who are sensitive to different learning requirements.

2   Train teachers by equipping them with the appropriate skills and materials to teach diverse student populations and meet the diverse learning needs of different categories of learners through methods such as professional development at the school level, pre-service training about inclusion, and instruction attentive to the development and strengths of the individual learner.

3   Support the strategic role of tertiary education in the pre-service and professional training of teachers on inclusive education practices through, inter alia, the provision of adequate resources.

4   Encourage innovative research in teaching and learning processes related to inclusive education.

5   Equip school administrators with the skills to respond effectively to the diverse needs of all learners and promote inclusive education in their schools.

6   Take into consideration the protection of learners, teacher and schools in times of conflict.

(http://www.ibe.unesco.org/en/ice/48th-session-2008/
conclusions-and-recommendations.html).

Clearly, given the global disparities in educational provision, and the differences in teacher qualifications and teacher education that exist within and between countries and regions of the world, these recommendations will have particular implications in different contexts. Yet in a global society there are also unprecedented opportunities for people to engage with these recommendations and to consider common themes. What are the implications of the UNESCO recommendations for those who prepare teachers? What does it mean to 'train teachers by equipping them with the appropriate skills and materials to teach diverse student populations'? Are there common meanings that transcend the boundaries of nation states and recognise that different groups of children may be vulnerable in different settings?

Questions about how well teachers are prepared, and the role they can play in reducing inequality, by virtue of the way in which they undertake their work, remain largely unexplored. Further, the traditional pattern of preparing teachers for different roles within schools by offering different courses, qualifications and certification are thought to result in systemic barriers to the development of inclusion. This poses particular challenges for the role of higher education as it attempts to merge separate teacher preparation programmes (Blanton and Pugach 2009) and embed issues of inclusion across courses that prepare primary and secondary school teachers (Florian and Rouse 2009).

Teacher education for inclusion: what do teachers need to know and be able to do?

It could be argued that there are two main strands in the debate about teacher preparation for working in mainstream inclusive settings. On one hand, there are those who claim that there is insufficient content knowledge about different types of disabilities and difficulties in teacher preparation courses (Hodkinson 2005; Jones 2006). In this view, which might be seen as an extension of special education approaches, the reason why inclusion is difficult to achieve is that new teachers do not know enough about disabilities and difficulties such as sensory impairments, dyslexia, autism, ADHD and other syndromes. It is argued that it is necessary to be able to 'diagnose' difficulties in learning in order to 'prescribe' particular teaching approaches, but that teachers are not sufficiently well trained in the specific teaching strategies that are thought to be associated with these types of difficulties. Those who subscribe to this view believe that specific training is required to implement the specialist teaching approaches that have been developed for children with particular kinds of disabilities.

However, questions about the usefulness of such specialist knowledge in the development of inclusion are widespread. For example, in an extensive review covering twenty-five years of work, Ysseldyke (2001) questions the evidence in support of 'diagnostic–prescriptive teaching'. Furthermore, the question of whether or nor there is a 'specialist pedagogy' has been addressed by several researchers (e.g. Cook and Schirmer 2003; Davis and Florian 2004; Kavale 2007; Lewis and Norwich 2005). Much of this work challenges simplistic assumptions about the nature and distinctiveness of diagnostic–prescriptive approaches to teaching children with disabilities and difficulties and increasingly there is a call for a new approach to the development of inclusive pedagogy (Florian and Kershner 2009).

The evidence suggests that content knowledge of optional courses in special needs is insufficient to improve practice in schools because too often it is not linked to the broader (mainstream) pedagogical and curriculum imperatives that the students have to learn and be able to apply. Because the content of special education courses is decontextualised and is seen as 'additional to and different from', students who attend such courses find it difficult to act upon this knowledge when teaching. Thus there may be a gap between what teachers know as a result of their training and what they do in their classrooms. Further, although there is evidence that teachers in training have positive attitudes to inclusion at the beginning of their courses, some researchers have found that student teachers' experiences on school placement can moderate this enthusiasm (Lambe and Bones 2006). In part this is because the realities of teaching and classroom life are challenging, but it is also associated with the tensions between what students learn in university and what they learn in school. Hagger and McIntyre (2006) make a powerful argument in favour of extending school-based teacher education, but in the area of inclusion and special educational needs there may be more complex factors at work. A recent report in England, *How Well New Teachers Are Prepared to Teach Pupils with Learning Difficulties and/ or Disabilities*, carried out by the Office for Standards in Education (Ofsted 2008) was critical of many aspects of initial teacher education in meeting special educational needs, particularly the quality of the input that student teachers receive while on school placements, because those responsible for providing the input in schools do not have the necessary expertise, nor do they have a sufficiently wide perspective on the that nature and purpose of the task.

Although we would argue that more expertise is needed about why some children have difficulties in learning, it is also important to recognise a serious, if unintended, consequence of thinking that only special needs teachers can teach special needs children: most mainstream teachers do not believe that they have the skills and knowledge to do this kind of work because they have not done the specialist course. Nor do they think they know about the appropriate pedagogies to teach special children. Further, they believe that there are 'experts' out there to deal with these students on a one-to-one basis or in small groups and so this work is not their responsibility. Clearly approaches based on these views are unsustainable and act as a major barrier to inclusion. Nevertheless, many experienced teachers do have concerns about inclusion and many surveys have found that teachers' attitudes towards inclusion are not particularly positive (Ellins and Porter 2005), in part because they claim not to know how to do it (Forlin 2008).

In contrast to those who call for more special education knowledge in teacher education courses, there are those, for example Slee (2001), who argue that inclusion cannot be created through the expansion of special education and a radical new approach is required based on the development of inclusive approaches to teaching and learning that do not depend on the identification of particular forms of disability or difficulty. In its most extreme form, this position can be criticised for denying important human differences.

We take a more pragmatic approach and would argue that the development of inclusive education should not involve a denial of difference, but we would question whether training separate cohorts of teachers to deal with children's difficulties in learning is the best way to proceed. Currently it is common for special needs and inclusion courses in initial teacher education to be offered as an optional extra, an elective available to some students. Typically these courses focus on the characteristics of particular kinds of learners, how they should be identified, specialist teaching strategies and the prevailing policy context. The main problem is that the content knowledge of such courses is often not well integrated into the broader curriculum and pedagogical practices of mainstream settings. Crucially only some, not all, teachers are able to take such courses, which in turn leads to a belief that they are not capable of teaching special children because they have not done the course. But in settings where teachers are encouraged to try out a range of teaching strategies they report that they knew more than they thought they knew and, for the most part, children learn in similar ways. Although some children might need extra support, teachers do not distinguish between 'types' of special need when planning this support (Florian and Rouse 2001), but knowledge of children's circumstances is important.

We believe that it is necessary to ask fundamental questions about what teachers need to know and be able to do when meeting special educational needs as the basis of providing guidance to teachers and teacher educators about the use of teaching strategies that can support all learners (see, for example, Kershner 2007). Therefore, development of inclusion requires new ways of thinking about the ways in which teachers are prepared and supported in this work.

One way of conceptualising this task might be to take the lead from Lee Shulman (2007), who, when talking about training and induction in many of the professions, claimed that they should consist of three essential elements. When President of the Carnegie Foundation for the Advancement of Teaching, Shulman was involved with the Foundation's 'Preparation for the Professions Programme', which investigates the preparation for various professions offered by academic institutions and compares across professions the approaches to teaching and learning that are used to ensure the development of three crucial areas: professional understanding, skills and integrity. He refers to these elements as the 'three apprenticeships' (Shulman 2007). The first is the 'apprenticeship of the head'; by this he means 'knowing that and knowing what'. This is the cognitive knowledge, the evidential base and theoretical foundations of the profession. The second is the 'apprenticeship of the hand'; this would include the technical and practical skills and ways of working that are required to carry out the essential tasks of the role. And finally there is 'apprenticeship of the heart'. This consists of the ethical and moral dimensions of a profession, the attitudes, values and beliefs that are crucial to a particular field and its ways of working.

Elsewhere (Rouse 2008; Florian 2008) we have suggested that developing effective inclusive practice is not only about extending teachers' knowledge, but also about encouraging them to do things differently and getting them to reconsider their attitudes and beliefs about children and schooling. Using Shulman's three apprenticeships might help us to consider how this task might be conceptualised and consider the relative contribution of 'knowing', 'doing' and 'believing'. We have expressed this as a reciprocal triangular relationship between three elements as shown in Figure 13.1.

In this model, there is a reciprocal relationship between knowing (the head), doing (the hand) and believing (the heart). Teachers are more likely to engage in inclusive practices if they have positive attitudes and believe that all children can learn. Equally teachers are more likely to believe all children can learn if they have the necessary pedagogical skills to run effective inclusive practice. Having only one of these elements in place is insufficient. For example, having a commitment to social justice is necessary but not sufficient, as is knowledge about children's impairments if other elements are ignored. We have argued elsewhere (Florian 2008; Rouse 2008) that at least two out of the three elements are necessary for the third to develop. The fundamental question is how we might help all teachers to develop the knowledge, beliefs and practices that support inclusion.

In the next sections we describe two projects that are designed to support the development of teacher education for inclusion. Both are supported by the Scottish Government and are based on the principles outlined above.

How might teacher education contribute to the development of teachers who can engage with inclusive practices? The Inclusive Practice Project

We have used many of the ideas outlined above in our work with colleagues at the University of Aberdeen on the Inclusive Practice Project to develop a new approach to training teachers to ensure that they:

- have a greater awareness and understanding of the educational and social problems/issues that can affect children's learning; and

Knowing (Head)

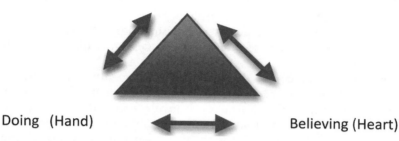

Doing (Hand)   Believing (Heart)

Figure 13.1 Knowing, believing and doing.

- have developed strategies they can use to support and deal with such difficulties.

To this end, the professional studies strand of the Professional Graduate Diploma in Education (PGDE) primary and secondary programmes have been combined into one single programme with an enhanced university-based curriculum designed to ensure issues of inclusion are fully addressed within the core of the programme for all student teachers rather than as an additional element or an elective selected by only some. The course begins with issues of inclusion and considers why inclusion is the responsibility of all teachers from the outset. It contains elements of 'knowing, doing and believing' and recognises that it is necessary to bridge the gap between what students learn in the university and what they learn in schools (Hagger and McIntyre 2006). The students are asked to consider what it is to be human and how human differences are socially constructed, and it also asks them to question their assumptions about human ability and how such views influence what happens in schools.

When asked, most student teachers have positive attitudes to inclusion and believe that they can make a difference to children's lives (Beacham and Rouse 2010), but many student teachers also have deeply embedded assumptions about human differences that are largely unacknowledged. Most of us are products of an educational system that systematically sorts children according to perceived abilities and aptitudes. This process starts early in primary school when children are placed in groups according to their 'level' for different subjects of the curriculum. By secondary school the process of sorting and shifting may have become part of an inflexible organisational structure. Grouping according to perceived ability remains a common organisational response despite the research evidence that it does not lead to improved outcomes (Ireson, Hallam and Huntley 2005). It is an organisational arrangement that student teachers will face when they are working in schools. It is necessary therefore to challenge the biological- and social-deterministic thinking (Gould 1996) that underpins such approaches. And so an important aspect of the course is based on the principles of learning without limits (Hart, Dixon, Drummond and McIntyre 2004), which involves an examination of deep-seated assumptions about human differences and an exploration of alternatives to deterministic thinking about human abilities.

Nevertheless, the course does not deny human differences but rather takes an ecological perspective to understand the circumstances in which children might experience difficulties. It involves an understanding of how many factors interact to produce individual differences (biology, culture, family, school), rather than focusing on explanations that stress a single cause. Inclusive practice involves understanding the relative contribution of each of these factors in determining appropriate responses when children experience difficulty (Florian 2008).

The students are given opportunities to explore approaches to inclusion in the schools in which they are placed and to consider their own individual responsibility in creating the conditions for promoting inclusion. In Scotland the universities have little control over where the students are placed, therefore it is important to work with the students to explain that they may find themselves in schools and classrooms in which inclusion is not seen as an important aspect of practice. In such settings the students have to negotiate their way through potentially difficult professional situations. This has resulted in an increased focus on 'doing', which has become an essential element of initial teacher education and professional learning. In many cases this involves supporting students to become 'activist professionals' (Sachs 2003). This also involves a greater emphasis on developing the skills of reflective practice and using evidence from their teaching to inform decision making.

The development of inclusive practice is about the things that staff do in schools, which give meaning to the concept of inclusive education (Florian 2009). It recognises that all teachers should accept the responsibility for all children in the classes that they teach, but it does not reject the notion of specialist knowledge and does not mean that teachers and learners are left on their own without support. Rather, it is the use of that support, the ways that teachers respond to individual differences during whole class teaching, the choices they make about group work and how they utilise specialist knowledge that matter. Thus it involves working with and through others. Therefore, training has to address the ways in which adults might develop the skills of working collaboratively to support children's learning and participation.

At the heart of this process is the development of positive relationships and optimistic views about learners. The development of inclusive practice depends to a large extent on teachers' attitudes and beliefs. Therefore it is important to consider how it might be possible for teachers to develop new ways of believing that all children are worth educating, that all children can learn, that they have the capacity to make a difference to children's lives and that such work is their responsibility and not only a task for specialists.

Teachers' professional identities are also important, as are their attitudes and beliefs about their roles and responsibilities. Inclusion threatens assumptions that some teachers have about many aspects of schools and schooling. In particular it can threaten teachers' identities. If responsibilities are to be shared and teachers are to take on new roles, then there have to be changes to the way inclusion is conceptualised and a realisation that it can only be achieved if all teachers are supported in the development of all aspects of this process: knowing, doing and believing.

In addition to changes to course structure and content, there is an ongoing programme of research, which is exploring many aspects of the project (for further details see Florian and Rouse 2009; Beacham and Rouse 2010; Florian and Linklater 2009; Florian and Young, in press).

This section of the chapter has described attempts in one university to reform teacher education for inclusion. In the next section we describe an ambitious national initiative designed to provide a framework to support the development of teacher education for inclusion.

What are the essential features of a framework for professional learning designed to support inclusion? Scottish Teacher Education Committee National Framework for Inclusion

The Scottish Government has recognised that inclusive education is of high priority for all those involved in education in Scotland. There has been recognition that teachers need to be well prepared and appropriately supported throughout their careers if they are to succeed in developing and sustaining inclusive practice to meet the increasingly diverse needs in Scottish schools. With the support of the government, the Scottish Teacher Education Committee (STEC) set up a working group consisting of course directors and inclusion specialists representing all seven universities involved in initial teacher education to develop the National Framework for Inclusion. The remit of the group was to develop a framework that would identify the values and beliefs, the professional knowledge and understanding, and the skills and abilities to be expected of student teachers and of qualified teachers at whatever stage of their career. The framework would also provide, through a web-based repository of resources, a source of additional information, advice, guidance and support for student teachers, teachers and teacher educators seeking further assistance with specific aspects of inclusive education.

The framework, which was launched in April 2009 (STEC 2009), high-lights the underpinning principles of inclusive practice – social justice, inclusion, and learning and teaching – in the context of current policy and legislation. The document provides a broad definition of inclusion that covers additional support needs, poverty, culture and language, also informed by relevant aspects of the UK Government's new Equality Bill (2009), in order to promote participation, achievement and equality. The aim is to link to Scotland's Curriculum for Excellence (Scottish Executive 2004) to ensure that ultimately all children and young people are successful learners, confi-dent individuals, effective contributors and responsible citizens.

The framework includes clear reference to the Standard for Initial Teacher Education (Scottish Executive 2006a,b) and the Standard for Full Registration (General Teaching Council for Scotland 2006, 2007). It aims to be comprehensive but not prescriptive, leaving the seven universities free to determine how best to turn the underlying principles into practice. It is question-based to encourage teachers to accept a shared responsibility for finding answers and further questions with the support of the web-based repository, which may be useful beyond Scotland. It attempts to promote inclusion as being the responsibility of all teachers in all schools and has tried to identify and to address the needs of teachers at all stages of their careers and to emphasise the need for career-long and life-long learning. It is an ambitious attempt to develop a coherent national approach to dealing with a fundamental issue in the promotion of inclusion and builds upon existing innovative practice within the universities of Scotland.

Conclusion

We believe that the elusiveness of inclusive education can be partly explained by the insufficient attention that has been paid to the ways in which teachers are prepared and supported to work in inclusive settings. By preparing only some teachers to deal with difference, remove the barriers to participation and develop inclusive practices, a climate is created in which other teach-ers can rightfully claim that these things are not their responsibility. This chapter has advanced the argument that inclusive practice has to be the task of all teachers if inclusive education is to be an effective strategy for achiev-ing EFA. To this end, Shulman's (2007) conceptualisation of professional learning as apprenticeships of the head (knowledge), hand (skill, or doing) and heart (attitudes and beliefs) was used to provide a framework for think-ing about the content and structure of teacher professional development so that there is a balance between the skills, knowledge, attitudes and beliefs necessary to promote inclusive practice. The chapter explored how these 'elements' might be integrated in teacher professional learning by describing two recent initiatives that were designed to support the initial preparation and professional development of teachers to work in inclusive schools where inclusive practices can thrive.

Examining how teachers are prepared to work in inclusive schools is an important step in ensuring that they are able to deal with difference, remove barriers to participation and implement inclusive practice. This requires not only a review of the ways in which all (not just some) teachers are prepared to enter the profession, but also the development of programmes of teacher education and professional learning that focus on inclusive practice as a pedagogical approach that empowers them to fulfil their obligations to all learners.

Bibliography

Ainscow, M., Dyson, A., Goldrick, S., Kerr, K. and Miles, S. (2008) *Equity in Education: Responding to Context.* Manchester: Centre for Equity in Education, University of Manchester.

Beacham, N. and Rouse, M. (2010) Student teachers' attitudes and beliefs about inclusive education. Paper presented to the American Educational Research Association Annual Meeting, Denver, May.

Blanton, L. and Pugach, M. (2009) A framework for conducting research on collaborative teacher education. *Teaching and Teacher Education,* 25 (4): 575–582.

Cook, B. G. and Schirmer, B. R. (2003) What is special about special education? Overview and analysis. *Journal of Special Education,* 37(3): 200–204.

Davis, P. and Florian, L. (2004) *Teaching Strategies and Approaches for Children with Special Educational Needs: A Scoping Study.* Research Report 516, London: DfES.

Ellins, J. and Porter, J. (2005) Departmental differences in attitudes to special educational needs in the secondary school. *British Journal of Special Education,* 32 (4): 188–195.

Florian, L. (2007) Reimagining special education. In L. Florian (Ed.) *The SAGE Handbook of Special Education.* London: Sage.

Florian, L. (2008) Special or inclusive education: future trends. *British Journal of Special Education,* 35(4): 202–208.

Florian, L. (2009) Towards inclusive pedagogy. In P. Hick, R. Kershner and P. Farrell (Eds) *Psychology for Inclusive Education: New Directions in Theory and Practice.* London: Routledge/Falmer.

Florian, L. and Rouse, M. (2001) Inclusive practice in secondary schools. In R. Rose and I. Grosvenor (Eds) *Doing Research in Special Education.* London: David Fulton.

Florian, L. and Kershner, R. (2009) Inclusive pedagogy. In H. Daniels, H. Lauder and J. Porter (Eds) *Knowledge, Values and Educational Policy: A Critical Perspective.* London: Routledge.

Florian, L. and Linklater, H. (2009) Enhancing teaching and learning: using 'Learning without Limits' to prepare teachers for inclusive education. Paper presented to the Annual Meeting of the American Association of Colleges for Teacher Education, Chicago, February.

Florian, L. and Rouse, M. (2009) The inclusive practice project in Scotland: teacher education for inclusion. *Teaching and Teacher Education,* 25 (4): 594–601.

Florian, L., Young, K. and Rouse, M. (in press) Preparing teachers for inclusive and diverse educational environments: studying curricular reform in an initial teacher education course. *International Journal of Inclusive Education*.

Forlin, C. (2008) Education reform for inclusion in Asia: what about teacher education? In C. Forlin and M.-G. J. Lian (Eds) *Reform, Inclusion & Teacher Education: Towards a New Era of Special Education in the Asia–Pacific Region*. Abingdon: Routledge.

General Teaching Council for Scotland. (2006) *The Standards for Full Registration*. Edinburgh: Author.

General Teaching Council for Scotland. (2007) *The Revised Standards for Full Registration*. Edinburgh: Author.

Gould, S. J. (1996) *The Mismeasure of Man*, revised edition. London: Penguin Books.

Hagger, H. and McIntyre, D. (2006) *Learning Teaching from Teachers: Realising the Potential of School-Based Teacher Education*. Maidenhead: Open University Press.

Hart, S., Dixon, A., Drummond, M. J. and McIntyre, D. (2004) *Learning without Limits*. Maidenhead: Open University Press.

Hodkinson, A. J. (2005) Conceptions and misconceptions of inclusive education: a critical examination of final year teacher trainees' knowledge and understanding of inclusion. *International Journal of Research in Education*, 73: 15–29.

Ireson, J., Hallam, S. and Huntley, C. (2005) What are the effects of ability grouping on GCSE attainment? *British Educational Research Journal*, 31 (4): 443–458.

Jones, P. (2006) They are not like us and neither should they be: issues of teacher identity for teachers of pupils with profound and multiple learning difficulties. *Disability & Society*, 19 (2): 159–169.

Kavale, K. (2007) Quantitative research synthesis: meta-analysis of research on meeting special educational needs. In L. Florian (Ed.) *The Sage Handbook of Special Education*. London: Sage.

Kershner, R. (2007) What do teachers need to know about meeting special educational needs? In L. Florian (Ed.) *The Sage Handbook of Special Education*. London: Sage.

Lambe, J. and Bones, R. (2006) Student teachers' perceptions about inclusive classroom teaching in Northern Ireland prior to teaching practice experience. *European Journal of Special Needs Education*, 22 (2): 167–186.

Lewis, A. and Norwich, B. (Eds). (2005) *Special Teaching for Special Children? Pedagogies for Inclusion*. Maidenhead, UK: Open University Press.

Lunt, I. and Norwich, B. (1999) *Can Effective Schools Be Inclusive Schools?* London: Institute of Education, University of London.

OECD (Organisation for Economic Cooperation and Development). (2007) *Quality and Equity of Schooling in Scotland*. Paris: Author.

Ofsted (Office for Standards in Education). (2008) *How Well New Teachers Are Prepared to Teach Pupils with Learning Difficulties and/or Disabilities*. London: Author.

Peters, S. (2007) Inclusive education as a strategy for achieving education for all. In L. Florian (Ed.) *The Sage Handbook of Special Education*. London: Sage Publications.

Pugach, M. and Blanton, L. (2009) A framework for conducting research on collaborative teacher education. *Teaching and Teacher Education*, 25 (4): 575–582.

Rouse, M. (2008) Developing inclusive practice. *Education in the North*, 16: 6–13.

Rouse, M. and Florian, L. (1997) Inclusive education in the marketplace. *International Journal of Inclusive Education*, 1 (4): 323–336.

Sachs, J. (2003) *The Activist Teaching Profession*. Maidenhead: Open University Press.

Scottish Executive. (2004) *A Curriculum for Excellence*. Glasgow: Learning and Teaching Scotland.

Scottish Executive. (2006a) *The Standard for Initial Teacher Education*. Edinburgh: Author.

Scottish Executive. (2006b) *The Guidelines for Initial Teacher Education Courses*. Edinburgh: Author.

Scottish Teacher Education Committee (STEC). (2009) *Framework for Inclusion*. Accessed 17 June 2009 at http://www.frameworkforinclusion.org

Shulman, L. (2007) Keynote lecture to American Association of Colleges for Teacher Education annual conference, New Orleans, February.

Slee, R. (2001) Inclusion in practice: does practice make perfect? *Educational Review*, 53 (2): 113–123.

United Kingdom Government. (2009) *Equality Bill*. Accessed 28 June 2009 at http://www.equalities.gov.uk/equality_bill.aspx

United Nations Educational, Scientific and Cultural Organisation (UNESCO). (2008) *Education for All, Global Monitoring Report*. New York: UNESCO. Accessed 18 December 2008 at http://www.ibe.unesco.org/en/ice/48th-session-2008.htmlSc

Ysseldyke, J. E. (2001) Reflections on a research career: generalizations from 25 years of research on assessment and instructional decision making. *Exceptional Children*, 67 (3): 295–309.

Section 5

Teaching and learning

Chapter 14

Developing inclusive approaches to teaching and learning

Meng Deng (Central China Normal University, Wuhan, China)

Moving towards inclusive education

The movement towards including all students in mainstream schools has gained unparalleled momentum in western societies since the 1950s and has continued into the new century (Brantlinger 1997; Villa and Thousand 2000). The mandate of the Education for All Handicapped Children Act in 1975 (P.L. 94–142, reauthorized as the Individuals with Disabilities Education Act of 1990, IDEA) in the United States (Meyen and Skrtic 1998) has profoundly influenced the levels of educational opportunity made available to students with disabilities (Zigmond 1995), and provided the initial legal impetus for inclusive education (Villa and Thousand 2000).

A variety of themes and terms with subtle differences in meaning, such as "normalization," "integration," "mainstreaming," "Regular Education Initiative," and most recently "inclusion," have emerged to address changes of philosophy and practices (Biklen 1991; Sale and Carey 1995). The concept of inclusive education has then become a flashpoint in the field of special education, and led to the transformation of education for students with disabilities from segregated placement (e.g., residential institutions, special schools and classes) to more inclusive educational settings through a continuum of services model which is composed of regular class, resource room, separate class, separate school facility, and homebound/hospital environment as presented by Crockett and Kauffman (1999) and a single full-time general classroom placement in many countries (Booth and Ainscow 1998). This movement reached a focal point in 1994, when delegates to the world conference on special education held in Spain announced a "framework for action" to advocate that all children be accommodated in ordinary schools, regardless of their physical, intellectual, social, emotional, linguistic or other conditions (UNESCO and Ministry of Education and Science 1994).

It is apparent that the movement toward inclusion has built a foundation on the philosophy of equality of opportunity and diversity risen from a liberal political system and a pluralistic culture (Foreman 1996). However, the debate on inclusive education has been intense during the last two decades and divided the field of special education into two camps: full inclusionists and a more cautious group of partial inclusionists or critics of full inclusion (Sage and Burrello 1994; Deng and Poon-McBrayer 2004). The full inclusionists advocate a restructuring of schools towards a unified system of general and special education in order to accommodate the diverse needs of all students (e.g. Sage and Burrelo 1994; Stainback and Stainback 1984, 1992; Villa and Thousand 1995, 2000); all students with disabilities should be educated in high-quality, age-appropriate, general education classrooms in their home schools and local communities without any discrimination (Salend 1998). The critics of full inclusion (e.g. Fuchs and Fuchs 1994; Kauffman 1993) do not support the "one size for all" approach, and they believe that a continuum of services should be available and that placement should be based on the severity of the disability. It is clear that the debate surrounding full inclusion is not about the rhetorical goal of high-quality and appropriate education for all (Chan 1998); it is about whether research supports the premise that these goals can be attained in the regular classroom (Nelson, Ferrante, and Martella 1999).

Best practice for inclusive teaching and learning

Providing meaningful instruction within the context of inclusive educational arrangements is a priority for students with diverse needs (Coutinho and Repp 1999; Foreman 1996). The unique instructional needs of many students with disabilities present a very real challenge to the ingenuity of general education teachers, and the movement towards an inclusive curriculum requires modifications to the existing curriculum, and to the teaching methods and practices used to implement it. A match between the student's learning and the instructor's teaching style has been considered important (Cohen and Lynch 1991). Many advocates of inclusive education urged that educators have to work collaboratively and communicate regularly with each other, and a series of the so-called best practice-related collaborations have been widely recommended to teachers working in inclusive settings. For example, Knackendoffel (2005) pointed out that team approaches have become increasingly popular for addressing diversity in schools, and collaborative teaming is aimed at improving services to students whose needs are not being met satisfactorily when professionals act alone rather than in concert with others. Salend (1998) stated that successful collaboration includes cooperative learning and collaborative consultation. Lipsky and Gartner (1997) recommended that best practice for inclusive education refers to cooperative learning, curricular adaptations, students supporting other students, using paraprofessional/classroom aids, and using instructional technology. Idol and West (1993) summarized that the most common alternatives of curricular and instructional arrangements include the format, sequence, content and materials for the curriculum, Individual Education

Plan (IEP) design, large and small group instruction, one-to-one instruction, peer tutoring, and collaborative/cooperative teaching. King-Sears (1997) summarized ten practices to build up the structure of inclusion: cooperative learning, strategy instruction, differentiation, self-determination, explicit instruction, curriculum-based assessment, generalization techniques, collaboration, proactive behavior management, and peer supports. Among these strategies, priorities of emphasis and research focus have been given to cooperative teaching, differentiation, and cooperative learning, and they are taken for granted to become the latest orthodoxy of "good teaching" that it is effective in raising students' attainments.

The literature indicates (e.g. Cook and Friend 1995; Lewis and Doorlag 1995; Idol and West 1993) that changing from traditional large group or whole class instruction into small group or collaborative/cooperative teaching has been seen as the most effective step towards facilitating the goals of inclusion. Cook and Friend (1995) defined cooperative teaching as "two or more professionals delivering substantive instruction to a diverse, or blended, group of students in a single physical space" (p. 2), and it includes models: one teaching, one assisting; station teaching; parallel teaching; alternative teaching; and team teaching. Friend (2007) stated that cooperative teaching is a direct and complementary outgrowth of a collaboration model, and it should be part of a school culture that encourages professionals to work together to achieve shared goals, and this is most effective when it is an integral component of a school's efforts to provide all students with the education to which they are entitled. Salend (1998) indicated that educators involved in cooperative teaching share responsibility and accountability for all activities related to planning and delivering instruction, and evaluating and disciplining students; it is designed to minimize problems associated with pull-out programs, and brings academic instruction and supportive services to students in the inclusive environment.

Second, the movement towards an inclusive curriculum requires modifications to the existing curriculum, and to the teaching methods and practices used to implement it. As Walters (1994) stated, students with disabilities may need to receive a more differentiated curriculum, and many researchers (Hoover and Patton 2005; Walters 1994) identify that successful differentiation of curriculum and instruction should be available for students with disabilities in mainstream classrooms. Curricular adaptations are modifications that relate specifically to instruction or curriculum content in general classrooms, and a curriculum adaptation is "any adjustment or modification in the environment, instruction, or materials used for learning that enhances a person's performance or allows at least partial participation in an activity" (Villa and Thousand 1995: 179). Teachers who successfully include students with disabilities have to constantly make decisions about what will be adapted in their curriculum and instruction.

Foreman (1996) pointed out that one of the key difficulties in mainstreaming students with disabilities is the existing curriculum in general education. In many countries the design of differentiated teaching addresses the reality that the population of a classroom is made up of students with varying skill levels and cognition, and it seeks to teach the same concepts while providing differing levels of complexity suited to particular learners (Hall, Strangman, and Meyer 2003; Tomlinson 2001). Westwood (2001) indicated that inclusion stands for an education system that provides differentiated education to serve a large diversity of students, and differentiation must be applied to "teaching strategies, to the curriculum content, to assessment methods, to the ways in which students are organised in the classroom, and to the ways in which the teacher interacts with individual students" (p. 6). Curricular or instructional differentiation could range from simple adjustment of performance standards or mastery criteria by the classroom teacher in a general classroom, to the use of an instructional program or curriculum that is totally separate and different in its goals and objectives from that taught in the classroom (Idol and West 1993). The current literature summarizes these practices as providing the same curriculum, multilevel curriculum, overlapping curriculum, or substitute curriculum to students with diverse needs, which should be put into practice, and IEPs used as a guide for determining appropriate modifications (King-Sears 1997; Lipsky and Gartner 1997).

Third, cooperative learning has been regarded as one of the most frequently recommended strategies for effecting the inclusion of students with disabilities in regular education classrooms (Jenkins and O'Connor 2003; Mastropieri, Scruggs, and Berkeley 2007). The use of cooperative learning has been extensively examined by many researchers; for example, Slavin (1995) identified that it is an integral part of a "success for all" model of effective instruction for enhancing student achievement. The essential components of cooperative learning include group goals, individual accountability, equal opportunities for success, team competition, task specialization, and adaptation to individual needs. Collaborative activity among children promotes their growth and mastery of critical concepts because children of similar ages are likely to be operating within one another's proximal zone of development based on Vygotsky's theory (Slavin 1995). Carter, Cushing, Clark, and Kennedy (2005) summarized that, stemming from classwide peer tutoring, cooperative learning, and other peer-mediated techniques, peer support interventions are emerging as an effective alternative to traditional models for supporting students with disabilities to access the general curriculum. While providing this assistance to their classmates, peers receive ongoing monitoring, feedback, and assistance from general education teachers, and thus contribute to higher levels of social interactions and academic improvement for students with and without disabilities (Cushing and Kennedy 2004). Jenkins, Antil, Wayne, and Vadasy (2003) concluded that peer tutors can clarify the nature of an assignment, interpret complex instructions, model performance, explain ideas, give feedback and corrections, scaffold problem-solving efforts, and provide encouragement to cooperative learners.

Is best practice of inclusive education best?

As portrayed by Westwood (2001), the advocates for inclusive education are likely to assure the public that a slightly more positive attitude, a bit more flexible and adaptable teaching approach (for example to do less direct teaching and to encourage more student-centered cooperative activity), and perhaps a little help from resource teachers will make all students fit comfortably in general classroom study. However, related research findings to date have not supported satisfactory or appropriate outcomes even in those pioneer nations advocating for inclusive education. A number of research studies (e.g. Cook, Semmel, and Gerber 1999; deBettencourt 1999; Zigmond and Baker 1995) revealed that inclusion's effectiveness is "inconclusive." Baker and Zigmond (1995) found that inclusive placements were not frequently associated with, or conducive to, improved outcomes; some key elements of effective instruction were missing or infrequent, including adaptations directed at a single student. Nelson *et al.* (1999) recorded negative academic results of inclusive programming and an effective pull-out service delivery model for students with disabilities. Daniel and King (1997) concluded that "consistent academic gains do not appear to be an advantage of students' participation in an inclusion classroom" (p. 77); thus, if enhancement of academic performance is the primary goal of inclusion, this goal may be unrealistic and inappropriate.

Many other studies (e.g. Scott, Vitale, and Masten 1998; Deng and Harris 2010) showed that, when students with disabilities were placed in their classroom, teachers were often unlikely to modify their traditional whole-classroom instructional methods, owing to a lack of the specific knowledge, skills, and continuing support to ensure inclusion's effectiveness despite favorable attitudes towards inclusion. Salend (1998) pointed out that co-operative teaching may not be effective as expected because educators may lack time for planning and implementation, be resisted by colleagues, and worry about increased workload. The most widely spread illusionary optimism about cooperative teaching has been that general and special education teachers will work and teach together happily and effectively once they are put in the same classroom. However, cooperative teaching is not always comfortable for all professionals. It needs willingness and skills to adjust to different teaching styles and personal dispositions, and work closely with others with respect and trust, and this represents serious challenges for many educators. Thus, cooperative teaching does not necessarily meet the needs of all students, and it seems that there are no recipes for the development and implementation of cooperative teaching despite the fact that training and resources are primary factors.

How to differentiate curriculum and instruction remains most challenging to many teachers and much opposition to inclusion from teachers has resulted from the failure to make successful differentiation. The biggest dilemma related to differentiation has been presented by Westwood (2001), who suggests that modifying or adapting the curriculum usually means a reduction in the content to be taught to some students and this seems to be against the principles of equity and social justice, and when we set different work and expectations for certain students we may increase the differences between the more able and less able students. This is an example of the well-known Matthew Effect in education, with the rich getting richer and the poor getting poorer.

In terms of cooperative learning, the similar illusion is that peers who do not have disabilities would be willing to initiate friendships with students with disabilities and provide needed tutoring and assistance in the right manner as required by teachers. Jenkins et al. (2003) regard the efficacy picture for cooperative learning with special education students as remaining cloudy, and it is hard to reconcile the inconsistency between research uncertainty and strong advocacy for using it. Salend and Duhaney (1999) reviewed the literature of inclusion programs and students with and without disabilities and their teachers. They concluded that, although some studies found that students with disabilities in inclusive programs interacted with others more often, received more social support, and developed more long-lasting and richer friendships with their general education peers, these interactions were often assistive in nature, and declined as the school year progressed. Sale and Carey (1995) used a positive and negative peer nomination strategy to assess the sociometric status of students with disabilities who attended an inclusive elementary school, and found that these students were less likely to be nominated as most liked, and more likely to be nominated as least liked, than their peers.

Although there have been many cases of successful collaborative teaching and learning, the curriculum integration, which is directly related to quality of instruction and has been assumed as the highest level of inclusion in the school, still remains as a challenge to inclusive practices across nations. Serious questions often confronting educators in general classrooms have been: Have general teachers been provided with adequate requisite expertise, training, and resources? How can students with disabilities participate in the general work of the class with or without adaptation, achieving the same basic outcome? How far should teachers differentiate between students in the use of instructional methods and materials if adaptation is necessary? Will the provision of differentiation for students with disabilities affect the academic outcomes of those without disabilities? How to ensure appropriate resources are made available? Would there be problems due to variation in teaching styles and behavior expectations or not? Obviously, future practice needs to address difficulties related to the efficient participation of students with disabilities in core instructional activities alongside their peers without disabilities in general schools.

Conclusion

The mixed results of inclusive practice reflect the dilemma that exists between the pursuit of academic excellence and the goal of education for all under the inclusive education initiatives across nations. It is encouraging that experimentation with inclusive education during the last two decades has provided educators with many valuable empirical insights into ways of teaching students with special needs in regular school settings (Westwood, 2001). However, as noted by Pijl, Meijer, and Hegarty (1997), there have been few countries, whether developed or developing, where high-quality, properly planned, and resourced inclusive education can be really in place, though a commitment to the education of disabled children in general schools has been expressed, however limited their services. There is no doubt that the final responsibility for the success of inclusion rests primarily with regular teachers, and their willingness and ability to use "best practice" to accommodate students with diverse needs have been put forward as decisive factors for the successful implementation of inclusion. Unless the teachers believe that they have the skills to respond to the needs of students, the outcome of inclusion will be anxiety rather than success (Villa and Thousand 2000). Thus, teachers' attitudes and beliefs, their ability to modify curriculum and instruction, and the availability of quality resources have been important prerequisites for educating students with disabilities effectively in general classrooms. Many nations were challenged by the shortage of expertise and qualified personnel to improve instructional quality in inclusive classrooms, and this signifies the importance of developing both well-planned teacher preparation systems (i.e., academic degree programs) and quality in-service training alternatives (e.g., mentorship programs) for the sustainable development of inclusive education (Deng and Harris 2010). Another key aspect of inclusive practice is that teachers should be encouraged to explore their own ways to address individual students' diverse needs, and their experiences should be shared and discussed in various situations. This particular type of phenomenological practice probably does not follow the current "best practice" model but may help to bridge the research-to-classroom chasm and fit in varying education conditions and contexts.

Bibliography

Baker, J. M. and Zigmond, N. (1995) The meaning and practice of inclusion for students with learning disabilities: themes and implications from the five cases. *Journal of Special Education*, 29 (2): 163–180.

Biklen, D. P. (1991) Social policy, social systems, and educational practice. In L. H. Meyer, C. A. Peck, and L. Brown (Eds.) *Critical Issues in the Lives of People with Severe Disabilities*. Baltimore: Brookes.

Booth, T. and Ainscow, M. (1998) *From Them to Us: An International Study of Inclusion in Education*. London: Routledge.

Brantlinger, E. (1997) Using ideology: cases of non-recognition of the politics of research and practice in special education. *Review of Educational Research*, 67 (4): 425–459.

Carter, E. W., Cushing, L. S., Clark, N. M., and Kennedy, C. H. (2005) Effects of peer support interventions on students' access to the general curriculum and social interactions. *Research & Practice for Persons with Severe Disabilities*, 30 (1): 15–25.

Chan, D. W. (1998) Education reform and special education in Hong Kong. In D. W. Chan (Ed.) *Helping Students with Learning Difficulties*. Hong Kong: Chinese University Press.

Cohen, S. B. and Lynch, D. K. (1991) An instructional modification process. *Teaching Exceptional Children*, 23 (4): 12–18.

Cook, B., Semmel, M., and Gerber, M. (1999) Attitudes of principals and special education teachers toward the inclusion of students with mild disabilities. *Remedial and Special Education*, 20 (4): 199–207.

Cook, L. and Friend, M. (1995) Co-teaching: guidelines for creating effective practice. *Focus on Exceptional Children*, 28 (3): 1–16.

Coutinho, M. J. and Repp, A. C. (1999) *Inclusion: The Integration of Students with Disabilities*. Belmont, CA: Wadsworth.

Crockett, J. B. and Kauffman, J. M. (1999) *The Least Restrictive Environment: Its Origins and Interpretations in Special Education*. Mahwah, NJ: Erlbaum.

Cushing, L. S. and Kennedy, C. H. (2004) Facilitating social relationships in general education settings. In C. H. Kennedy and F. M. Horn (Eds.) *Including Students with Severe Disabilities*. Boston: Allyn & Bacon.

Daniel, L. G. and King, D. A. (1997) Impact of inclusive education on academic achievement, student behaviour and self-esteem, and parental attitudes. *Journal of Educational Research*, 91 (2): 67–80.

Debettencourt, L. (1999) General educators' attitudes toward students with mild disabilities and their use of instructional strategies. *Remedial and Special Education*, 20 (1): 27–35.

Deng, M. and Harris, K. (2010) Teacher training strategies for meeting the needs of students with disabilities in Chinese general education classrooms: toward better instruction. *Teacher Education and Special Education*.

Deng, M. and Poon-McBrayer, K. F. (2004) Inclusive education in China: conceptualisation and realization. *Asia-Pacific Journal of Education*, 24 (2): 143–156.

Foreman, P. (1996) *Integration and Inclusion in Action*. Sydney: Harcourt Brace.

Fraenkel, J. R. and Wallen, N. E. (1993) *How to Design and Evaluate Research in Education*, 2nd edition. New York: McGraw-Hill.

Friend, M. (2007) The co-teaching partnership. *Educational Leadership*, 64 (5): 48–52.

Fuchs, D. and Fuchs, L. S. (1994) Inclusive schools movement and the radicalization of special education reform. *Exceptional Children*, 60 (4): 294–309.

Hall, T., Strangman, N., and Meyer, A. (2003) *Differentiated Instruction and Implications for UDL Implementation*. National Center on Accessing the General

Curriculum. Accessed 2 November 2006 at http://www.k8accesscenter.org/training_resources/udl/documents/DifferentiatedInstructionUDL_000.pdf

Hoover, J. J. and Patton, J. R. (2005) Differentiating curriculum and instruction for English-language learners with special needs. *Intervention in School and Clinic*, 40 (4): 231–235.

Idol, L. and West, J. F. (1993) *Effective Instruction of Difficult-to-Teach Students: An In-Service and Pre-Service Professional Development Programme for Classroom, Remedial and Special Education Teachers*. Austin, TX: Pro-ed.

Jenkins, J. R. and O'Connor, R. E. (2003) Cooperative learning for students with learning disabilities: evidence from experiments, observations, and interviews. In S. Graham, K. Harris, and L. Swanson (Eds.) *Handbook of Learning Disabilities*. New York: Guilford.

Jenkins, J. R., Antil, L. R., Wayne, S. K., and Vadasy, P. F. (2003) How co-operative learning works for special education and remedial students. *Exceptional Children*, 69 (3): 279–292.

Johnson, B. and Christensen, L. (2000) *Educational Research: Quantitative and Qualitative Approaches*. Boston: Allyn and Bacon.

Kauffman, J. M. (1993) How we might achieve the radical reform of special education. *Exceptional Children*, 60, (1): 6–16.

King-Sears, M. E. (1997) Best academic practices for inclusive classrooms. *Focus on Exceptional Children*, 29 (7): 1–23.

Knackendoffel, E. A. (2005) Collaborative teaming in the secondary school. *Focus on Exceptional Children*, 37 (5): 1–16.

Lewis, R. B. and Doorlag, D. H. (1995) *Teaching Special Students in the Mainstream*, 4th edition. Englewood Cliffs, NJ: Merrill.

Lipsky, D. K. and Gartner, A. (1997) *Inclusion and School Reform: Transforming America's Classrooms*. Baltimore: P. H. Brookes.

Mastropieri, M. A., Scruggs, T. E., and Berkeley, S. L. (2007) Peers helping: with support from their peers, students with special needs can succeed in the general classroom. *Educational Leadership*, February: 54–58.

Meyen, E. L. and Skrtic, T. (1998) *Exceptional Children and Youth*, 3rd edition. Denver: Love Publishing.

Nelson, J., Ferrante, C., and Martella, R. (1999) Children's evaluations of the effectiveness of in-class and pull-out service delivery models. *International Journal of Special Education*, 14 (2): 77–91.

Pijl, S. J., Meijer, C. J. W., and Hegarty, S. (1997) *Inclusive Education: A Global Agenda*. London: Routledge.

Sage, D. D. and Burrello, L. C. (1994) *Leadership in Educational Reform: An Administrator's Guide to Changes in Special Education*. Baltimore: Paul H. Brookes.

Sale, P. and Carey, D. M. (1995) The sociometric status of students with disabilities in a full-inclusion school. *Exceptional Children*, 62 (1): 6–19.

Salend, S. J. (1998) *Effective Mainstreaming: Creating Inclusive Classrooms*, 3rd edition. Upper Saddle River, NJ: Prentice-Hall.

Salend, S. J. and Duhaney, G. (1999) The impact of inclusion on students with and without disabilities and their teachers. *Remedial and Special Education*, 20 (2): 114–126.

Scott, B. J., Vitale, M. R., and Masten, W. G. (1998) Implementing instructional adaptations for students with disabilities in inclusive classrooms. *Remedial and Special Education*, 19 (2): 106–119.

Slavin, R. E. (1995) *Cooperative Learning: Theory, Research, and Practice*, 2nd edition. Boston: Allyn & Bacon.

Stainback, W. and Stainback, S. (1984) A rationale for the merger of special and regular education. *Exceptional Children*, 51 (2): 102–111.

Stainback, S. and Stainback, W. (1992) Schools as inclusive communities. In W. Stainback and S. Stainback (Eds.) *Controversial Issues Confronting Special Education: Divergent Perspectives*. Boston: Allyn & Bacon.

Tomlinson, C. A. (2001) *How to Differentiate Instruction in Mixed-Ability Classrooms*. Upper Saddle River, NJ: Pearson Education.

UNESCO and Ministry of Education and Science. (1994) *Final Report*. World Conference on Special Needs Education: Access and Quality, Salamanca, Spain, 7–10 June.

Villa, R. A. and Thousand, J. S. (1995) *Creating an Inclusive School*. Alexandria, VA: Association for Supervision and Curriculum Development.

Villa, R. A. and Thousand, J. S. (2000) *Restructuring for Caring and Effective Education: Piecing the Puzzle Together*. Baltimore: Paul H. Brookes.

Walters, B. (1994) *Management for Special Needs*. London: Cassell.

Westwood, P. (2001) Differentiation as a strategy for inclusive classroom practice: some difficulties identified. *Australian Journal of Learning Disabilities*, 6 (1): 5–11.

Zigmond, N. (1995) An exploration of the meaning and practice of special education in the context of full inclusion of students with learning disabilities. *Journal of Special Education*, 29 (2): 109–115.

Zigmond, N. and Baker, J. M. (1995) Concluding comments: current and future practices in inclusive schooling. *Journal of Special Education*, 29 (3): 245–250.

Chapter 15

Overcoming barriers to the acquisition of literacy in twenty-first-century inclusive classrooms

Thérèse McPhillips (St Patrick's College Dublin, Ireland), Sheena Bell (University of Northampton, UK) and Mary Doveston (University of Northampton, UK)

Literacy is an essential skill for participation in education and the workplace and has therefore become the focus of international concern. In all languages and cultures there will be some children who find the acquisition of reading and writing difficult, an area of concern for governments around the world (United Nations Educational, Scientific and Cultural Organisation 2008).

To provide inclusive learning opportunities, education professionals are grappling with issues of how and when to identify those who fall behind expectations of literacy attainments. Students who struggle to acquire literacy may be identified with a particular label such as 'dyslexia', 'specific learning difficulties' or 'learning disability'. (In this chapter, for ease of referencing, we have chosen to use the term 'dyslexia'.) However, issues around identification are acknowledged to be a possible area of contention, as discussed later in the chapter. A controversy exists around the usefulness of the label 'dyslexia' and how this impacts on expectations of children's literacy development and the resourcing of appropriate interventions for learners with literacy difficulties. There is a growing appreciation of the need to locate a student's difficulties in the context of their learning environment. Alongside this, findings from neuro-psychological research have begun to illustrate distinct learning differences and inform approaches to the teaching of literacy.

Dyslexia is increasingly interpreted as a result of cognitive functioning differences which lead to particular learning preferences (Blakemore and Frith 2005). There is a growing recognition of the co-morbidity of specific learning difficulties, such as dyslexia and autism (Reid 2003). It is vitally important that teachers are trained to recognise these potential barriers to learning (McPhillips, Bell and Doveston 2009). Teacher knowledge of how children learn is an important factor in effective literacy pedagogy. Equally, their conceptualisation of learner difficulties is a crucial part of their values and beliefs and has a direct influence on their teaching interactions (Regan and Woods 2000).

In the inclusive classroom, interventions or inclusive teaching approaches are based on the belief that every student can learn, and achieve his/her potential. Rather than focusing on deficits within the student and the causes for these difficulties, the emphasis is on quality teaching and learning for all. The approach taken addresses the learning task, the learning environment and the interaction between student, instruction and task. Key elements include differentiation of teaching, building up the student's self-esteem, encouraging independence of the student and developing the skills needed to continue learning.

In this chapter we draw on our own recent research and that of others and give examples from our contact with classroom teachers who currently support learners with literacy difficulties.

Neurodiversity and personalised learning

In the twenty-first century, a growing scientific understanding of neurobiological differences is fuelling a shift from the identification and subsequent categorisation of learners with literacy difficulties towards an appreciation of neurodiversity in the classroom. Rather than a simplistic view of the individual child neatly labelled with a single learning difficulty, the educational establishment is now being invited to cultivate an appreciation of biological and cultural diversity and identify and respond to individualised learner profiles. For example, teachers in both England and Ireland identified areas of strength in students with dyslexia, who were seen to be 'good problem solvers, often lateral thinkers, think outside the box'. Another teacher observed that 'Usually they have good general knowledge and conversation – this often masks literacy difficulties.' One teacher recognised that students with dyslexia 'may also bring strengths, spatial awareness, artistic or musical aptitude' (McPhillips et al. 2009: 74).

There has been an increasing interest at classroom level in the notion of multiple intelligences (Gardner 1993) and learning styles (Mortimore 2008), particularly in relation to literacy acquisition. Amongst the teachers we work with in England and Ireland, there is a growing appreciation that all learners have their particular learning preferences. One teacher in England described dyslexia as 'a learning style with distinctive patterns of strengths and weaknesses'.

The potential of every child to learn and the way in which they do this can no longer be viewed as a static phenomenon, becoming just another label to attach to a learner (Coffield, Moseley, Hall and Ecclestone 2004). Through an understanding of each individual's unique profile and the implications of cognitive functioning differences, teachers have the potential to encourage and develop metacognitive skills (Flavell 1979), which may empower students to maximise effective learning and develop their individual strengths. For example, this teacher identified metacognition as an important outcome of a one-to-one teaching programme:

At first, Luke was a little uncomfortable with being asked to articulate his thinking and method of completing a task. . . . he did as he was asked and was able to see the value for himself of metacognitive learning. There were occasions when he told me without prompting what he was doing and was not adverse to stating if he found something too difficult or of little use to him.

Children identified as at risk of impaired literacy acquisition have been shown to have underlying difficulties in processing oral and written language regardless of innate intelligence (Hatcher and Snowling 2002). Phonological processing is proposed as a key deficit for dyslexic-type difficulties regardless of language background (Zeigler and Goswami 2006). In phonetic languages, linguistic structure can make literacy learning more or less challenging for learners. Learning to read and write in English is relatively difficult compared with other European languages because of its deep orthography (Goswami 2008). In addition, learners with dyslexia and their teachers face additional challenges if they are taught in a language that is not their mother tongue (Cline and Shamsi 2000), a situation that is becoming more common with increasingly fluctuating cross-cultural mobility (United Nations 2005).

Although learners with dyslexia may have their academic and practical strengths recognised and celebrated by their teachers, the way in which this is recognised must be considered in order to achieve qualifications which will help them progress though an educational system and into suitable employment. Despite competence in a range of subjects, weaknesses such as writing at speed, fast and automatic information processing, and memory may mean that learners with dyslexia find it difficult to perform in examinations. There is a risk that accreditation of their true skills and knowledge is elusive or unattainable. The evolution of special arrangements (also known as accommodations or concessions for examinations), such as giving extra time in exams or using readers and scribes, seeks to redress this imbalance by enabling all students to demonstrate competence and cognition in a variety of subjects. However, whilst this reflects an attempt to embrace a range of learning preferences, it can give rise to a different interpretation. It can be seen as a response to educational systems that use exams needing literacy (in the narrow sense of secretarial skills) as almost the sole medium for demonstration of knowledge.

An important characteristic of special provision has also been the consideration of the affective dimension (social and emotional needs) of individual pupils. Our understanding of the neural bases for learning is now increasing and we can recognise more clearly how affective factors such as anxiety, low self-esteem, attention and concentration difficulties can impinge on learning for dyslexic students in common with any other learners who find literacy difficult (Miles and Varma 1995).

Despite the research at a biological level, it is also recognised that dyslexia and other learning difficulties cannot be divorced from the social context of the learner. Ecological models of child development encourage us to view the literacy learner in a social context (Poole 2003). Teachers and educational psychologists take a holistic and dynamic view of a child before identifying their behaviour as a disability. This view is illustrated by a teacher who recognises that environmental influences could be impacting on individuals:

> Many of our children's difficulties *might* be due to lack of input at home . . . and currently due to our social/economic area.

However, there is a potential tension between the need to understand the whole child and accessing resources for extra support, which could be dependent on a professional diagnosis of a special educational need. The identification of dyslexia and literacy difficulties is therefore highly significant to all stakeholders.

Identification: issues and dilemmas

Current definitions of dyslexia (International Dyslexia Association 2002) focus on dyslexia manifesting itself as difficulties in reading and spelling at word level. A dilemma has been in conceptualising students with dyslexia as distinct from 'garden variety poor readers' (Stanovich 1988). Although there is agreement about the importance of early intervention and this is enshrined in recent government policy in countries around the world (Commonwealth of Australia 2005; Rose 2006; Thirumurthy and Jayaraman 2007) the identification of dyslexia remains controversial (Steubing, Fletcher, Reid Lyon, Shaywitz and Shaywitz 2002). The issues have centred on how dyslexia is defined and whether a separate dyslexia label is useful in the identification and teaching of learners with literacy difficulties (Vellutino, Fletcher, Snowling and Scanlon 2004).

The fact that dyslexia is accepted to be a 'spectrum of difficulties' (Miles 1983: 54) and its developmental nature (Vellutino and Fletcher 2007) can make it difficult to identify at different stages. One dilemma in terms of identification has been the age at which children are diagnosed, which may be due to a reluctance to attach labels to children at an early age. However, this comment by a teacher in England reflects the recognition that early identification is important:

> We would always test for SpLD (Specific learning difficulties: dyslexia) from Yr 1 [age 5–6] onwards if pupil wasn't making progress in literacy/ acquiring age related skills.

Some would argue that identification of dyslexia is less important than identifying specific barriers. As definitions of dyslexia often focus on word-level difficulties many assessment procedures focus on reading and spelling at word level with the result that the holistic view of purposeful reading for meaning is marginalised, which may have implications for how teaching programmes are planned and implemented. Some tests focus on underlying difficulties such as phonological awareness or short-term/working memory (McPhillips *et al.* 2009). In effect, a wide variety of tools can be used ostensibly to test for dyslexia depending on the conceptualisation of dyslexia held by whoever is responsible for testing. One teacher told us:

> We try to identify potential SpLD pupils early in KS2 (Age 7–11). Occasionally they slip through – some learn to compensate and it is not until we test them with LASS Junior [a dyslexia screening test] that we realise the difficulties they have been working with.

The link between IQ and dyslexia is highly complex and contested (Jiménez, Siegel, O'Shanahan and Ford 2009). Current research tells us that the discrepancy model of dyslexia, which defines it as a significant difference between cognitive ability and literacy attainments, is no longer helpful in the identification of learners with specific literacy difficulties because it can rule out children with reading difficulties who do not show this discrepancy but have cognitive processing difficulties (Steubing *et al.* 2002). In England and Ireland, dyslexia diagnosis has traditionally been the remit of the educational psychologist. However, there is a danger that intervention can be delayed by the process of identification when teachers rely on an 'expert's' diagnosis in order to draw down funding. Many teachers encountered by the writers have shown awareness that more training is needed to enable them to screen appropriately.

> This is an area that as SENCO (Special Educational Needs Co-ordinator) I should look into further and revise in line with best practice.

Effective teaching requires a clear understanding of where the students are now in their learning and where they are headed. This is described as 'day-to-day' assessment or 'assessment for learning' (Black and Wiliam 1998: 6). Detailed knowledge of the underlying difficulties for learners and a clear notion of their current attainment levels are essential in order to plan and implement an appropriate teaching programme. Diagnostic teaching is based on reflective evaluation of the learning process which responds to a learner's strengths and needs at a micro-systemic level. This means, in practice, more responsive models of teaching, for example using running records (Clay 1979) or miscue analysis (Goodman 1967) in the teaching of reading; these methods are not novel but are likely to be under-used without teacher

training and practice. Many of the adults involved in individual support interventions may not have the specialist skills acquired through training and
professional development to undertake these methodologies (McPhillips *et
al.* 2009).

Interventions and inclusive teaching approaches

Towards the end of the twentieth century there was international concern
to include all learners in education (UNESCO 1995). Models of inclusive
support vary across the world, and in many countries learners identified as
having specific learning difficulties, including dyslexia, are taught in mainstream settings.

Despite the interventions and efforts of successive governments worldwide, there has not been a magic bullet leading to 100 per cent literacy
acquisition. However, scientific research only confirms the immensity of
the task. Reading has not yet evolved as an innately acquired brain process (Milne 2005) although the fact that it becomes an automatic skill for
the majority of populations with access to teaching leads to the assumption
that it should be easily achievable for everyone – this is about as logical as
predicting that everyone can be expected to play a sport at a competent
level. Because reading difficulties are so individual, it is not surprising that,
in order to address this, teachers need to use focused assessment to plan
teaching programmes.

Difficulties in reading at word level have been associated with dyslexia
(International Dyslexia Association 2002); alongside this there has been
a renewed focus on phonic teaching (Commonwealth of Australia 2005;
Torgerson, Brooks and Hall 2006) which has been re-evaluated and integrated into classrooms across the world. In our research, teachers in England
and Ireland identified phonics as the most frequently used teaching methodology (McPhillips *et al.* 2009).

However, research points us to the fact that reading involves a range of
skills (NICHD 2000). The danger of focusing solely on word level is that
learners forget why they are doing the task. In England, there are concerns
that the National Literacy Strategy (DfEE 1998) has created better readers
but children read less (Sainsbury and Schagen 2004), a point recognised by
this English teacher: 'Reading is seen as decoding words not building a story.'

In the past ten years our current understanding of best practice in literacy
teaching has broadened to a richer and more 'balanced' model of the reading
process (Pressley 2006). Every literacy lesson needs to address literacy skills
at the word, sentence and text levels. Pupils need to apply word-level skills
within continuous text and relate this to the rest of the curriculum. Although
a student who struggles with spelling or phonological awareness skills may
need more stand-alone phonics teaching, this work needs to be embedded in
and supported with context-rich and exciting reading material. The student

needs this support and not just instruction in separate discrete skills. There is a danger that a predominantly skills-based or 'bottom-up' approach of identifying letters and sounds and building individual words overshadows the more complex bigger picture of learning to read and write. Making sense of print is what reading is all about (Goodman 1967). Good readers use the 'big four' comprehension strategies of *predicting, visualising, connecting* and *questioning* to aid comprehension (Pressley 2000). Yet there is evidence that the explicit teaching of comprehension strategies is frequently neglected (Department of Education and Science Inspectorate 2005; RAND Reading Study Group 2002).

For learners who may be adequate decoders but have a difficulty comprehending text, *reciprocal teaching* and *inference training* are effective approaches that support holistic and inclusive literacy teaching (Brooks 2007).

Inclusive teaching approaches

There is currently a trend away from categories of special educational need and specialist teaching approaches, and a renewed emphasis on the teaching and learning context of the student (Davis and Florian 2004; Lewis and Norwich 2001). For children with specific literacy learning difficulties, there is little evidence of a need for distinctive teaching approaches although responding to individual difference is crucial. The notion of a *continuum* of teaching approaches is useful (Lewis and Norwich 2005) as this keeps the profile of the individual learner in mind and the teacher can adapt accordingly. Research on effective literacy teaching has shown that the critical element is the teacher (Hall 2003). Effective literacy learning has more to do with teachers combining knowledge, skills and understanding to suit the needs of individual learners than expertise in delivering a particular programme. Some children benefit from more explicit teaching, reinforcement, structure, detail and continuous assessment of their learning than others. Although no single specific strategy will provide a support model for all teachers, there has been some conclusive research on the effectiveness of classroom practices in some areas.

A number of useful strategies have been identified (Brooks 2007). Partnership approaches for reading and writing such as pairing one pupil with another, one becoming the tutor and the other the tutee, are effective. For example, Paired Reading (Topping and Lindsay 1992) has been shown to improve reading ability, social skills and self-esteem. Pairing students within the same class can also help students access the curriculum, although training and school support are needed if this practice is to be effective.

All learners can benefit from working in small groups, not least the student with additional learning needs or literacy difficulties (Johnson and Johnson 1994). The cooperative working approach uses the concept of multiple intelligences and learning preference in a group setting. There are some key concepts common to effective learning in groups. The teacher directs the organisation and structure while fostering positive interdependence and accountability. Effective teachers of literacy have been found to balance whole class, small group and individual instruction (Taylor, Pressley and Pearson 2003). Recent reports suggest that flexible group work in class is a challenge to many teachers (Department of Education and Science Inspectorate 2005; NCCA 2005). This is illustrated in the writers' recent cross-cultural study of students receiving dyslexia support; in England, teachers highlighted the importance placed on individual work. These teachers preferred 'individualised, regular and short teaching sessions' *for* learners with dyslexia within a mainstream setting.

Teachers are now combining different experiences to provide for the learning preferences among students. By providing a multisensory learning environment, the teacher provides a variety of opportunities for the student to access learning through their preferred modality and also to encourage students to move outside of their learning preference or their 'comfort zone' (Mackay 2003: 34). This approach engages multiple senses simultaneously. The learner should be able to see, hear, say and touch the materials to be learned. In a recent study, teachers described using multisensory strategies and materials when supporting students with dyslexia; for example: 'Very visual, lots of colour, animation. Regular repetition, frequent practice in multi sensory methods.' Games such as 'word bingo', Snap, 'Fish in the Pond' and nursery rhymes can also form part of multisensory learning (McPhillips *et al.* 2009). A multisensory approach supports the specific needs of particular learners without being qualitatively different from the approaches used in mainstream pedagogy (Lewis and Norwich 2005). These methods therefore benefit all learners and not just those with specific learning difficulties.

Because of the difficulties associated with dyslexia such as short-term memory, automaticity and phonological awareness skills, considerable reinforcement of learning is considered necessary for many learners. In an inclusive classroom the teacher will be aware of the need to constantly revisit and consolidate the development of literacy skills for all students. However, some students will need a higher level of practice and repetition to ensure mastery of the literacy skills. When teachers were asked how they organised their dyslexia support teaching, they reported 'Frequent short sessions which allow for the re-learning and over-learning of specific skills' (McPhillips *et al.* 2009: 74).

Building self-esteem and encouraging confidence as a reader is linked with improved outcomes in reading. The teaching approach of combining literacy instruction with building pupils' self-esteem is supported by recent studies (Brooks 1999, 2007). It was found that intervention in reading failure undertaken with strategies designed to improve self-esteem was the most effective. Research emphasises the importance of building confidence and self-esteem as a crucial part of support and inclusion (Humphrey 2003). As one teacher observed: 'With support they can become more confident at building strategies to overcome their difficulties.'

Given the great interest both nationally and internationally in students' literacy achievements, with international ranking of literacy levels across countries (OECD 2006; PIRLS 2001), it is no surprise that the huge number and variety of published literacy interventions and programmes continues to grow. The notion of 'caveat emptor' or 'buyer beware' readily applies to schools and teachers in selecting literacy materials for pupils who need additional support. Confusion may arise between literacy programmes designed for all learners, catch-up programmes for some learners and individualised programmes. Caution is also recommended regarding a single approach to phonics teaching (Lewis and Ellis 2006). The power of publishing companies cannot be underestimated in prescribing programmes based on a selective interpretation of research findings (e.g. neuroscience). Brooks (2007) reported that good literacy intervention schemes can deliver at least twice the normal rate of progress and it is reasonable to expect this. However, there is frequently a gap between evidence and policy. Teachers must link their choice of materials to their informed professional judgement and the needs of the learner.

Conclusions: implications for training and professional development

Teachers in all schools will encounter students with barriers to literacy acquisition. In order for them to provide appropriate teaching and support they need to have relevant training and professional development opportunities. An inclusive approach to supporting learners must be focused at the classroom level and involve both specialist and class teachers. Training and continuing professional development should not focus on the delivery of particular programmes, but should inform teachers of the underlying learning processes which can impede literacy development. Teachers need to have knowledge of the range of methodologies available in order to choose the most effective intervention for specific learners. Once trained, teachers should be enabled to apply their skills specifically to *teach* learners with literacy difficulties and not just organise and monitor support. Furthermore, they should have opportunities to work with non-specialist teachers to develop inclusive classroom practice. All those involved in the teaching and support of dyslexic learners should receive specialist training.

The organisation of teaching and support will inevitably vary according to cultural variations and available funding. However, the social context of learning is important and needs to be considered, not least because of issues of self-esteem. Literacy learning can never be divorced from the learners' main school programme and is an aid to accessing the whole curriculum and gaining accreditation of skills and knowledge.

Because literacy is so important to all our lives in the twenty-first century, it is not surprising that the failure of some students to achieve efficient skills is still a cause of controversy. However, research has provided us not only with a growing understanding of the underlying difficulties which impede literacy development, but also with a clear view of a variety of ways in which teachers can support dyslexic students in inclusive settings. The importance of linking ongoing assessment to planning learning programmes cannot be underestimated. Learning goals and targets must be viewed as part of a wider, holistic view of the learner. The classroom context and the learning opportunities provided by the teacher can minimise the difficulties experienced by the student with dyslexia. It is up to educational communities worldwide, and the governments that fund them, to support efforts to enhance inclusive classroom practices if we are to ensure effective learning for students with literacy difficulties.

Bibliography

Black, P. and Wiliam, D. (1998) Inside the Black Box: raising standards through classroom assessment. *Phi Delta Kappan*, 5 (1): 7–74.

Blakemore, S. J. and Frith, U. (2005) *The Learning Brain: Lessons for Education*. Oxford: Blackwell.

Brooks, G. (1999) What works for slow readers? *Support for Learning*, 14 (1): 27–31.

Brooks, G. (2002) *What Works for Children with Literacy Difficulties? The Effectiveness of Intervention Schemes*. NFER Research Report RR380. London: DfES.

Brooks, G. (2007) *What Works for Children with Literacy Difficulties: The Effectiveness of Intervention Schemes*, 3rd edition. Slough: DfCSF/NfER.

Clay, M. (1979) *Reading; The Patterning of Complex Behaviour*, 2nd edition. Portsmouth: Heinemann Educational.

Cline, T. and Shamsi, T. (2000) *Language Needs or Special Needs? The Assessment of Learning Difficulties in Literacy among Children Learning English as an Additional Language: A Literature Review*. RR 1894. London: DfEE.

Coffield, F., Moseley, D., Hall, E. and Ecclestone, K. (2004) *Learning Styles and Pedagogy in Post 16 Learning: A Systematic and Critical Review*. Learning and Skills Research Centre. Accessed 19 February 2009 at http://www.lsneducation. org.uk/research/reports/

Commonwealth of Australia. (2005) *Teaching Reading: Report and Recommendations. National Inquiry into the Teaching of Literacy December 2005*. Accessed 19 February 2008 at http://www.dest.gov.au/nitl/documents/report_recommendations.pdf

Davis, P. and Florian, L. (2004) *Teaching Strategies and Approaches for Pupils with Special Educational Needs: A Scoping Study*. Research Report 516. Nottingham: DfES Publications.

Department for Education and Employment (DfEE). (1998) *The National Literacy Strategy: A Framework for Teaching*. London: HMSO.

Department of Education and Science Inspectorate. (2005) *An Evaluation of Curriculum Implementation in Primary Schools*. Dublin: Stationery Office.

Flavell, J. H. (1979) Metacognition and cognitive monitoring: a new area of cognitive-developmental inquiry. *American Psychologist*, 34: 906–911.

Gardner, H. (1993) *Frames of Mind: The Theory of Multiple Intelligences*, 2nd edition. London: Fontana.

Goodman, K. (1967) A linguistic study of cues and miscues. *Elementary English*, 42 (6): 369–643.

Goodman, Y. M. and Goodman, K. S. (1994) To err is human: learning about language processes by analyzing miscues. In R. B. Ruddell, M. R. Ruddell and H. Singer (Eds) *Theoretical Models and Processes of Reading*, 4th edition. Newark, DE: International Reading Association.

Goswami, U. (2008) Reading, complexity and the brain. *Literacy*, 42 (2): 67–74.

Hall, K. (2003) *Listening to Stephen Read: Multiple Perspectives on Literacy*. Buckingham: Open University Press.

Hatcher, J. and Snowling, M. J. (2002) The phonological representations hypothesis of dyslexia: from theory to practice. In G. Reid and J. Wearmouth (Eds) *Dyslexia and Literacy: Theory and Practice*. London: John Wiley & Sons.

Humphrey, N. (2003) Facilitating a positive sense of self in pupils with dyslexia: the role of teachers and peers. *Support for Learning*, 18 (3): 130–136.

International Dyslexia Association. (2002) *What is Dyslexia?* Accessed 17 February 2009 at http://www.interdys.org/FAQWhatIs.htm

Jiménez, J. E., Siegel, L., O'Shanahan, I. and Ford, L. (2009) The relative roles of IQ and cognitive processes in reading disability. *Educational Psychology*, 29 (1): 27–43.

Johnson, D. W. and Johnson, R. T. (1994) *Learning Together and Alone: Cooperative, Competitive and Individualistic Learning*, 4th edition. Englewood Cliffs, NJ: Prentice Hall.

Lewis, A. and Norwich, B. (2001) Mapping a pedagogy for SEN. *British Educational Research Journal*, 27 (3): 313–330.

Lewis, A. and Norwich, B. (2005) *Special Teaching for Special Children? Pedagogies for Inclusion*. Buckingham: Open University Press.

Lewis, M. and Ellis, S. (2006) *Phonics Practice, Research and Policy*. London: Paul Chapman Publishing.

Mackay, N. (2001) *Removing Dyslexia as a Barrier to Achievement: The Dyslexia Friendly Schools Toolkit*. Wakefield: SEN Marketing.

Mackay, N. (2003) Dyslexia friendly schools. In L. Peer and G. Reid (Eds) *Dyslexia – Successful Inclusion in the Secondary School*. London: David Fulton Publishers.

McPhillips, T., Bell, S. and Doveston, M. (2009) Identification and intervention for primary pupils with dyslexia in Ireland and England: finding a path through the maze. *REACH Journal of Special Needs Education in Ireland*, 22 (2): 67–81.

Miles, T. R. (1983) *Dyslexia: The Pattern of Difficulties*. London: Collins Educational.

Miles, T. R. and Varma, V. P. (1995) *Dyslexia and Stress*. London: Whurr.

Milne, D. (2005) *Teaching the Brain to Read*. Hungerford: SK Publishing.

Mortimore, T. (2008) *Dyslexia and Learning Style: A Practitioner's Handbook*, 2nd edition. Chichester: John Wiley.

NCCA (National Council for Curriculum and Assessment). (2005) *Primary Curriculum Review Phase 1: Summary of Findings and Recommendations*. Dublin: Author.

NICHD (National Institute of Child Health and Human Development). (2000) *Teaching Children to Read: An Evidence-Based Assessment of the Scientific Research Literature on Reading and Its Implications for Reading Instruction: Reports of the Subgroups*. (Report of the National Reading Panel, NIH Publication No. 00–4754). Washington, DC: U.S. Government Printing Office.

OECD. (2006) *Education at a Glance*. New York: OECD.

PIRLS (Progress in International Reading Literacy Study). (2001) *Reading All over the World*. London: DfES.

Poole, J. (2003) Dyslexia: a wider view: the contribution of an ecological paradigm to current issues. *Educational Research*, 45 (2): 167–180.

Pressley, M. (2000) What should comprehension instruction be the instruction of? In M. L. Kamil, P. Mosenthal, R. Barr and P. D. Pearson (Eds) *Handbook of Reading Research*, Vol. 3. Mahwah, NJ: Erlbaum.

Pressley, M. (2006) *Reading Instruction that Works: The Case for Balanced Teaching*, 3rd edition. New York: Guildford Press.

RAND Reading Study Group. (2002) *Reading for Understanding: Toward an R&D Programme in Reading Comprehension*. Santa Monica, CA: RAND.

Regan, T. and Woods, K. (2000) Teachers' understandings of dyslexia: implications for educational psychology practice. *Educational Psychology in Practice*, 16 (3): 333–347.

Reid, G. (2003) *Dyslexia: A Practitioner's Handbook*, 3rd edition. Chichester: Wiley.

Riddick, B. (1996) *Living with Dyslexia*. London: Routledge.

Rose, J. (2006) *Independent Review of the Teaching of Early Reading*. Nottingham: Department for Education and Skills.

Sainsbury, M. and Schagen, I. (2004) Attitudes to reading at ages nine and eleven. *Journal of Research in Reading*, 27 (4): 373–386.

Stanovich, K. E. (1988) Explaining the difference between the dyslexic and the garden variety poor readers: the phonological core model. *Journal of Learning Disabilities*, 21 (10): 590–604.

Steubing, K., Fletcher, J., Reid Lyon, G., Shaywitz, S. and Shaywitz, B. (2002) Validity of IQ-discrepancy classifications of reading disabilities: a meta-analysis. *American Educational Research Journal*, 39 (22): 469–518.

Taylor, B. M., Pressley, M. and Pearson, D. (2003) Research-supported characteristics of teachers and schools that promote reading achievement. In B. M. Taylor and P. D. Pearson (Eds) *Effective Schools and Accomplished Teachers*. Hillsdale, NJ: Erlbaum.

Thirumurthy, V. and Jayaraman, B. (2007) Special education in India at the crossroads. *The Free Library*. Accessed 17 February 2009 at http://www.thefreelibrary.com/Special education in India at the crossroads.-a0168163372

Topping, K. A. and Lindsay, G. A. (1992) Paired reading: a review of the literature. *Research Papers in Education*, 7 (3): 199–246.

Torgerson, C. J., Brooks, G. and Hall, J. (2006) *A Systematic Review of the Research Literature on the Use of Phonics in the Teaching of Reading and Spelling*. London: DfES.

United Nations. (2005) *World Population Prospects: The 2004 Revision.* New York: United Nations. Accessed 17 February 2009 at http://www.un.org/esa/population/publications/WPP2004/2004Highlights_finalrevised.pdf

United Nations Educational, Scientific and Cultural Organisation (UNESCO). (1995) *The Salamanca Statement and Framework for Action on Special Needs Education.* World Conference on Special Needs Education: Access and Quality, Salamanca, Spain, 7–10 June 1994. Accessed 19 February 2009 at http://portal.unesco.org/education/en/ev.php-URL_ID=8412&URL_DO=DO_TOPIC&URL_SECTION=201.html#fulltext

United Nations Educational, Scientific and Cultural Organisation (UNESCO). (2008) *International Literacy Statistics: A Review of Concepts, Methodology and Current Data.* Montreal: Institute for Statistics.

Vellutino, F. R. and Fletcher, J. (2007) Developmental dyslexia. In M. Snowling and C. Hulme (Eds) *The Science of Reading: A Handbook.* Oxford: Blackwell.

Vellutino, F. R., Fletcher, J. M., Snowling, M. J. and Scanlon, D. M. (2004) Specific reading disability (dyslexia): what have we learned in the past four decades? *Journal of Child Psychology and Psychiatry and Allied Disciplines*, 45 (1): 2–40.

Zeigler, J. C. and Goswami, U. (2006) Becoming literate in different languages: similar problems, different solutions. *Developmental Science*, 9 (5): 429–453.

Chapter 16

The development of inclusive teaching and learning

A European perspective?

Amanda Watkins and Cor Meijer (European Agency for Development in Special Needs Education)

The focus of this chapter is upon presenting a European perspective on the development of inclusive teaching and learning. The title has been deliberately phrased as a question, not a statement, as the authors hope the information presented explores rather than just describes the situation in Europe.

All of the original data presented in this chapter have been gathered within the framework of the European Agency for Development in Special Needs Education, an independent and self-governing organisation established by its member countries to act as their platform for collaboration regarding the exchange of information on development of provision for learners with special educational needs (SEN). The ultimate goal for the Agency is to improve educational policy and practice for these learners.

The Agency currently has national networks in twenty-seven European countries[1] and is financed by the member countries' ministries of education and the European Commission Lifelong Learning Programme, as one of the six institutions pursuing an aim of European interest in the field of education (Jean Monnet Programme).[2]

Within this chapter, work conducted within the twenty-seven member countries of the European Agency for Development in Special Needs Education will be drawn upon to explore whether there is a European perspective on inclusive teaching and learning. Specifically, project work dealing with assessment and classroom practice will be examined to identify common factors across countries in their developing approaches to providing inclusive teaching and learning experiences for all learners.

Special needs education (SNE) and inclusion: the European Union policy framework

The European Union is arguably the most diverse formal alliance of countries in the world: the EU has twenty-seven full member states and twenty-three official languages (plus at least five unofficial ones). Each of the member states has its own laws, policies and systems for all aspects of society, including education. At least five of the member and other European partner states – Belgium, Germany, Spain, Switzerland and the UK – can be loosely described as federal; that means they actually comprise small 'national units' which have their own legislative and decision-making powers (again including education).

This diversity aside, there are two levels of internationally agreed statements and resolutions on education and specifically education and provision for people with special needs and disabilities that all European countries have ratified to one degree or another.

At the international – that is global – level, the majority of EU member states have ratified the United Nations *Standard Rules on the Equalisation of Opportunities for Persons with Disabilities* (1993), the UNESCO *Dakar Framework for Action, Education for All: Meeting our Collective Commitments* (2000) and the United Nations *Convention on Rights of People with Disabilities* (2006). Within the Convention, Article 24 is crucial for guiding work in educational policy and practice:

> States Parties recognise the right of persons with disabilities to education. With a view to realising this right without discrimination and on the basis of equal opportunity, States Parties shall ensure an inclusive education system at all levels . . . The full development of human potential and sense of dignity and self-worth, and the strengthening of respect for human rights, fundamental freedoms and human diversity . . .

Most European countries have signed the Convention (although it must be noted they have not necessarily ratified the Convention or signed or ratified the optional protocol – please see http://www.un.org/disabilities/countries.asp?navid=17&pid=16 for more details).

At the European Union level, there are a number of statements and resolutions (ministerial-level agreements that, without being legally binding upon member states, do give an agreed direction for policy formation) on disability and special education that underpin national policies. The first of these dates from 1990 with the Resolution of the Council of Ministers of Education concerning *Integration of children and young people with disabilities into ordinary systems of education*. In 1996, the Council published the *Resolution on the human rights of disabled people* and the European Commission published a Communication (a statement asking for Council action) on the *Equality of opportunity for people with disabilities*. 2001 saw the European Parliament Resolution *Towards a barrier-free Europe for people with disabilities* and in 2003 the Parliament published the resolution *Towards a United Nations legally binding instrument to promote and protect the rights and dignity of persons with disabilities*.

The Council Resolution of 2003 on *Promoting the employment and social integration of people with disabilities* and the Council Resolution, 2003, on *Equal opportunities for pupils and students with disabilities in education and training* are two of the main EU-level statements that guide member states' policies for special education.

These principles are echoed in the 2007 *Lisbon Declaration – Young People's Views on Inclusive Education* (Portuguese Ministry of Education and the European Agency for Development in Special Needs Education 2007), which outlines a number of proposals agreed upon by young people with special educational needs from twenty-nine countries attending secondary, vocational and higher education. The declaration outlines the young people's views on their rights, needs, challenges they face and recommendations in order to achieve successful inclusive education.

Most importantly, all European countries have ratified the UNESCO *Salamanca Statement and Framework for Action on Special Needs Education* (1994). This collective statement is a major focal point for special needs education work in Europe – it is still a keystone in the conceptual framework of many countries' policies. One extract from the statement is used repeatedly as a guiding principle in policy-level debates:

> Regular schools with an inclusive orientation are the most effective means of combating discriminatory attitudes, creating welcoming communities, building an inclusive society and achieving education for all; moreover, they provide an effective education to the majority of children and improve the efficiency and ultimately the cost-effectiveness of the entire education system.
>
> (p. 8)

All European countries agree that the key principles encompassed in the Salamanca Statement of equal opportunities in terms of genuine access to learning experiences that respect individual differences and quality education for all, focused upon personal strengths rather than weaknesses, are those principles that should underpin all education policies – not just those specifically dealing with special needs education.

Inclusive education – shared definitions?

At the international policy level, all European countries agree that the key international statements and resolutions on inclusion and special education provide the main principles regarding equal opportunities that underpin national policies and provide a frame of reference for their work. Such guidelines highlight the need for teaching to promote genuine access to learning experiences that respect individual differences and high-quality education for all focused upon personal strengths rather than weaknesses.

However, how these key principles are then translated into policy that directs practice for teaching and learning in inclusive settings in European countries differs greatly.

A first point to note is the terminology used in European Union and national-level policy statements. There are various debates, at policy-making and practitioner levels, regarding the use of the words 'integration' and 'inclusion' (and of course their respective translations in the twenty-three languages of the EU). At the EU level, official statements are only recently beginning to refer to 'inclusion' rather than 'integration'.

However, for the majority of national-level policies, the term 'inclusion' is the only one used, as this is seen to reflect an important change in thinking about provision for learners with special needs: inclusion referring to a learner being a part of their local educational community from the beginning – a part from the start; integration implying that the goal is to integrate a learner back into the mainstream school, because at some point they have been excluded from it.

Despite this shift in thinking towards educational inclusion as an agreed goal for European countries, agreements on what settings are considered 'inclusive' are not so clear. In key areas of Agency work (for example) an operational definition of inclusive settings has been employed: 'those educational settings where pupils with special needs follow the largest part of the curriculum in the mainstream class alongside peers without special educational needs' (Meijer 2003a: 9).

However, the range of settings and types of provision evident in countries emphasises the enormous difficulties in comparing situations across Europe. All countries are at 'different points of the journey to inclusion signposted by the Salamanca statement' (Peacey 2006). The term 'inclusion' has itself been on a journey since it was initially introduced within an educational context.

First, it is now understood to concern a far wider range of pupils vulnerable to exclusion than those identified as having SEN. Second, for many people the introduction of the term was an explicit attempt to move ideas of education for all beyond 'mainstreaming'. In its most basic form, mainstreaming can be seen as the physical co-existing of pupils with and without SEN in the same place.

Third, most typically the early use of the term in European countries was characterised by the belief that pupils with SEN should have 'access to the curriculum'. This implied that 'the curriculum' was a fixed and static entity and that pupils with SEN require different types of support to access the mainstream curriculum. The current use of the term 'inclusion' usually starts from the proposition that pupils with SEN have a right to a curriculum that is appropriate to their needs and that education systems have a duty to provide this.

Alongside these ideas are three key propositions:

1   A curriculum for all considers academic and social learning. Curriculum goals and implementation should reflect this dual focus.

2   Inclusion is a process and not a state. Educators will always need to move their work forward to enable the learning and participation of all pupils.

3   As mainstream schools are the main means of educating the vast majority of pupils in Europe, 'mainstreaming' in terms of 'location' of pupils with SEN is still a vital part of inclusion.

At a European level, it is fair to say that the term 'inclusive settings' usually refers to mainstream educational provision in schools and classes that:

- Has pupils with or without SEN learning together;
- Works to develop a curriculum that enables the learning and participation of all pupils.

(Watkins 2007)

In Europe, the policy aim for most countries is generally agreed to be inclusion of learners with SEN within compulsory mainstream education – although this is not universally agreed to be appropriate for all SEN pupils. It is therefore important to bear in mind that the issue of *quality in education* is not addressed by only considering developments in the proportion of learners with SEN who are educated separately. Placement in an inclusive setting does not necessarily guarantee high-quality provision; conversely, placement in a separate setting does not result in inappropriate educational provision for some pupils.

Inclusive education is not a static phenomenon. It has been developing in different ways and it continues to develop. Conceptions of, policies for, and practice in inclusive education are constantly undergoing change in all countries (Kyriazopoulou and Weber 2009). Inclusive education is a goal all countries are working towards and countries' policies and practice are at different stages in this process of development.

Provision for pupils with special educational needs in European countries

Provision for pupils with special educational needs in all countries across Europe includes education and placement in special schools or classes (separate provision), as well as in mainstream settings. National governments all have financial commitments to segregated, as well as inclusive, systems of special educational provision. Two aspects of this fact will be considered here: the population of pupils identified as having SEN and the types of policies that direct their educational placement.

Population of pupils with SEN

As a biennial activity, the Agency member countries provide ministerial-level statistical data on numbers of pupils formally identified as having SEN in their countries. All data are provided by ministries of education, but data are not independently assessed or verified and it is generally understood that practice can differ from official data.

Using the most recent data from the Agency member countries – collected during 2008 – it is possible to get an overview of the population of pupils recognised as having SEN. Based on the information provided by the thirty-one states[3] considered in the 2008 analysis, it is possible to say that:

- Of the 63.5 million pupils in compulsory schooling, around 3.5 per cent are officially recognised as having some form of SEN that requires additional support to be made available.
- The range of percentages of pupils officially recognised as having SEN across the countries is from 1.5 per cent to almost 20 per cent.
- Around 2 per cent of pupils with SEN in compulsory education are educated in segregated settings: special schools or classes where they spend more than 80 per cent of their school time away from mainstream peers.
- The percentage of pupils placed in segregated settings varies widely between countries, ranging from below 1 per cent to over 5 per cent.

An examination of numerical data on pupils with SEN reflects more divergence than convergence in countries' policy approaches that direct provision:

1   All data refer to pupils officially identified as having SEN as *defined in the country in question*. The data use the country-based, legal definitions of SEN, as there are no accepted definitions of SEN available to use comparatively.

2   Within country definitions, different 'categories' of special needs may or may not be covered: disabilities (sensory, physical, psychological); learning difficulties; behaviour problems; gifted learners; health problems; socially disadvantaged etc.

3   The age range of compulsory school education is not the same in all countries.

4   Parental choice of placement in a mainstream or segregated setting may or may not be an entitlement in policy.

5   Country policies may or may not include a 'definition' of what is meant by inclusive education and a segregated setting.

6   Countries may or may not 'count' only those learners who have an official 'recognition' (decision, certificate, statement or other

legal document) of SEN. Many countries do not collect data on the numbers of learners in fully inclusive settings that receive SEN support. Many countries indicate that their data relate to learners 'officially recognised' as having SEN. Other learners also receive support, but are not 'counted'.

The points above have led Agency member countries to conclude that is it not useful to compare the overall numbers and/or percentages of pupils officially recognised as having SEN (as different definitions are being applied) or to compare the numbers or percentages of pupils with SEN in fully inclusive settings, as the data are not always available and, when they are available, they are not comparable. It is agreed that the only comparable set of data is the percentage of pupils who are educated in segregated settings.

In summary, the patterns of pupils identified as having SEN in inclusive and separate provision are determined by the systems and methods of identifying and assessing pupils' needs. These differences reflect differences in assessment procedures and funding arrangements rather than differences in the actual incidence of SEN across countries (Meijer 1999, 2003b; Watkins 2007).

Given that the way in which SEN is defined and consequently the types of provision that have been developed in relation to SEN are different for each country, direct comparisons between countries are not possible. However, the trends in the proportion of pupils educated separately are a useful indication of developments towards inclusion for SEN pupils.

Policies directing placement

Using the 2008 dataset (available in Watkins 2009), it is possible to group countries according to the percentage of pupils with SEN educated in segregated settings (calculated against the overall school population).

- *Below 1 per cent* – Cyprus, Greece, Ireland, Italy, Malta, Norway, Portugal, Slovenia, Spain.
- *Between 1 per cent and 3 per cent* – Austria, Bulgaria, France, Hungary, Iceland, Lithuania, Luxembourg, Netherlands, Poland, Sweden, UK (England), UK (Scotland), UK (Wales).
- *Above 3 per cent* – Belgium (Flemish-speaking community), Belgium (French-speaking community), Czech Republic, Denmark, Estonia, Finland, Germany, Latvia, Switzerland.

These 'bands' of placement can be loosely mapped onto clearly defined policy approaches for inclusion. Country policies can be divided into three categories according to their approach to including pupils with SEN in mainstream education (Meijer 2003).

- In a *one-track approach* – where countries place fewer than 1 per cent of pupils in segregated settings – countries develop policy and practice geared towards the inclusion of almost all pupils within mainstream education. This type of inclusion is supported by a wide range of services focusing on the mainstream school.
- In a *multi-track approach*, countries have a multiplicity of approaches to inclusion. They offer a variety of services between the two systems, mainstream and special needs education. Countries using this approach generally place between 1 per cent and 3 per cent of pupils in segregated settings.
- In a *two-track approach*, there are two distinct educational systems. Pupils with SEN are usually placed in special schools or special classes. Generally, the vast majority (i.e. 3 per cent or more) of the pupils officially registered as having SEN do not follow the mainstream curriculum among non-disabled peers.

(It should be noted that for all countries there is not an exact match of all provision to these tracks, but this pattern generally holds for the majority of countries.)

Work conducted in the Agency member countries – notably by Meijer (2003a, 2005) – indicates that there are some common trends in countries. The first of these relates to legislative progress regarding inclusion in many countries. This applies especially to countries with a highly developed segregated special needs education system, where new legislative frameworks concerning SEN within the mainstream school are being developed.

Second, some countries have made changes within their funding system in order to achieve more inclusive services. In other countries, there is a growing awareness of the importance of a flexible funding system that allows for a variety of placements and provision to be considered for individual pupils.

Finally, there is a movement in which countries with a clear two-track system of special needs education (relatively large SNE system beside the mainstream system) are developing a continuum of services between the two systems. Furthermore, special schools are more and more defined as resources for mainstream schools.

These movements in policy and systems have not resulted in all countries' policies for inclusion converging towards an accepted approach. There are still obvious differences as a result of the fact that the education systems (policies and practice) in countries have evolved over time, within very specific contexts, and therefore remain highly individual.

However, policy movements coupled with ongoing changes in the conceptions of inclusion and teaching and learning generally can be seen to result in some similarities across European countries in the practice and the implementation of inclusive education. There are some identifiable approaches that countries agree are beneficial in all situations and that do not appear to be country context specific. These approaches are the focus of the following sections, where the key principles that emerge from across Europe as being critical in the development of inclusive teaching and learning will be highlighted.

Developing inclusive teaching and learning – common approaches

The information presented here draws upon two European projects conducted by the European Agency for Development in Special Needs Education:

- *Inclusive Education and Classroom Practice* (http://www.european-agency.org/iecp/iecp_intro.htm). The project was focused on revealing, analysing, describing and disseminating apparently successful classroom practice in inclusive settings. The project involved fourteen European countries and was divided into two phases investigating primary and secondary education.
- *Assessment in Inclusive Settings* (http://www.european-agency.org/site/themes/assessment/index.shtml). The overall goal for the project was to examine how assessment policy and practice can support effective decision making about teaching and learning approaches, methods and steps in the best possible ways. Twenty-five countries were involved in the project work overall.

Inclusive approaches in teaching and classroom practice

The first main conclusion from the three-year study confirmed that inclusive classrooms do exist throughout European countries. However, in all countries, behaviour, social and/or emotional problems are the most challenging within the area of inclusion of pupils with SEN and practically dealing with differences or diversity in the classroom forms one of the biggest problems within European schools.

The study showed that the following approaches appear to be effective in all school situations:

- *Cooperative teaching* – teachers need support from, and to be able to cooperate with, a range of colleagues within the school and professionals outside the school.
- *Cooperative learning* – peer tutoring or cooperative learning is effective in cognitive and affective (social–emotional) areas of pupils' learning and development. Pupils who help each other, especially within a system of flexible and well-considered pupil grouping, profit from learning together.

- *Collaborative problem solving* – for all teachers, but specifically those who need help in including pupils with social/behavioural problems, this is a systematic way of approaching undesired behaviour in the classroom and is an effective tool for decreasing the amount and intensity of disturbances during the lessons. Clear class rules and a set of borders, agreed with all the pupils (alongside appropriate incentives), have proven to be effective.
- *Heterogeneous grouping* – heterogeneous grouping and a more differentiated approach in education are necessary and effective when dealing with a diversity of pupils in the classroom. Targeted goals, alternative routes for learning, flexible instruction and the abundance of homogeneous ways of grouping enhance inclusive education.
- *Effective teaching* – the arrangements outlined above should take place within an overall effective school/teaching approach wherein education is based on pupil assessment and teaching evaluation, high expectations, direct instruction and feedback for learners and teachers. All pupils – including those pupils with SEN – improve with systematic monitoring, assessment, planning and evaluation of their learning. A curriculum geared to meeting individual needs and providing additional support can be outlined in an Individual Educational Plan (IEP). This IEP should fit within the 'normal' curriculum offered to all pupils.

The factors described above are important at both primary and secondary education level. However, for secondary schools two additional effective approaches emerged:

- *Home area system* – in some schools the organisation of the delivery of the curriculum has been changed drastically: students stay in a common area consisting of two or three classrooms where nearly all teaching takes places. Within such systems, a small team of teachers is responsible for the education provided in the home area.
- *Alternative ways of learning* – to support the inclusion of students with special needs, several models that focus on learning strategies and metacognition have been developed over the past few years. Such programmes aim to teach students how to learn and how to solve problems. Furthermore it is argued that giving students greater responsibility for their own learning can contribute to the success of inclusion in schools.

The specific case studies considered in the project – please see the project web area for more details: www.european-agency.org/iecp/iecp_intro.htm – highlighted the importance of each of these factors. However, it should be emphasised that some case studies appear to have demonstrated that *the combination* of these approaches is important for effective classroom practice within inclusive schools.

Inclusive approaches to assessing learning

A main challenge facing all European countries centres upon developing their systems of pupil assessment so that they facilitate and do not act as a potential barrier to inclusion. With the Agency project, the key question for consideration was how assessment in inclusive classrooms informs decision making about teaching and learning approaches, methods and steps in the best possible ways.

Three areas of challenges were identified:

1   using assessment information to inform monitoring of educational standards in the most appropriate way;
2   ensuring assessment used within initial identification of SEN informs teaching and learning;
3   developing assessment policies and procedures that promote ongoing assessment.

A main conclusion of the project was the identification of the concept 'inclusive assessment'. This was defined as:

An approach to assessment in mainstream settings where policy and practice are designed to promote the learning of all pupils as far as possible. The overall goal of inclusive assessment is that all assessment policies and procedures should support and enhance the successful inclusion and participation of all pupils vulnerable to exclusion, including those with SEN.

(Watkins 2007: 47)

Inclusive assessment is based on the general principle of celebrating diversity by identifying and valuing all pupils' progress and achievements in mainstream settings. It involves legislative measures that take into account the needs of pupils with SEN, ensuring that all pupils are entitled to take part in all assessment procedures in a way that meets their learning needs. It also very clearly links into and supports the strategies and approaches identified as being effective in inclusive classroom practice.

Inclusive assessment requires that:

• teachers in mainstream classrooms should have the appropriate attitudes, training, support and resources for assessment;
• mainstream schools should promote an 'inclusive culture', plan for inclusive assessment and be appropriately organised;
• the work of all specialist support staff involved in assessing pupils with SEN should effectively contribute to inclusive assessment in mainstream classrooms;

- all educational policies concerned with assessment – both general and SNE specific – should aim to promote inclusive assessment practice and take into account the needs of all pupils vulnerable to exclusion, including those with SEN.

The provision of feedback on pupils' learning is a vital strategy within effective classroom practice. Within the Agency assessment project the concept of providing feedback to pupils about their learning was seen as the crucial element in understanding the difference between the use of assessment methods and procedures *for* learning (formative assessment), or the use of methods and tools in order to engage in assessment *of* learning (summative assessment).

Assessment *for* learning is concerned with collecting evidence about learning that is used to adapt teaching and plan next steps in learning. Evidence about learning is crucial as it indicates if there has been a shift (or not) in a pupil's learning progress and possibly learning processes. On the basis of such evidence, teachers can formulate targets/goals and are able to provide pupils with feedback about their learning (see Hattie and Timperly 2007), clearly indicating to a pupil not just what they have learned, but also giving them information on how they may have learned it and how best they can learn in the future. The feedback provided during assessment *for* learning contributes to pupils' reflection on their own learning.

However, within the research literature, the consideration of the concept assessment *for* learning has considered pupils with SEN only in a limited way (for example Lynn *et al.* 1997). All of the contributions from the project experts were unanimous: the concept of assessment *for* learning is valid for all pupils – including those with SEN.

This argument can be developed further: assessment *for* learning concerns all pupils and from an inclusive perspective there should not be any need to differentiate between pupils with or without SEN, but rather to differentiate classroom practice to meet all pupils' requirements. Assessment *for* learning can and should be applied to all pupils, including those with SEN, provided that the relevant and necessary changes and modifications are made in order to ensure the individual pupil's full participation in the assessment process.

Two conditions for inclusive approaches to teaching and learning

Across the Agency member countries' work, it is possible to highlight a number of common factors for implementing inclusive approaches to teaching and learning. These are factors within educational environments involved in the various European projects conducted by the Agency that appear to underpin the work of teachers and other professionals and stakeholders in inclusion.

These are general factors that are not always related to classroom practice as such. These factors have more to do with the overall educational environment and how this environment can support (or not) successful inclusion. The factors of the educational environments that appear to support inclusive assessment can be grouped into two aspects of inclusion policy and practice:

- infrastructure: the structures, policies and support systems for inclusion;
- shared value systems: the attitudes, professional values and beliefs that underpin a school's educational culture and approach.

It has been possible to identity the main characteristics of both educational infrastructure and shared value systems that appear to support inclusive practice. Although each is considered separately here, it was clear that each of the characteristics is highly dependent upon the others.

Educational policy that facilitates innovative practice

Despite the differences in national and regional policies represented within the Agency, it is possible to see that the following elements within policy are crucial for providing the preconditions necessary for innovation leading to inclusive practice:

- participation in local decision making that involves all stakeholders in inclusion;
- flexibility within policies and systems that encourages innovation and change in the implementation of inclusive policy and practice;
- the active involvement of policy makers in the identification and mobilisation of existing human, physical and financial resources to ensure that local decision making and innovation in policy and practice can occur.

Overall, these characteristics of policy must be underpinned by a political commitment to support innovation, creativity and degrees of freedom for practitioners to innovate in their work. One concrete example of such political commitment is where innovators in inclusion are directly involved in informing changes to educational policies.

Interdisciplinary support structures

Pupils, parents and teachers make complex demands of specialist support staff and services in inclusive settings. A move towards *inter*disciplinary rather than just *multi*disciplinary working has been identified through a number of projects (for example Soriano 2005; Watkins 2007). Interdisciplinary working integrates the knowledge and perspectives of different areas of professional expertise in order to consider issues holistically. This is not the same as a multidisciplinary approach whereby professionals from different disciplines work alongside each other, but not necessarily within an integrated and agreed single approach. Interdisciplinary working requires cooperation and collaboration at all levels, between all stakeholders in inclusion: it is to a large extent guided by the local decision making outlined in the previous section.

The following factors drive moves towards interdisciplinary working:

- it is seen as an efficient use of limited public resources;
- it results in better workload management for specialists and allows more meaningful work with pupils, parents and teachers;
- it leads to more flexible support options and a range of possible responses to requests and demands.

The participatory nature of interdisciplinary work also appears to imply a change in the locus of control for support and input from specialists. Decision making not only involves, but also becomes increasingly led by, those in schools, including mainstream class teachers with parents and pupils, working in partnership with professionals who are external to the pupil's immediate educational environment. Such a change in working approach requires a major attitudinal shift on the part of specialist professionals, as well as changes to their practice.

Leadership and vision

Policies that facilitate innovation have to be initiated and formulated by key groups or individuals who have a vision of inclusive education generally. Similarly, the key individuals responsible for the work of specialist assessment teams are most often the driving forces behind the move from multi- to interdisciplinary working. Such influential individuals not only initiate change in practice, but also give a lead in what values and principles should underpin policies and support systems.

Within Agency project work it is clear that the role of school or resource centre leaders and senior managers in shaping shared value systems for inclusion is critical in developing professional environments that allow innovation and change. Key educational leaders:

- have a personal vision for inclusive practice, which is then developed into a shared vision within their staff or team;
- actively promote a school or organisational culture that supports pupil and parental participation;
- either initiate change in practice, or actively support other staff who can initiate such change;

- establish organisational systems that do not just support but actively require teamwork, collaborative problem solving and shared approaches to teaching and learning;
- secure the necessary flexibility in physical, financial and time resources to allow possibilities for 'innovating', that is developing and trialling new methods and approaches to inclusion;
- provide various opportunities for teacher and educational staff training and development in inclusive approaches;
- establish effective communication structures based upon a 'shared language' for teaching and learning that is understood and used by pupils, parents and all educational professionals.

Positive attitudes towards meeting diversity in education

At the core of a shared value system that supports inclusive practice is the view that diversity in education is a beneficial thing that all school stakeholders should acknowledge. A positive approach to meeting a diverse range of needs in education is perhaps the most critical element of a school's educational culture and approach that can be seen to promote inclusive practice. Work to avoid segregation in all forms and promote a school for all appears to be characterised by a view of learning itself being process based, not content or subject based, and a main goal for all pupils' learning as being developing learning to learn skills, not just subject knowledge.

Successful approaches and techniques for supporting the learning of pupils with special educational needs can also be useful for promoting the social and educational inclusion of other groups (for example pupils from different social or ethnic backgrounds). In consequence, meeting a diverse range of needs is increasingly seen within Agency member countries as an approach to developing education for all pupils generally, rather than being focused upon specific groups.

Concluding comments

It is clear from the Agency's work that in order to implement inclusive approaches to teaching and learning there are no clear-cut solutions that 'work' for all school or class situations. Each country, region, school and class involved in the various Agency projects has developed different approaches to their practice and focused upon different aspects of what was felt as being crucial for the development of inclusion at that moment. These changes depend on local challenges, but mainly on the school culture (or shared value systems) and the educational policies (or infrastructure) directing their work.

In addition, various aspects of Agency work (Meijer, Soriano and Watkins 2006; Watkins 2007; Kyriazopoulou and Weber 2009) suggest that there are a number of areas for policy development requiring further attention:

- the *ongoing tension* between the need for schools to demonstrate increasing academic achievements and the position of pupils with special education needs;
- the development of systematic *monitoring and evaluation procedures* within the framework of special needs education in inclusive and segregated settings;
- the development of flexible *frameworks of provision* that support inclusive practice applied to all sectors of educational provision, including the secondary sector, transition from school to employment phase, post-compulsory, higher and adult education (with the same degree of focus being given as within the pre-primary and primary sectors).

That said, however, it is possible to identify common approaches to in-clusive teaching and learning that are useful across differing country and regional contexts, as are described in the preceding sections.

In conclusion two further arguments as a result of Agency work can be put forward:

- Special teaching approaches designed to meet the needs of pupils with specific needs and or disabilities is *good specialised teaching for all* – the only difference being that it should include special methods and tools as appropriate for particular needs.
- All the evidence suggests that *what is good for pupils with SEN is good for all pupils* in inclusive settings. Good teaching approaches benefit all pupils.

Notes

1 Austria, Belgium (Flemish- and French-speaking communities), Cyprus, Czech Republic, Denmark, Estonia, Finland, France, Germany, Greece, Hungary, Iceland, Ireland, Italy, Latvia, Lithuania, Luxembourg, Malta, Netherlands, Norway, Poland, Portugal, Slovenia, Spain, Sweden, Switzerland, United Kingdom (England, Northern Ireland, Scotland and Wales).

2 The Action Programme in the field of Lifelong Learning for 2007–2013 en-tered into force on 14 December 2006. Source: http://ec.europa.eu/education/programmes/llp/structure/monnet_en.html

3 Austria, Belgium (Flemish-speaking community), Belgium (French-speaking community), Bulgaria, Cyprus, Czech Republic, Denmark, Estonia, Finland, France, Germany, Greece, Hungary, Iceland, Ireland, Italy, Latvia, Lithuania, Luxembourg, Malta, Netherlands, Norway, Poland, Portugal, Slovenia, Spain, Sweden, Switzerland, UK (England), UK (Scotland) and UK (Wales).

Bibliography

European Union. (1990) Resolution of the Council and the Ministers of Education meeting with the Council of 31 May 1990 concerning *Integration of children and young people with disabilities into ordinary systems of education*. Official Journal C 162, 03/07/1990, pp. 2–3.

European Union. (1996) *Resolution on the human rights of disabled people*. Official Journal C 17, 22/10/1996, p. 196.

European Union. (1996) *Communication of the Commission on equality of opportunity for people with disabilities*. COM (96)406 final of 30 July 1996. Accessed 22 December 2009 at http://europa.eu.int/comm/employment_social/news/2001/jul/1996406_en.html

European Union. (2001) European Parliament Resolution on the Communication from the Commission to the Council, the European Parliament, the Economic and Social Committee and the Committee of the Regions – *Towards a barrier-free Europe for people with disabilities* adopted on the 4 March 2001. COM (2000) 284 – C5–0632/2000–2000/2296 (COS).

European Union. (2003a) Council Resolution of 15 July 2003 on *Promoting the employment and social integration of people with disabilities* (2003/C 175/01). Accessed 22 December 2009 at http://europa.eu.int/comm/employment_social/news/2003/oct/crs_175_03_en.html

European Union. (2003b) Council Resolution of 5 May 2003 on *Equal opportunities for pupils and students with disabilities in education and training* (2003/C 134/04). Official Journal C 134, 07/06/2003, pp. 6–7. Accessed 16 November 2009 at http://europa.eu.int/comm/employment_social/news/2003/oct/crs_134_04_en.html

European Union. (2003c) European Parliament Resolution on the Communication from the Commission to the Council and the European Parliament *Towards a United Nations legally binding instrument to promote and protect the rights and dignity of persons with disabilities* (COM(2003) 16 – 2003/2100 (INI)).

Hattie, J. and Timperly, H. (2007). The power of feedback. *Review of Educational Research*, 77 (1): 81–112.

Kyriazopoulou, M. and Weber, H. (Eds). (2009) *Development of a Set of Indicators for the Conditions of Inclusive Education in Europe*. Odense: European Agency for Development in Special Needs Education.

Lynn, S. F., Fuchs, L. S., Fuchs, D., Karns, K., Hamlett, C. L., Katzaroff, M. and Dutka, S. (1997) Effects of task-focused goals on low-achieving students with and without learning disabilities. *American Educational Research Journal*, 34: 513–543.

Meijer, C. J. W. (Ed.). (1999) *Financing of Special Needs Education*. Middelfart: European Agency for Development in Special Needs Education.

Meijer, C. J. W. (Ed.). (2003a). *Inclusive Education and Classroom Practices*. Middelfart: European Agency for Development in Special Needs Education.

Meijer, C. J. W. (Ed.). (2003b) *Special Education across Europe in 2003: Trends in Provision in 18 European Countries*. Middelfart: European Agency for Development in Special Needs Education.

Meijer, C. J. W. (Ed.). (2005) *Inclusive Education and Classroom Practice in Secondary Education*. Middelfart: European Agency for Development in Special Needs Education.

Meijer, C. J. W., Soriano, V. and Watkins, A. (Eds). (2006) *Special Needs Education in Europe: Provision in Post-Primary Education.* Middelfart: European Agency for Development in Special Needs Education.

Peacey, N. (2006) *Reflections on the Seminar.* Presentation given at the Agency Assessment Project meeting, 20 May 2006, Vienna, Austria.

Portuguese Ministry of Education and the European Agency for Development in Special Needs Education. (2007) *Lisbon Declaration – Young People's Views on Inclusive Education.* Odense: European Agency for Development in Special Needs Education.

Soriano, V. (Ed.). (2005) *Early Childhood Intervention: Analysis of Situations in Europe – Key Aspects and Recommendations.* Middelfart: European Agency for Development in Special Needs Education.

UNESCO. (1994) *Salamanca Statement and Framework for Action on Special Needs Education.* Paris: UNESCO. Accessed 22 December 2009 at http://unesdoc. unesco.org/images/0009/000984/098427eo.pdf

UNESCO World Education Forum. (2000) *Dakar Framework for Action, Education for All: Meeting our Collective Commitments.* Accessed 14 February 2010 at http://unesdoc.unesco.org/images/0012/001202/120240e.pdf

United Nations. (1993) *Standard Rules on the Equalisation of Opportunities for Persons with Disabilities.* Accessed 14 February 2010 at http://www.un.org/esa/socdev/enable/dissre00.htm

United Nations. (2006) *Convention on Rights of People with Disabilities.* Accessed 14 February 2010 at http://www.un.org/disabilities/convention/conventionfull.shtml

Watkins, A. (Ed.). (2007) *Assessment in Inclusive Settings: An overview of Policy and Practice across Europe.* Odense: European Agency for Development in Special Needs Education.

Watkins, A. (Ed.). (2009) *Special Needs Education: Country Data 2008.* Odense: European Agency for Development in Special Needs Education.

Watkins, A. and D'Alessio, S. (Eds). (2009) *Putting Inclusive Assessment into Practice.* Odense: European Agency for Development in Special Needs Education.

All of the Agency documents listed above are available to download free of charge in various European languages from http://www.european-agency.org/site/info/publications/agency/index.html

In addition each thematic project has a dedicated web area with all country as well as Agency information. These databases can be accessed from the Information Resources section of the Agency website: http://www.european-agency.org/site/info/index.html

The majority of the key guiding principle documents providing international statements and resolutions on special needs education can be accessed from http://www.european-agency.org/site/about/index.html#guide

Section 6

Support in the classroom

Chapter 17

Supporting students with disabilities in inclusive classrooms

Personnel and peers

Michael F. Giangreco (University of Vermont, USA), Erik W. Carter (University of Wisconsin-Madison, USA), Mary Beth Doyle (Saint Michael's College, Vermont) and Jesse C. Suter (University of Vermont, USA)

Over the past few decades, educating students with the full range of disabilities has progressed from denying services outright to delivering education primarily in segregated settings (e.g. institutions, special schools, special classes) to providing instruction within general education classes with access to the same curriculum as classmates without disabilities. Regardless of the terminology in vogue in any particular place or point in time (e.g. mainstreaming, integration, inclusive education), there has been slow but steady progress toward more inclusive educational opportunities. Advocacy for inclusive education has been rooted in human rights efforts to ensure equitable and just opportunities and supports so that people with disabilities have access to the full benefits of citizenship accorded to people without disabilities (Mittler 2000; UNESCO 1994). Simultaneously, the professional literature documents both successful approaches to inclusive education and its positive impact on students with and without disabilities (Downing 2008; Hick and Thomas 2009; Hunt and Goetz 1997; McGregor and Volgelsberg 1998; Ryndak and Fisher 2003).

Despite trends toward greater school inclusion, too many students, particularly those with intensive support needs, remain unnecessarily segregated in special education schools and classes. Some are even segregated *within* general education classes. Yet for every student who remains educationally segregated there are other students with similar attributes, abilities, and needs who are successfully included. This simple fact suggests that whether a student with a disability is meaningfully included may have less to do with his or her characteristics and more to do with the attitudes, skills, structure, and practices of the adults responsible for providing education. Therefore, this chapter focuses on actions within our collective sphere of control, namely *appropriate supports in the classroom*. After sharing our conceptualization of inclusive education, the remainder of the chapter presents evidence-based approaches regarding (a) the roles of various personnel (i.e. administrators, classroom teachers, special educators, related services providers, teacher assistants) and (b) the roles of peers.

Elements of inclusive education

In the absence of a single, agreed-upon definition of inclusive education, we offer a set of elements demonstrating that inclusion is more than mere physical presence in general education classes. Inclusive education refers to an interrelated set of values from which we make decisions and a set of practices designed to support equitable and appropriate education (Doyle 2008; Giangreco 2006). Inclusive education exists when each of the following elements occurs on an ongoing, daily basis:

1   *All* students are welcomed in general education. The first placement options considered are the general education classes in the school the students would attend if they did not have a disability.
2   Disability is recognized as a form of human diversity. As such, students with disabilities are accepted as individuals and not denied access based on disability.
3   Appropriate supports are available, regardless of disability label or severity. Given their portability, supports are provided in typical environments, rather than sending students to specialized settings to receive needed supports.
4   Students are educated in classes reflecting the naturally occurring proportion of students with and without disabilities. Therefore, the percentage of students without disabilities in each class would be substantially higher than those with disabilities.
5   Students, irrespective of their developmental or performance levels, are educated with peers in the same age groupings available to those without disability labels rather than with younger students. Students with disabilities need not function at or near the same academic level as their classmates (though some do) to benefit from a chronologically age-appropriate, inclusive placement.
6   Students with and without disabilities participate in shared educational experiences while pursuing individually appropriate learning outcomes with necessary supports. Educational experiences are designed to enhance valued life outcomes that seek an individualized balance between both the academic–functional and the social–personal aspects of schooling.

Inclusive education does not mean enrolling students in classes with inadequate supports, sink-or-swim approaches, "reverse mainstreaming" whereby a small number of students without disabilities spend some time in special class settings, or placement in special classes that are euphemistically labeled (e.g. "Learning Space"). Any such fragmented, partial, disjointed, or inaccurately labeled approach delays the advance of thoughtfully designed, appropriately supported, inclusive education (Davern *et al*. 1997).

Implementing inclusive education at the classroom level requires thoughtful attention to at least four interrelated components, including ongoing access to (a) inclusive environments, (b) individualized curriculum, (c) purposeful instruction, and (d) necessary supports (Giangreco 2006). Across each component teams are encouraged to seek contextually valid approaches that are chronologically age appropriate and encourage self-determination (Wehmeyer *et al*. 2007). Within this framework students with disabilities need not earn the right to access inclusive environments. Instead, they gain access by virtue of their status as children and youth who are eligible for schooling. Although some students may not be able to participate in every aspect of typical class activities in the same ways or at the same level as classmates, they are not denied access. Rather than an all-or-nothing approach based on the unduly restrictive notion that if a student cannot do everything he or she will not have access to anything, inclusive education encourages partial participation (Ferguson and Baumgart 1991). Partial participation is based on the notion that, even if a student cannot do everything, he or she can still benefit from participating in some parts of all class activities when appropriately designed or adapted. By following the principle of the least dangerous assumption (Donnellan 1984), teams seek to identify a balance between learning outcomes based on assessed needs and opportunities for students to surprise us with their yet-to-be-discovered abilities and talents. This helps avoid underestimating students with disabilities – a problem that continues to impede their progress and obscure their potential.

Personnel supports in the classroom

The attitudes and skills of school personnel are central to how well inclusive education is implemented. In the following sections, we describe key roles of school personnel that contribute to inclusive classrooms. Research suggests that the impact of personnel rests largely on their collaboration with each other and with the families of the students they serve (Villa, Thousand, Nevin, and Malgeri 1996; Wallace, Anderson, and Bartholomay 2002).

Administrator support

Administrators are the only school personnel described in this chapter who do not typically engage in the daily instructional life within inclusive classrooms, yet still exert a major influence on classroom functioning (Crockett 2002). Research consistently reports that the leadership and commitment to inclusive education displayed by school administrators are critical factors in its success (Riehl 2000; Salisbury and McGregor 2002). Conviction about the value of inclusion for all students is necessary to sustain administrators through the resistance they are likely to encounter as they attempt to create a general education system that is inclusive, rather than an add-on or special education responsibility (McLeskey and Waldron 2002).

By establishing expectations of inclusion for all students and collaboration among school personnel, school leaders' credibility is bolstered when they operationalize inclusive attitudes with practical actions (DiPaola and Walther-Thomas 2003; Hines 2008). In part, this means (a) scheduling opportunities for collaboration among teachers, special educators, teacher assistants, and other services providers; (b) providing relevant staff development related to inclusive practice (e.g. co-teaching, universal design for learning, peer supports); and (c) ensuring constructive working conditions (e.g. caseload, staffing ratios, reducing paperwork burden). Recent research on special education service delivery reminds us that the contemporary emphasis on evidence-based curriculum and instruction will be helped or hindered by the quality of service delivery (Suter and Giangreco 2010; Giangreco, Broer, and Suter in press). Special and general education administrators can be influential in creating inclusive service delivery models that provide tangible evidence of support to their staff, and thus increase the likelihood of serving students better and retaining quality personnel (Billingsley 2003).

Classroom teacher support

The importance of classroom teacher support to the success of inclusive placements for students with disabilities cannot be overstated. As the only credentialed professional typically in the classroom throughout the entire school day, the primary adult role model for students, and the curriculum content specialist, classroom teachers are the linchpin to ensuring access to the general education curriculum. Teachers' social and academic interactions with their students who have disabilities send powerful messages to all students about the value of classmates with disabilities and their status as members of the classroom community (Schnorr 1997).

Teachers who successfully include students with disabilities demonstrate ownership for these students' education by becoming instructionally engaged (Giangreco, Broer, and Edelman 2001; Idol 2006; Olson, Chalmers, and Hoover 1997), meaning that teachers (a) are knowledgeable about the student's performance levels and individualized learning outcomes, (b) spend time directly providing instruction to the student with a disability, (c) retain a prominent role in instructional planning and decision making with special education personnel, (d) mentor and co-direct the work of any teacher assistants who are present in the classroom, and (e) advance their own learning to improve their inclusive skills.

Research highlights the differing attitudes general education teachers have about including students with varying types of disabilities in their classes and the complexity of their relationships with special educators (Carter and Hughes 2006; Soodak, Podell, and Lehman 1998). Close collaboration between teachers and special educators is widely acknowledged as essential to successful inclusive education, yet implementing collaboration is easier said than done (Idol 2006; Scruggs, Mastropieri, and McDuffie 2007). As we acknowledge the essential nature of supports *provided by* classroom teachers to students with disabilities, so must we acknowledge that supports *provided to* classroom teachers also are essential.

Although staff development pertaining to inclusive practices may be among the more obvious supports provided to teachers, we encourage those who question their current capacity or training to meet the educational needs of students with disabilities to remain cognizant of two important points. First, classroom teachers are not expected to have all the answers or undertake the tasks of inclusive education alone; individually determined supports from other team members representing different disciplines should be available. Second, it may be helpful to remind teachers that their fundamental skills are well suited to educating students with disabilities. The foundational principles of teaching and learning do not change because a student has a disability label, though those principles may need to be applied differently or used more systematically. Therefore, a qualified classroom teacher with an inclusive attitude can expect to be successful in teaching students with disabilities in his or her classroom and to extend that success with ongoing collaborative teamwork and targeted staff development.

Special educator support

The ways in which special educators support students who are taught in inclusive classrooms (e.g. in-class support, co-teaching, pull-out remediation, case management) is open to a debate that, at present, tends to be more conceptual than research-based (Fisher, Frey, and Thousand 2003; Hoover and Patton 2008). Logically, special educators have some different roles when they shift from being the teacher of a special education class into inclusive environments (e.g. consulting with general education teachers, designing curriculum adaptations to suit typical class activities and more heterogeneous groups, facilitating interactions with peers who do not have disabilities). What is essential is that their roles match the inclusive context.

Being responsive to the inclusive context includes shifting away from deficit-driven approaches that too often have been over-reliant on remedial, pull-out approaches. Such approaches often establish a main part of the special educator's role as "getting the student to grade level" so he or she can benefit from typical classroom instruction. The frequently unspoken inference of this approach, one we challenge as detrimental, is that students with disabilities need to function at or near grade level to gain access to or benefit from learning in an inclusive classroom. Thus, such pull-out services may inadvertently set up unnecessary "either–or" scenarios in which the student with a disability can *either* be included *or* learn, as if these options were mutually exclusive (Kluth 2005). As stated by Rea, McLaughlin, and Walther-Thomas (2002: 221), "The assumption that segregation from typical peers is the price that students with disabilities have to pay in order to learn must be seriously questioned."

Inclusion-oriented special educators are encouraged to reject "either–or" options. They instead adapt and invent ways to apply their skills creatively and collaboratively so that students with disabilities can be included *and* learn (Jorgensen, Shuh, and Nisbet 2006; Thousand, Villa, and Nevin 2002). Pursuing inclusive opportunities and quality instruction simultaneously provides a promising path to progress in our field while seeking to ensure the educational and civil rights of individual students.

Regardless of setting, special educators share a variety of common roles (e.g. assessment, collaboration with team members, case management, service coordination, instruction, data collection, communication with families, positive behavior supports, transition planning). Here we focus on six supports provided by special educators that are unique to inclusive classrooms (Fisher *et al.* 2003). Not all special educators currently working in inclusive classrooms possess the knowledge and skills overviewed, though we propose these roles are foundational for successful inclusion.

First, an overarching support special educators can bring to inclusive classrooms is the application of creative problem-solving principles to extend the power of a team's collaborative efforts (Giangreco, Cloninger, Dennis, and Edelman 2002). As the variations across inclusive classrooms are numerous, being skillful in a generic problem-solving approach allows special educators to lead efforts to address the many novel challenges they will probably encounter on a regular basis. Second, inclusion-oriented special educators work with classroom teachers to adapt and modify curriculum and instruction in ways that facilitate participation of students with disabilities in typical class activities. This involves applications of differentiation, universal design, multilevel instruction, and curriculum overlapping so that students who perform at substantially different levels can pursue individually determined learning outcomes within shared class activities (Giangreco 2007; Peterson and Hittie in press; Thousand, Villa, and Nevin 2007).

Third, special educators can support inclusive classrooms by providing instruction in a variety of formats such as co-teaching with the classroom teacher (Villa, Thousand, and Nevin 2004), teaching small mixed-ability groups, or individual tutoring. Ensuring that the combination of individually determined instructional formats is implemented in concert with classroom teachers and the classroom context is the element that sets inclusive instructional options apart from merely providing instruction in the physical classroom space in ways that may be disconnected from its overall operation. Fourth, special educators provide supports that facilitate interactions between peers with and without disabilities. This occurs through combined efforts to teach students with disabilities pro-social behaviors, apply positive behavior supports, and teach students without disabilities how to interact with their classmates who have learning differences.

Fifth, special educators play a unique role in co-directing the work of teacher assistants along with classroom teachers (Giangreco and Doyle 2004). Unlike separate classes, where special educators typically spend their entire school day in close proximity to their assistants, in inclusive schools special educators tend to serve more than one classroom and therefore are separated from some of the teacher assistants for substantial periods of time. Directing the work of teacher assistants includes (a) orientation to the student's characteristics, educational program, and related needs (e.g. personal care, assistive technology); (b) orientation to the school and classroom (e.g. expectations, procedures); (c) training related to teacher assistant roles as described in a clear job description (e.g. research-based literacy approaches, positive behavior supports) through a variety of options (e.g. workshops, teacher modeling, online learning); (d) planning for teacher assistant interactions with students so that assistants are not inappropriately expected to make pedagogical decisions; and (e) monitoring teacher assistant performance and communicating with them about their work in both formative and summative ways.

Sixth, special educators can support inclusive classrooms by keeping abreast of the continually expanding assistive technology options available to support students who experience orthopedic, learning, memory, sensory, health, and/or behavioral challenges. This role can provide a vital support that can benefit students with and without disabilities. The roles of special educators in inclusive classrooms will continue to evolve as we challenge ourselves to include a broader range of students in a wider array of general education classes and other integrated learning environments. Ultimately, the goal is for special educators to carefully match their roles to the needs of students in inclusive classrooms.

Related services support

Working together, special educators and classroom teachers possess the knowledge and skills to address the educational needs of many students with disabilities. However, a subset of students with more complex or low-incidence disabilities may require the involvement of one or more related services providers (e.g. speech/language pathologist, physical therapist, occupational therapist, school psychologist, orientation and mobility specialist, assistive technology specialist) who possess specialized skills in various areas and can be essential to student success. When related services providers offer supports in inclusive classrooms, it is foundational for all team members to understand the purpose of their participation on the team and for their involvement to be educationally supportive. The potential positive impact of related services providers is diminished if they (a) operate as isolated or parallel services without regard to potential overlaps or gaps with other providers; (b) develop separate, discipline-specific goals that are largely disconnected from the student's educational goals; or (c) make service decisions without sufficient regard to the educational context (Giangreco, Edelman, and Dennis 1991).

In inclusive classrooms, related services are provided only when they are both educationally relevant and necessary within the context of a shared framework that has the student's education at its core (Giangreco, Prelock, Reid, Dennis, and Edelman 2000). In other words, students do not attend school to get certain therapies; they get certain therapies at school if those services are required in order for them to receive an appropriate education. The educational team collaboratively decides which services are needed and specific specialist involvement is explicitly referenced to existing components of the student's educational plan (Giangreco, Edelman, Nelson, Young, and Kiefer-O'Donnell 1999).

Once a team has decided that a related service is needed, providers may engage in a variety of functions through a combination of direct and consultative services, such as (a) selecting or developing adaptive equipment that allows for active participation or prevents negative outcomes (e.g. regression, discomfort, pain); (b) transferring information and skills to others (e.g. positioning a student for learning, programming an alternative or augmentative communication device); (c) serving as a resource or support to the family; and (d) applying discipline-specific skills that address a student's educational needs (e.g. teaching Braille). When deployed thoughtfully within a team framework that accounts for the educational context, related services providers offer essential supports to students, teachers, special educators, and families.

Teacher assistant support

Teacher assistants are known by many titles such as paraprofessionals, paraeducators, and learning support assistants. They are widely acknowledged as important contributors in inclusive classrooms (Doyle 2008). The literature indicates that, despite their perceived value, a substantial number are undertrained, inadequately supervised, and increasingly expected to undertake questionable roles (e.g. lesson planning, adapting curriculum, providing a substantial amount of primary instruction; Giangreco and Broer 2005; Giangreco, Edelman, Broer, and Doyle 2001; Riggs and Mueller 2001).

Rather than proactively developing equitable models of inclusive education to ensure all students have access to qualified general and special educators, some schools have reactively assigned the least qualified staff (i.e. teacher assistants) to provide the bulk of instruction for some students with the most complex learning characteristics. Misuse and overuse of teacher assistants have been associated with a host of inadvertent detrimental effects (e.g. interference with teacher engagement, interference with peer interactions, unnecessary dependence, stigmatization, provocation of behaviors, inadequate instruction; Broer, Doyle, and Giangreco 2005; Carter, Sisco, Brown, Brickham, and Al-Khabbaz 2008; Giangreco, Broer *et al.* 2001; Giangreco, Edelman, Luiselli, and MacFarland 1997; Malmgren and Causton-Theoharis 2006).

Teacher assistants can play important support roles in inclusive classrooms by engaging in tasks that create opportunities for general and special educators to spend more time instructing all students and collaborating with each other. Some of these support roles include doing clerical tasks; engaging in follow-up instruction or homework help; supervising in group settings (e.g. cafeteria, playground, bus boarding); assisting students with personal care needs (e.g. bathroom use, dressing); facilitating peer interactions; and assisting in implementing positive behavior support plans. Research suggests that when instruction is delivered by teacher assistants it should be (a) supplemental, rather than primary or exclusive; (b) planned by a qualified professional (e.g. teacher, special educator) so that it does not require paraprofessionals to plan lessons, determine accommodations, or make other pedagogical decisions; (c) based on explicit and intensive training in research-based practices; and (d) followed by ongoing supervision to ensure implementation fidelity (Causton-Theoharis, Giangreco, Doyle, and Vadasy 2007). By ensuring that teacher assistants have appropriate roles, corresponding training, and ongoing supervision, they are poised to provide valued supports in inclusive classrooms.

Peer supports in the classroom

We address personnel and peer supports concurrently in this chapter because *both* are critical to the success of inclusive classrooms. Peer support strategies communicate high expectations for all students and presume that students with disabilities can and should learn from and with their peers without disabilities. Peers without disabilities offer practical, promising, and powerful avenues for supporting students with disabilities in inclusive classrooms. Ensuring students with disabilities benefit from the rich array of learning and social opportunities that exist in typical classrooms is not only enhanced by the active involvement and receptivity of peers in these settings, but may actually be dependent on it.

Contributions of peers

Although having peers support one another is not novel, adults still represent the primary, sometimes exclusive, source for supporting the inclusion of students with disabilities, especially those with intensive support needs (Mastropieri, Scruggs, and Berkeley 2007; Roseth, Johnson, and Johnson 2008). Yet peers offer a ready avenue for enhancing social and academic learning, both planned and incidental, that happens within shared classroom experiences. Classmates typically exchange academic, social, emotional, and other supports as they work together. Creating opportunities for students with disabilities to access and exchange these same supports is a natural extension of how all students learn within inclusive classrooms.

Positive peer relationships and a sense of belonging are central to class-room success, school engagement, and quality of life. When students with disabilities receive all of their support from adults and have few opportunities for interacting with classmates, valued and durable peer relationships often remain elusive (Carter *et al.* 2008). Although some students with disabilities have specific social goals in addition to academic and functional goals, these social goals are unlikely to be met without intentional efforts that include the active involvement of peers. Students without disabilities can effectively provide an array of supports to their classmates with disabilities, usually provided by adults, in ways that enhance educational experiences (Carter, Cushing, and Kennedy 2009). Therefore, schools should consider the con-tributions of peer supports rather than the common response of relying too heavily or unnecessarily on extra adult supports (e.g. one-to-one teacher assistants).

Peer support strategies

Peer support strategies typically involve one or more students without disabil-ities providing academic or social support to their classmates with disabilities while receiving needed guidance from teachers and assistants (Carter and Kennedy 2006). The supports that peers provide range from informal and occasional to structured and sustained. For example, students with and with-out disabilities might be paired together on a single class project, collaborate within cooperative groups, work together within classwide peer-tutoring arrangements, or interact daily within formal peer support arrangements (Harper and Maheady 2007; Janney and Snell 2006). The supports peers provide may focus on educational goals related to communication (e.g. mod-eling social skills, reinforcing communication attempts; Weiner 2005), social interactions (e.g. initiating conversations, making introductions, discussing shared interests; Hunt, Soto, Maier, and Doering 2003), classroom partici-pation (e.g. sharing materials, teaching self-management; Gilberts, Agran, Hughes, and Wehmeyer 2001), and academics (e.g. completing assignments together, reviewing work, explaining key concepts; Carter, Sisco, Melekoglu, and Kurkowski 2007; Jameson, McDonnell, Polychronis, and Risen 2008).

Effective peer support strategies require the active and ongoing support of personnel to (a) identify students with and without disabilities who might benefit from involvement in peer support arrangements; (b) orient students to their roles and responsibilities; (c) provide opportunities for students to work and interact together; (d) offer ongoing support to students so they feel confident and well prepared in their roles; and (e) monitor all students' progress to ensure they are reaping the intended academic and social benefits (Carter *et al*. 2009). As peers make more contributions to each other, adults providing one-to-one support to students with disabilities can then fade their proximity and support, thus broadening their potential roles to other classroom needs. Peer support strategies are meant to be embedded within good-quality inclusive practices; they are not designed to supplant support from educators.

Research-based benefits

The empirical literature is clear that well-designed peer support strategies can have a substantial impact on learning and social outcomes of students with disabilities *and* their peers who provide support (Carter *et al*. 2009). Research involving students with disabilities (Broer *et al*. 2005), their peers (Copeland *et al*. 2004; Kamps *et al*. 1998), and educators (Carter and Pesko 2008) indicates that peer support strategies are endorsed by students and fit well within inclusive classrooms. In other words, good support strategies can be good for *all* students.

For students with disabilities, particularly those with intensive support needs (e.g. intellectual disabilities, autism, multiple disabilities), peer support strategies offer distinct advantages over an exclusive reliance on adult-delivered strategies, such as improving engagement in classroom instruction, access to general education curricular content, academic achievement, and attainment of individually determined goals for students with disabilities (Carter and Kennedy 2006; Carter *et al*. 2007; Jameson *et al*. 2008). Socially, peer support strategies can expand students' communication skills, peer interactions, social support, peer networks, and friendships (Bellini, Peters, Brianner, and Hopf 2007; Carter and Hughes 2005). Decreasing students' dependence on teacher assistants as the first source for assistance and instruction can also encourage students' independence and foster self-determination (Wehmeyer *et al*. 2007).

Substantive academic and social benefits also appear available for peers without disabilities who provide support. Peers have been shown to be as or more engaged academically when they provide support to a classmate with disabilities (Cushing and Kennedy 1997; Shukla, Kennedy, and Cushing 1999). Similarly, the academic responsibilities, support responsibilities, and additional adult attention these peers receive have translated into higher grades, particularly for students who are struggling in class, unengaged in school, or at risk for school failure (Carter *et al*. 2009). The increased opportunities peers have to interact and work with their classmates with disabilities can break down attitudinal barriers, foster personal growth, promote greater appreciation of diversity, and expand their own social networks (Copeland *et al*. 2004; Siperstein, Norins, and Mohler 2007). Collectively, the mutual benefits of peer supports, for students both with and without disabilities, should challenge schools to consider whether they are putting sufficient emphasis on this aspect of improving their inclusive classrooms.

Conclusion

When considering personnel and peer supports in inclusive classrooms, the information presented in this chapter may be summarized as encouraging attention to the four "Cs": collaboration, coherence, context, and challenge. Given the wide-ranging needs of students with disabilities, no single discipline embodies all of the knowledge and skills required to meet their educational and related needs. Yet merely having many disciplines involved in a student's program is insufficient. Therefore, *collaboration* is essential among all team members. Having school personnel, students, and families collaboratively working together with a shared vision toward common goals is clearly a foundation for success.

Second, there must be *coherence* in ways that personnel and peer supports are applied in inclusive classrooms. In other words, these supports must fit together with other essential elements (e.g. curriculum content, instructional practices, age-appropriate materials) in a way that makes sense, forming a coherent (and hopefully beautiful) mosaic. Actively pursuing coherence among the various aspects of inclusive classrooms avoids disjointed applications that continue to plague well-intended efforts.

The success of supports in inclusive classroom requires attention to the *context*. This means we cannot simply use all the same approaches in the same ways that we used in special classes. Our approaches must be suited to the culture of the classroom. We need to be especially conscious of providing supports that are chronologically age appropriate and to be mindful of unnecessarily overspecializing supports. Within inclusive contexts we should ask ourselves whether the supports we are offering draw undue negative attention to our students with disabilities or cause them to be perceived negatively by their peers. Minimally, personnel and peer supports should be status-neutral; preferably they should be status-enhancing. Last, we need to *challenge* ourselves to do more to facilitate quality inclusive opportunities and to do so more quickly. While our field debates the merits of inclusive education, how to do it better, and how fast to change, too many students with disabilities are missing out on the incredible opportunities available to them in inclusive classrooms.

Bibliography

Bellini, S., Peters, J. K., Brianner, L., and Hopf, A. (2007) A meta-analysis of school-based social skills interventions for children with autism spectrum disorders. *Remedial and Special Education*, 28 (3): 153–162.

Billingsley, B. S. (2003) *Special Education Teacher Retention and Attrition: A Critical Analysis of the Literature*. COPSSE Document No. RS-2. Gainesville, FL: University of Florida, Center on Personnel Studies in Special Education. Accessed 25 January 2009 at http://www.coe.ufl.edu/copsse/docs/RS-2/1/RS-2.pdf

Broer, S. M., Doyle, M. B., and Giangreco, M. F. (2005) Perspectives of students with intellectual disabilities about their experiences with paraprofessional supports. *Exceptional Children*, 71 (4): 415–430.

Carter, E. W. and Hughes, C. (2005) Increasing social interactions among adolescents with intellectual disabilities and their general education peers. *Research and Practice for Persons with Severe Disabilities*, 30 (4): 179–193.

Carter, E. W. and Hughes, C. (2006) Including high school students with severe disabilities in general education classes: perspectives of general and special educators, paraprofessionals, and administrators. *Research and Practice for Persons with Severe Disabilities*, 31 (2): 174–185.

Carter, E. W. and Kennedy, C. H. (2006) Promoting access to the general curriculum using peer support strategies. *Research and Practice for Persons with Severe Disabilities*, 31 (4): 284–292.

Carter, E. W. and Pesko, M. J. (2008) Social validity of peer interaction intervention strategies in high school classrooms: effectiveness, feasibility, and actual use. *Exceptionality*, 16 (3): 156–173.

Carter, E. W., Sisco, L. G., Melekoglu, M., and Kurkowski, C. (2007) Peer supports as an alternative to individually assigned paraprofessionals in inclusive high school classrooms. *Research and Practice for Persons with Severe Disabilities*, 32 (4): 213–227.

Carter, E. W., Sisco, L. G., Brown, L., Brickham, D., and Al-Khabbaz, Z. A. (2008) Peer interactions and academic engagement of youth with developmental disabilities in inclusive middle and high school classrooms. *American Journal on Mental Retardation*, 113 (6): 479–494.

Carter, E. W., Cushing, L. S., and Kennedy, C. H. (2009) *Peer Support Strategies for Improving All Students' Social Lives and Learning*. Baltimore: Paul H. Brookes.

Causton-Theoharis, J., Giangreco, M. F., Doyle, M. B., and Vadasy, P. F. (2007) Paraprofessionals: the "sous chefs" of literacy instruction. *Teaching Exceptional Children*, 40 (1): 57–62.

Copeland, S. R., Hughes, C., Carter, E. W., Guth, C., Presley, J., Williams, C. R. *et al.* (2004) Increasing access to general education: perspectives of participants in a high school peer support programme. *Remedial and Special Education*, 26 (6): 342–352.

Crockett, J. B. (2002) Special education's role in preparing responsive leaders for inclusive schools. *Remedial and Special Education*, 23 (3): 157–168.

Cushing, L. S. and Kennedy, C. H. (1997) Academic effects on students without disabilities who serve as peer supports for students with disabilities in general education classrooms. *Journal of Applied Behaviour Analysis*, 30 (1): 139–152.

Davern, L., Sapon-Shevin, M., D'Aquanni, M., Fisher, M., Larson, M., Black, J., and Minondo, S. (1997) Drawing distinctions between coherent and fragmented efforts at building inclusive schools. *Equity and Excellence in Education*, 30 (3): 31–39.

DiPaola, M. F. and Walther-Thomas, C. (2003) *Principals and Special Education: The Critical Role of School Leaders*. COPPSE Document No. IB-7. Gainesville, FL: University of Florida, Center on Personnel Studies in Special Education. Accessed 25 January 2009 at http://www.personnelcenter.org/pdf/copsse_principals.pdf

Donnellan, A. (1984) The criterion of the least dangerous assumption. *Behaviour Disorders*, 9 (2): 141–150.

Downing, J. E. (2008) *Including Students with Severe and Multiple Disabilities in Typical Classrooms: Practical Strategies for Teachers*, 3rd edition. Baltimore: Paul H. Brookes.

Doyle, M. B. (2008) *The Paraprofessional's Guide to the Inclusive Classroom*, 2nd edition. Baltimore: Paul H. Brookes.

Ferguson, D. L. and Baumgart, D. (1991) Partial participation revisited. *Journal of the Association for Persons with Severe Handicaps*, 16 (4): 218–227.

Fisher, D., Frey, N., and Thousand, J. (2003) What do special educators need to know and be prepared to do for inclusive schooling to work? *Teacher Education and Special Education*, 26 (1): 42–50.

Giangreco, M. F. (2006) Foundational concepts and practices for educating students with severe disabilities. In M. E. Snell and F. Brown (Eds.) *Instruction of Students with Severe Disabilities*, 6th edition. Upper Saddle River, NJ: Pearson Education/ Prentice-Hall.

Giangreco, M. F. (2007) Extending inclusive opportunities. *Educational Leadership*, 64 (5): 34–37.

Giangreco, M. F. and Doyle, M. B. (2004) Directing paraprofessional work. In C. H. Kennedy and E. M. Horn (Eds.) *Including Students with Severe Disabilities*. Boston: Allyn & Bacon.

Giangreco, M. F. and Broer, S. M. (2005) Questionable utilization of paraprofessionals in inclusive schools: are we addressing symptoms or causes? *Focus on Autism and Other Developmental Disabilities*, 20 (1): 10–26.

Giangreco, M. F., Edelman, S., and Dennis, R. (1991) Common professional practices that interfere with the integrated delivery of related services. *Remedial and Special Education*, 12 (2): 16–24.

Giangreco, M. F., Edelman, S. W., Luiselli, T. E., and MacFarland, S. Z. C. (1997) Helping or hovering? Effects of instructional assistant proximity on students with disabilities. *Exceptional Children*, 64 (1): 7–18.

Giangreco, M. F., Edelman, S., Nelson, C., Young, M. R., and Kiefer-O'Donnell, R. (1999) Improving support service decision-making: consumer feedback regarding updates to VISTA. *International Journal of Disability, Development and Education*, 46 (4): 463–473.

Giangreco, M. F., Prelock, P., Reid, R., Dennis, R., and Edelman, S. (2000) Roles of related services personnel in inclusive schools. In R. Villa and J. Thousand (Eds.) *Restructuring for Caring and Effective Education: Piecing the Puzzle Together*, 2nd edition. Baltimore: Paul H. Brookes.

Giangreco, M. F., Broer, S. M., and Edelman, S. W. (2001) Teacher engagement with students with disabilities: differences between paraprofessional service delivery models. *Journal of the Association for Persons with Severe Handicaps*, 26 (2): 75–86.

Giangreco, M. F., Edelman, S. W., Broer, S. M., and Doyle, M. B. (2001) Paraprofessional support of students with disabilities: literature from the past decade. *Exceptional Children*, 68 (1): 45–63.

Giangreco, M. F., Cloninger, C., Dennis, R., and Edelman, S. (2002) Problem-solving methods to facilitate inclusive education. In J. Thousand, R. Villa, and A. Nevin (Eds.) *Creativity and Collaborative Learning: A Practical Guide to Empowering Students and Teachers*, 2nd edition. Baltimore: Paul H. Brookes.

Giangreco, M. F., Broer, S. M., and Suter, J. C. (in press) Guidelines for selecting alternatives to overreliance on paraprofessionals: field-testing in inclusion-oriented schools. *Remedial and Special Education*.

Gilberts, G. H., Agran, M., Hughes, C., and Wehmeyer, M. (2001) The effects of peer delivered self-monitoring strategies on the participation of students with severe disabilities in general education classrooms. *Journal of the Association for Persons with Severe Handicaps*, 26 (1): 25–36.

Harper, G. F. and Maheady, L. (2007) Peer-mediated teaching and students with learning disabilities. *Intervention in School and Clinic*, 43 (2): 101–107.

Hick, P. and Thomas, G. (Eds.) (2009) *Inclusion and Diversity in Education*. London: Sage.

Hines, J. T. (2008) Making collaboration work in inclusive high school classrooms: recommendations for principals. *Intervention in School and Clinic*, 43 (5): 277–282.

Hoover, J. J. and Patton, J. R. (2008) The role of special educators in a multitiered instructional system. *Intervention in School and Clinic*, 43 (4): 195–202.

Hunt, P. and Goetz, L. (1997) Research on inclusive educational programmes, practices, and outcomes for students with severe disabilities. *Journal of Special Education*, 31 (1): 3–29.

Hunt, P., Soto, G., Maier, J., and Doering, K. (2003) Collaborative teaming to support students at risk and students with severe disabilities in general education classrooms. *Exceptional Children*, 69 (3): 315–332.

Idol, L. (2006) Toward inclusion of special education students in general education: a programme evaluation of eight schools. *Remedial and Special Education*, 27 (2): 77–94.

Jameson, J. M., McDonnell, J., Polychronis, S., and Risen, T. (2008) Embedded, constant time delay instruction by peers without disabilities in general education classrooms. *Intellectual and Developmental Disabilities*, 46 (5): 346–363.

Janney, R. and Snell, M. E. (2006) *Social Relationships and Peer Support*, 2nd edition. Baltimore: Paul H. Brookes.

Jorgensen, C. M., Schuh, M. C., and Nisbet, J. (2006) *The Inclusion Facilitator's Guide*. Baltimore: Paul H. Brookes.

Kamps, D. M., Kravits, T., Lopez, A. G., Kemmerer, K., Potucek, J., Harrell, L. G., and Garrison, L. (1998) What do the peers think? Social validity of peer-mediated programmes. *Education & Treatment of Children*, 21 (2): 107–134.

Kluth, P. (2005) *Special Education Is Not a Place: Avoiding Pull-Out Services in Inclusive Schools*. Accessed 25 January 2009 at http://www.paulakluth.com/articles/pulloutsvc.html

McGregor, G. and Volgelsberg, R. T. (1998) *Inclusive Schooling Practices: Pedagogical and Research Foundations: A Synthesis of the Literature that Informs Best Practices about Inclusive Schooling*. Baltimore: Paul H. Brookes.

McLeskey, J. and Waldron, N. L. (2002) School change and inclusive schools: lessons learned from practice. *Phi Delta Kappan*, 84 (1): 65–72.

Malmgren, K. W. and Causton-Theoharis, J. N. (2006) Boy in the bubble: effects of paraprofessional proximity and other pedagogical decisions on the interactions of a student with behaviour disorders. *Journal of Research in Childhood Education*, 20 (4): 301–312.

Mastropieri, M. A., Scruggs, T. E., and Berkeley, S. L. (2007) Peers helping peers. *Educational Leadership*, 64 (5): 54–58.

Mittler, P. (2000) *Working toward Inclusive Education: Social Contexts*. London: David Fulton.

Olson, M. R., Chalmers, L., and Hoover, J. H. (1997) Attitudes and attributes of general education teachers identified as effective inclusionists. *Remedial and Special Education*, 18 (1): 28–35.

Peterson, J. M. and Hittie, M. M. (2010) *Inclusive Teaching: The Journey towards Effective Schools for All Learners*, 2nd edition. Columbus, OH: Merrill.

Rea, P. J., McLaughlin, V. L., and Walther-Thomas, C. (2002) Outcomes for students with learning disabilities in inclusive and pullout programmes. *Exceptional Children*, 68 (2): 203–223.

Riehl, C. J. (2000) The principal's role in creating inclusive schools for diverse students: a review of normative, empirical, and critical literature on the practice of educational administration. *Review of Educational Research*, 70 (1): 55–81.

Riggs, C. G. and Mueller, P. H. (2001) Employment and utilization of paraeducators in inclusive settings. *Journal of Special Education*, 35 (1): 5.

Roseth, C. J., Johnson, D. W. and Johnson, R. T. (2008) Promoting early adolescents' achievement and peer relationships: the effects of cooperative, competitive, and individualistic goal structures. *Psychological Bulletin*, 134 (2): 223–246.

Ryndak, D. L. and Fisher, D. (Eds.) (2003) *The Foundations of Inclusive Education: A Compendium of Articles on Effective Strategies to Achieve Inclusive Education*, 2nd edition. Baltimore: TASH.

Salisbury, C. L. and McGregor, G. (2002) The administrative climate and context of inclusive elementary schools. *Exceptional Children*, 68 (2): 259–274.

Schnorr, R. F. (1997) From enrollment to membership: "belonging" in middle and high school classes. *Journal of the Association for Persons with Severe Handicaps*, 22 (1): 1–15.

Scruggs, T. E., Mastropieri, M. A., and McDuffie, K. A. (2007) Co-teaching in inclusive classrooms: a meta-synthesis of qualitative research. *Exceptional Children*, 73 (4): 392–416.

Shukla, S., Kennedy, C. H., and Cushing, L. S. (1999) Intermediate school students with severe disabilities: supporting their social participation in general education classrooms. *Journal of Positive Behaviour Interventions,* 1 (3): 130–140.

Siperstein, G. N., Norins, J., and Mohler, A. (2007) Social acceptance and attitude change: fifty years of research. In J. W. Jacobson, J. A. Mulick and J. Rojahn (Eds.) *Handbook of Intellectual and Developmental Disabilities*. New York: Springer.

Soodak, L. C., Podell, D. M., and Lehman, L. R. (1998) Teacher, student, and school attributes as predictors of teachers' responses to inclusion. *Journal of Special Education*, 31 (4): 480–497.

Suter, J. C. and Giangreco, M. F. (2010) Numbers that count: exploring special education and paraprofessional service delivery in inclusion-oriented schools. *Journal of Special Education*. Accessed 22 May 2008 at doi: 10.1177/0022466907313353

Thousand, J. S., Villa, R. A., and Nevin, A. (2002) *Creativity and Collaborative Learning: A Practical Guide to Empowering Students and Teachers*, 2nd edition. Baltimore: Paul H. Brookes.

Thousand, J. S., Villa R. A., and Nevin, A. (2007) *Differentiating Instruction: Collaborative Planning and Teaching for Universally Designed Learning*. Thousand Oaks, CA: Corwin.

UNESCO. (1994) *The Salamanca Statement and Framework for Action on Special Needs Education*. Accessed 8 January 2009 at http://www.unesco.org/education/pdf/SALAMA_E.PDF

Villa, R. A., Thousand, J. S., Nevin, A., and Malgeri, C. (1996) Instilling collaboration for inclusive schooling as a way of doing business in public schools. *Remedial and Special Education*, 17 (3): 169–181.

Villa, R. A., Thousand, J. S., and Nevin, A. (2004) *A Guide to Co-teaching: Practical Tips for Facilitating Student Learning*. Thousand Oaks, CA: Corwin.

Wallace, T., Anderson, A. R., and Bartholomay, T. (2002) Collaboration: an element associated with the success of four inclusive high schools. *Journal of Educational and Psychological Consultation*, 13 (4): 349–381.

Wehmeyer, M. L., Agran, M., Hughes, C., Martin, J., Mithaug, D. E., and Palmer, S. (2007) *Promoting Self-Determination in Students with Intellectual and Developmental Disabilities*. New York: Guilford Press.

Weiner, J. S. (2005) Peer-mediated conversational repair in students with moderate and severe disabilities. *Research and Practice for Persons with Severe Disabilities*, 30 (1): 26–37.

Chapter 18

Identifying core competencies and skills for assistants

Implications for training to support inclusive classrooms

Áine O'Neill (Church of Ireland College of Education, Dublin)

The deployment of additional adults working in collaboration with teachers to support the inclusion of students with special educational needs (SEN) in mainstream and special schools has become increasingly common internationally over the past two decades. Trends relating to increase in numbers as well as issues relating to the most effective use of these adults have been well recorded in the literature. In a summary of literature relating to the work of 'teacher assistants' from the USA Giangreco and Doyle (2007) report that, although additional adults have been identified as a support to the inclusion of students with SEN, they have also been identified as creating barriers to inclusion. Lack of clarity relating to their role, especially in relation to the teaching and learning process, and lack of appropriate training are identified across jurisdictions as contributing to practices that may have negative consequences for the students who are being supported.

This chapter reflects on the issue of initial training for adults who are supporting students with SEN in schools. The discussion is informed by international research, which identifies the challenges relating to the effective use of this kind of support. It is also informed by the author's experience working with teachers who are engaged in a postgraduate training programme in special educational needs, and with training programmes for special needs assistants (SNAs) in Ireland. The term 'assistant' will be used throughout to describe support personnel.

The discussion presented here is predicated on a number of understandings. The first is that the rationale for deployment of assistants is to support the inclusion of students with SEN in schools. The second is that they have a role in supporting the work of teachers. The third is that assistants are not intended as substitutes for trained class or special education teachers.

One of the difficulties relating to role definition for assistants is the variety of contexts in which they work and consequently the wide range of tasks carried out by them. Assistants working with students with severe, profound or multiple disabilities, perhaps in special settings, are engaged in very different tasks from those working in classrooms supporting students with less complex or temporary needs. This presents a challenge for those involved in designing training programmes for assistants. Training could be approached from two perspectives. The first is that training should be provided for particular settings or to support students with specific needs. The second is that by examining common issues that emerge relating to the role of assistants working with children with special educational needs across settings it should be possible to identify areas of knowledge and skills that would inform initial training providing the same foundation knowledge for all assistants. This training would prepare them to work in all types of schools. The former view has implications that may limit the learning possibilities for assistants and restrict flexibility in relation to deployment. The latter view reflects a similar path to the professional preparation which teachers and other professionals follow whereby the study of relevant areas of knowledge provides a foundation for competencies and skills appropriate to that profession.

The role of assistant and teacher

The document that currently outlines the role or 'duties' of assistants (called special needs assistants or SNAs) in Ireland stipulates that their duties relate to the 'care needs' of students with SEN and must be 'non-teaching' in nature (DES 2002: 16). Evidence from Irish research, however, indicates that assistants in Irish schools are involved in the teaching and learning process (Lawlor and Cregan 2003; Logan 2006). Similar trends are to be found in international literature and discussion of this trend in the literature often relates it to a lack of clarity in relation to the role of the assistant (Egilson and Traustadottir 2009; Moran and Abbott 2002; Rose and O'Neill 2009). Although this is indeed the case, it is also fair to argue that it may also be influenced by different interpretations of what constitutes teaching. It is useful, therefore, to reflect briefly on this before attempting to define roles.

Reflecting on what constitutes teaching inevitably leads to reflection on education and what happens in schools. If we start from the premise that the purpose of schools is to educate students and the vehicle for this is the curriculum then we need to define what we mean by curriculum. Rose (2007) points out that 'curriculum' may be defined in different ways. It may be defined narrowly as a prescribed syllabus to be followed and taught by teachers. It may also be considered more broadly as everything the child experiences in school and the formal and informal learning that occurs through these experiences. If the latter is true, then the school environment and all of the people who work within it may provide learning opportunities for students and as such are involved in the teaching and learning process. What is often described as the hidden curriculum can be as powerful an influence on the students learning as is the prescribed one.

An exercise carried out with teachers and SNAs who are course participants on the training programmes referred to earlier asks them to define 'teaching'. Having observed students engage in this task over the years, it is possible to say that there is a high level of predictability in group responses. Participants will generally identify a very wide variety of activities and skills. These include what might be described as core elements of teaching, for example planning, selecting content, instruction and assessment. They also include what might be considered as nurturing aspects of teaching such as listening, encouraging, motivating, supporting, explaining, modelling, enabling, facilitating, mediating, to name but a few. These, it is generally agreed, are essential elements of the teaching process. In the discussions that follow this exercise, participants struggle to define teaching and 'non-teaching' roles. Attempts to separate the parts of 'encouraging', 'modelling', 'listening', 'assisting' and 'supporting' into teacher and assistant roles quite quickly becomes an exercise in semantics and generally a consensus emerges that these nurturing aspects of teaching are shared between teachers and assistants. Initially, participants reflecting on 'core' elements of teaching tend to ascribe these elements to the domain of the teacher. However, when invited to reflect on areas such as assessment and planning it is generally acknowledged that the observations of assistants are invaluable and should contribute to these important aspects of teaching.

What is clear from this exercise is that trying to set absolute lines of de-marcation between teachers and assistants as a starting point in establishing the role of the assistant is not possible. In order to train assistants for an identifiable role, that role needs a clear identity. So far we have established that assistants have a role in the teaching and learning process. The question is what kind of role this is. Do students with SEN need some kind of 'semi-teacher' who does exactly what teachers do but without the formal training, or is there a place for a related role, discrete, but with a clear identity and purpose?

Establishing a common identity for assistants

Much of the evidence relating to the effective deployment of assistants focuses on their relationship with teachers and on the importance of estab-lishing teams and collaborative partnerships to support the needs of students with SEN. In examining issues relating to effective partnerships, Lacey (2001) comments on the 'more or less equal status' of teachers and other professionals when working together. She also suggests that a less than equal status may exist between teachers and assistants when they collaborate. This difference relates to the fact that professionals come to teamwork with a well-established identity, bestowed on them by the specialist knowledge and training they have gained in professional preparation. Teachers working in teams also share a knowledge base, a language and common skills. The fact that assistants do not bring a clearly identifiable knowledge base and set of skills to their work inevitably brings a level of randomness to the nature of the partnerships that may develop with teachers and to the quality of the collaboration that might ensue. A teacher working with a number of assistants in a school may find the variation in skills and levels of knowledge relating to the work of classrooms difficult to accommodate (Wilson, Schlapp and Davidson 2003). In considering role definition, therefore, it might be more logical first to explore an agreed identity for assistants through the exploration of an appropriate knowledge base and set of skills which would form the basis of training prior to taking up positions in schools. This might give a better understanding of the possibilities for the assistant's role in the school team. Lacey (2001) makes the point that 'status becomes of little importance if everyone feels that they have a role that is particular to them and they are appreciated when they carry it out' (p. 101). A critical vehicle for the establishment of this *particular* role should be initial training.

In examining the issue of an appropriate role for a teaching assistant in England, Petrie's (2005) exploration of the European 'pedagogic' approach to supporting children and young people in a variety of different circumstances offers an interesting perspective on how the identity of assistants might be developed. With this approach the 'pedagogue', a trained professional, supports children's 'overall development: physical, cognitive, social and creative' in a range of settings, including schools (p. 177). Training and education for work in the field of pedagogy largely takes place in universities and colleges and takes three to four years. This training is described as a combination of placement and study with the areas of study related to the behavioural and social sciences: a body of skills that the 'pedagogue' will need when working with children and skills relevant to working in teams (p. 178). The 'pedagogue' is described as highly respected, with a professional status parallel to that of the teacher but with a distinct identity and also as 'a necessary component of the whole school team' (p. 180). This identity is developed through professional pre-service training. Although working in a very different education system from that of England, Petrie identifies some similarities between the work of assistants and that of the 'pedagogue'. These would relate in particular to instruction in social skills training and in the nurturing aspects of teaching identified earlier as listening, encouraging and motivating students (Giangreco and Doyle 2007; Moran and Abbott 2002; Logan 2006). There is precedent therefore in education systems for a professional with a distinctly different professional identity to that of teachers, but working as a team member in schools. What needs to be explored now is, first, whether assistants need a distinct set of knowledge and skills in order to do their work. Second, can we identify these clearly enough to discuss the possibility of a broad, common pre-service training similar to the model described for the 'pedagogue' earlier? Finally, following from that, would this training enable us to clarify boundaries between teacher and assistant and to become comfortable with the possibility of some overlap between the two?

Identifying areas of knowledge and appropriate skills

In identifying areas of knowledge and skills appropriate to the work of assistants, a reasonable starting point would be to refer back to the rationale stated at the outset for the deployment of assistants. This is to support the inclusion of students with SEN and, by implication, support the work of the teacher and the school. Much of the criticism relating to the deployment of assistants for this purpose is drawn from research in which findings indicate that support may serve to exclude students by creating dependency and inhibiting the development of autonomy and independence. This experience may affect the students' social, personal and academic development (Moran and Abbott 2002; Howes 2003). The theme of assistants inhibiting independence and contributing to feelings of exclusion also comes through very clearly when students are asked to speak about their school experiences (Shevlin and Rose 2003; Skar and Tamm 2001; Broer, Doyle and Giangreco 2005). Whereas some of the behaviours and factors that result in exclusive practices are caused by factors that are outside the control of assistants, it is clear from the literature that there are core competencies and understandings that, if developed through training, would enable assistants to work more effectively to promote inclusion rather than the reverse.

Identifying knowledge and competencies that support inclusion

Child and adolescent development

Assistants are employed to work in mainstream primary, post-primary and special schools. They will therefore find themselves working with very young children who are beginning their formal education, adolescents or possibly even young adults. An appropriate starting point in training therefore would be that assistants coming to work in schools should have an understanding of child and adolescent development. Prioritising knowledge in this area would have important implications for assistants when working with students and teachers. An understanding of the need and the entitlement of all students to develop an appropriate level of control over their lives, their learning and their relationships with peers would seem essential. Concomitant with this should be an understanding of the consequences of impeding progress towards independence in terms of the student's overall development. In an exploration of the identities ascribed to assistants, Skar and Tamm (2001) identify inappropriate identities such as mother and best friend, but also discover what students describe as the 'professional assistant'. This identity was ascribed by students to those assistants who understood their needs as children or adolescents first, who were able to stand back, observe and make appropriate judgements about how and when to intervene and offer support.

Understanding the learning process

A second important possible outcome of the study of child and adolescent development relates to assistants' understanding of the work of the teacher. An understanding of patterns of development in relation to physical, cognitive, social, emotional and aesthetic development provides a foundation for understanding of the organisation of learning and curriculum, particularly at primary school level. An understanding of child and adolescent development would help assistants to understand the rationale for different approaches to teaching selected by the teacher. An understanding of how children learn informs the selection of methodologies and the role of the adult in that process. This is the case regardless of whether the assistant is engaged in supporting students in core aspects of the curriculum or in the incidental learning that is happening throughout the school day in the classroom, the corridors or the playground.

Howes (2003) reports from research evidence that, in supporting learning, assistants may lack an understanding of the importance of the learning process and focus on 'outcomes' instead of process. Calder and Grieve (2004) also express concerns about the involvement of assistants who do not understand the processes of learning in the teaching of young children. Supporting children's learning through play and activities requires skill and training. De Valenzuela (2007) reflects on the influence socio-cultural theory has had in the areas of pedagogy, in particular in relation to special education. This influence can also be seen on general curricula (Ireland 1999) where language is given a central place in learning and methodologies that engage children in questioning and reflective learning behaviours are prioritised (p. 15). The role of the more competent other (be they adult or peer) in this approach is worth close examination when considering the role of assistants in the learning process. Purposeful training in scaffolding behaviours that facilitate students to be proactive in their own learning would position the assistant well to support the work of the teacher in the classroom. An understanding of this approach would also enable the assistant to support peers in group and cooperative learning approaches. Skills such as observation, listening, encouraging, assisting and modelling are all pertinent to this approach. We know from the literature that assistants currently draw on these skills in their work (Rose 2000; Logan 2006). There is a sense, however, that when they demonstrate these skills they are regarded as positive personal qualities rather than skills and competencies to be developed and fine-tuned as part of their role.

Inclusion

A survey of the literature would indicate that many assistants come to their work with no prior training and that where they do have 'qualifications' they may not quite match the needs of the school (Moran and Abbott 2003;

Giangreco and Doyle 2007). If the rationale for employing assistants is to promote the inclusion of students with disabilities, then an opportunity to explore the concept of 'inclusion' would seem be a priority area in the professional development of assistants. An attitudinal study in Ireland of perceptions and attitudes to disability in the general population reports very mixed understandings and levels of acceptance of people with disabilities (NDA 2008). In this study, respondents' perceptions were found to be shaped by personal experiences of someone with a disability in family or social settings. Given that assistants generally do not come to their work with any specialist training, it is possible that their perceptions and attitudes to disability are influenced by personal experience and that these are further shaped by their experiences in schools. Experience, referred to earlier, of working with SNAs on training programmes in Ireland indicates that participants have little awareness of the broad issues relating to inclusion. Rose and Forlin (2010) also report this to be the case with education assistants in Hong Kong participating in an advanced training programme. There, assistants 'expressed a desire for a greater understanding of what was meant by inclusion' (p. 10). Although we may find the task of defining what is meant by inclusion a challenge in itself, we can identify behaviours, attitudes and environmental factors, both physical and social, that may lead to the exclusion of students from learning experiences in school. Students themselves cite overprotection and misconceptions about their ability, for example. This emanates from a deficit view of disability and results in practices that prohibit students from taking risks in the learning process and consequently limits independence (Skar and Tamm 2001; Shevlin and Rose 2003; NDA 2008). Providing opportunities to explore the assistants' personal perceptions and attitudes to disability, as well as those prevalent in society, would increase awareness of how measures and behaviours intended to help students might instead become a hindrance. Empowering assistants by providing them with a robust understanding of social models of inclusion and allowing them to question and to reflect on their work would enable them to see competencies rather than deficits in the students they work with. It would also enable them to reflect on practices required of them and the possible obstacles to inclusion. This is particularly important given that assistants may find themselves working in situations that espouse a social model in policy statements but through practices and attitudes present a different reality. These understandings, complemented by skills in observation, listening and communication, would enable assistants to play a valuable role in school teams whose purpose is to support the inclusion of students with SEN.

Advocacy

The voice of students in research has enabled us so far to identify important areas of knowledge that would help assistants to support them more effectively. Unfortunately, another theme that emerges in the same research is the fact that students find it difficult to have their voices heard in school settings. They experience having adults, including assistants, presume that they know them well enough to make decisions without consulting them. They also report being spoken to through their assistants. Skar and Tamm (2001) include one student's experience stating that 'sometimes they ask the assistant whether he wants to take part before they ask me, and that's no fun' (p. 925). On the other hand, there is evidence that students may talk to assistants about issues and concerns that they may not discuss with other adults in school and that they appreciate being listened to.

From the assistants' perspective Howes (2003) cites evidence that they act as 'mediators' or 'connectors' (p. 150). There is plenty of evidence of assistants bringing to teachers observations relating to students and this is seen as very appropriate to planning for and evaluation of student learning (O'Neill and Rose 2008). This is done informally and formally with school teams through the Individual Educational Plan (IEP) process. The mediating role may relate to mediation between students when enabling them to interact socially or in the words of one student to 'stay out of trouble' (Logan 2006: 94). It may also refer to mediation with other adults on behalf of the student, for example through involvement in resolution of difficulties such as bullying for the student (Broer, Doyle and Giangreco 2005). The role and responsibility of the assistant in relation to these different communication roles needs careful consideration.

The term 'advocate' has been used in relation to some of the roles described above (Broer, Doyle and Giangreco 2005). Advocacy can be defined as the act of speaking on behalf of or for another person. It carries with it a responsibility to be absolutely faithful to the concerns and wishes of that person. The principles that underpin advocacy are described as 'empowerment, autonomy, inclusion and citizenship' (Comhairle 2004). Although these principles as stated pertain to wider society, they can easily translate to the school situation. The work of the advocate begins with the presumption of competence on the part of the individual being represented. This starting point suggests that, regardless of the level of disability, each person has competence to indicate choice and preference. Assistants working closely with students with disabilities are in a position to develop a communicative relationship that can empower the student to speak for him- or herself or, if that is not possible, to communicate on their behalf. Whether assistants are in a position to become advocates in the truest sense of that role is a question that deserves a chapter in itself. It is arguable, for example, that it is not possible for someone who is working within the school structure to achieve the level of independence required in that role. It is realistic, however, to say that assistants are in a position to enable students to be heard, by enabling them to speak for themselves or by representing their views faithfully. They are also in a position to make observations about the physical and social environment, which may need adjustment in order to meet the needs of students with SEN. In order to do this it would seem important that they be prepared for this role. Providing an opportunity for assistants to explore the principles of advocacy, and to develop and practice the related skills such as observation and communication, would place them in a position where they might be better able to support inclusion.

Identifying and developing appropriate skills

In the discussion so far, particular skills that might enable assistants to support inclusion have been identified. The experience of students with SEN has informed this. Although it is the case that assistants do observe and do listen and engage in communications regarding students, it is through reflection and practice that assistants perfect these skills. Assistants may come to their work with intuitive behaviours that are very supportive of students with disabilities. However, an analysis of the skills identified will illustrate that, regardless of the natural abilities of assistants, specific training is required to ensure that these important skills are used positively to include rather than exclude.

Observation

Observation is a skill that requires specific training, continuous practice and evaluation. Through skilled observation, the observer may learn about the student and about the challenges presented to the student in the school environment. In assessing the needs of students with SEN, many individuals my contribute observations and these may or may not be influenced by valid perceptions of the child. The quality of observations therefore may vary. In developing observation skills the single most important issue is developing the capacity to observe accurately and present objective information.

In describing the skills needed to become efficient observers Hayes (2005) describes observation as a process or a series of steps. In our daily living, we as human beings are equipped to continuously use our senses to observe and make judgements that inform our actions. We observe, interpret quickly, and react or ignore information, selecting that which is relevant and appropriate to the task in hand. In other words, in order to function we need to be selective and subjective about the information we assimilate and process. For objective observation, Hayes suggests, we need to adjust our natural tendency to select particular aspects and reject others and insert a new step into the series: '*observe, record, interpret* and *react* (or *ignore*)' (p. 35). Recording information precisely, either in writing or in memory, and interpreting it objectively at a later stage ensures that opinion and individual perceptions do not influence or create a bias in the information delivered.

In addition to this adjustment in behaviour, the skilled observer needs to develop the ability to use a range of different methods to record observations. Furthermore, techniques and competencies need to be developed that enable assistants to make objective observations while they are participating in an activity with the student or observing from a distance.

The student and teacher benefit from effective observation and indeed so does the school. As Broer, Doyle and Giangreco (2005) point out, the school benefits when assistants can identify difficulties that the students with special needs encounter, as it is very likely that other students are encountering these also.

Effective communication skills

Listening

Effective communication skills are, along with observation, critical skills that support the areas of knowledge outlined above. The important skill of listening can enable the assistant to support the student, the teacher and the whole school community. Whereas we might consider listening to be a natural human behaviour, for many professionals it is a critical skill that needs to be developed over time and also requires practice. Different situations may require different kinds of listening. For example, passive listening allows for a total focus on listening as it does not involve responding and thus offers an opportunity to observe the speaker closely. The listener may offer non-verbal encouragement: the fact that she or he is not composing a response or interaction of any kind allows for focused listening. This kind of listening can support observation and would support the observation of social and communication skills of students. Active listening on the other hand requires the listener to know when to support the speaker and to do so appropriately. It involves what Weitzman and Greenberg (2002) describe as the 'observe, wait, listen or OWL' strategy (pp. 72–74). Active listening also involves encouraging behaviours such as restating ('so what you are saying is . . . ?'), clarifying ('can you explain . . . ?' or 'say a little bit more about . . . ?'), reflecting ('you feel that . . . ?') and summarising to enable the speaker the opportunity to check that he or she has been understood.

This kind of listening would support the student in a number of ways. The individual student's own listening and communication skills can only be enhanced by being supported in this way. The assistant is also in a stronger position to scaffold and support the learning process outlined earlier. This would also support the work of the assistant as a participant in team planning and collaboration with other adults who work with the student.

Communication

Effective communication skills complement good listening and are similarly developed through training and practice. Effective use of the body, the face, the eyes and the voice to communicate is as important as the spoken message. Training in communication skills is part of the initial training of many professionals. Assistants working with students with disabilities need expertise in effective communication with the students in their care and with the other adults with whom they collaborate. In their role supporting the inclusion of students with disabilities they are called upon to display many different communication skills. With their students they may be involved in supporting learning and using language and communication skills that require subtlety and knowledge of the student's own communication style and level. It may be that the assistant has to use alternative or augmentative systems.

Different communications may be required to work effectively as a team member or to work as an advocate for students with SEN. Representing the student in a clear, direct and honest way may not be easy in every circumstance. Developing assertive communication skills through professional training would support this work.

Conclusion

In the past decade questions have been raised about the efficacy of the employment of assistants to support the inclusion of students with SEN in schools. Concerns that their deployment may work to exclude rather than include students have been justified through evidence from research. In addition, defining appropriate roles for teachers and assistants in the teaching and learning process continues to be a challenge. A question was raised at the outset about the 'identity' ascribed to the role of assistant. In the discussion that followed, it was suggested that discrete skills can be identified which, if developed, might help assistants to prevent or remove some of the barriers to inclusion encountered by students with SEN. Initial training in these skills might also identify the role of assistant as one that complements rather than compromises the work of the teacher. Anecdotal evidence from working with assistants in Ireland suggests that they appreciate how these competencies and skills enhance and clarify their role. Whether teachers would fully appreciate their value and avail of them might be dependent on training. This raises the issue of training in collaborative practice for assistants and teachers and this is a topic for another discussion.

Bibliography

Broer, S., Doyle, M. B. and Giangreco, M. (2005) Perspectives of students with intellectual disabilities about their experiences with paraprofessional support. *Exceptional Children*, 71 (4): 415–430.

Calder, I. and Grieve, A. (2004) Working with other adults: what teachers need to know. *Educational Studies*, 30 (2): 113–126.

Comhairle: Citizens Advice Board. (2004) *Developing an Advocacy Service for People with Disabilities*. Accessed date at http://www.oasis.irlgov.ie/publications/advocacy.advocacy.index.html

Department of Education and Science (DES). (2002) *Applications For Full-time or Part-time Special Needs Assistant Support to Address the Special Care Needs of Children with Disabilities*. Circular Sp. ED 07/02. Dublin: DES.

De Valenzuela, J. S. (2007) Sociocultural views of learning. In L. Florian (Ed.) *The Sage Handbook of Special Education*. London: Sage Publications.

Egilson, S. T. and Traustadottir, R. (2009) Assistance to pupils with physical disabilities in regular schools: promoting inclusion or creating dependency? *European Journal of Special Needs Education*, 24 (1): 21–36.

Giangreco, M. F. and Doyle, M. B. (2007) Teacher assistants in inclusive schools. In L. Florian (Ed.) *The Sage Handbook of Special Education*. London: Sage Publications.

Hayes, N. (2005) *Early Childhood: An Introductory Text*. Dublin: Gill & MacMillan.

Howes, A. (2003) Teaching reforms and the impact of paid adult support on participation and learning in mainstream schools. *Support for Learning*, 18 (4): 147–153.

Lacey, P. (2001) *Support Partnerships: Collaboration in Action*. London: David Fulton.

Lawlor, L. and Cregan, A. (2003) The evolving role of the special needs assistant: towards a new synergy. *REACH, Journal of Special Needs Education in Ireland*, 16 (2): 82–93.

Logan, A. (2006) The role of the special needs assistant supporting pupils with special educational needs in Irish mainstream primary schools. *Support for Learning*, 21 (2): 92–98.

Moran, A. and Abbott, L. (2003) Developing inclusive schools: the pivotal role of teaching assistants in promoting inclusion in special and mainstream schools in Northern Ireland. *European Journal of Special Educational Needs*, 17 (2): 161–173.

NDA (National Disability Authority). (2008) *The Experiences of Students with Physical Disabilities in 2nd Level Schools*. Dublin: NDA.

O'Neill, A and Rose, R, (2008) The changing roles of teaching assistants in England and special needs assistants in Ireland: a comparison. *REACH, Journal of Special Needs Education in Ireland*, 22 (1): 48–58.

Petrie, P. (2005) Schools and support staff: applying the European pedagogic model. *Support for Learning*, 20 (4): 176–180.

Rose, R. (2000) Using classroom support in a primary school: a single school case study. *British Journal of Special Education*, 27 (4): 205–210.

Rose, R. (2007) Curriculum considerations in meeting special educational needs. In L. Florian (Ed.) *The Sage Handbook of Special Education*. London: Sage Publications.

Rose, R. and O'Neill, A. (2009) Classroom support for inclusion in England and Ireland: an evaluation of contrasting models. *Research in Comparative and International Education*, 4 (3): 250–261.

Rose, R. and Forlin, C. (2010) Impact of training on change in practice for education assistants in a group of international private schools in Hong Kong. *International Journal of Inclusive Education*, 14 (1): 1–15.

Shevlin, M. and Rose, R. (2003) *Encouraging Voices: Respecting the Insights of Young People Who Have Been Marginalised*. Dublin: National Disability Authority.

Skar, L. and Tamm, M. (2001) My assistant and I: disabled children's and adolescents' roles and relationships to their assistants. *Disability and Society*, 16 (7): 917–931.

Weitzman, E. and Greenberg, J. (2002) *Learning Language and Loving It: A Guide to Promoting Children's Social, Language, and Literacy Development in Early Childhood Setting*. Toronto: Hanen Centre.

Wilson, V., Schlapp, U. and Davidson, J. (2003) An 'extra pair of hands'? Managing classroom assistants in Scottish primary schools. *Educational Management Administration & Leadership*. Accessed 17 February 2009 at http://ema,sagepub.com

Chapter 19

Classroom support for including students with challenging behaviour

Sue Roffey (University of Western Sydney, Australia)

This chapter will address conceptualisations of children and young people whose behaviour is hard to manage in school and the practical responses that follow alternative ways of positioning both students and their behaviour. There is an increasing emphasis on student well-being in Australia, which encompasses a focus on resilience and the protective factors that enhance this. These include positive relationships, a sense of belonging, social and emotional learning, a focus on strengths and solutions, student participation, building a sense of community and restorative practices. Although a medical 'within child' model persists in some educational jurisdictions, this is increasingly being questioned as it does not sit well with the 'whole child/ whole school' approach advocated by the research.

Introduction

Although inclusion for students with special educational needs is commonly advocated as in the best interests of the child there is often less enthusiasm when pupils manifest their needs in emotional and behavioural difficulties. These students may struggle with learning and have other needs but it is their behaviour that becomes the primary focus of concern. The argument is often about how the education of other students will be affected and how teachers are not equipped to deal with such difficulties.

Children and young people from families who neglect or harm them, who have role models that promote conflict and violence and/or those with a background which is unsupportive of an inclusive educational philosophy are likely to be a challenge for teachers in the classroom. The behaviour of such students may be uninterested, disruptive, defiant or simply uncontrolled. Their emotions may be volatile and both their intra- and interpersonal skills at a basic level of development. Their main focus is likely to be on getting their psychological needs met – not on learning or on establishing healthy relationships with either teachers or peers.

Alternative theoretical positions

> We do not see the way things are, we see the way we are.
>
> (Jewish proverb)

There are many ways of conceptualising such students in the classroom. How children are discussed, perceived and positioned impacts on how teachers position themselves in relation to their pupils and informs how they respond (Laws and Davies 2000; Roffey 2006a). The 'bad' and 'mad' models place difficult behaviour squarely 'within' the young person. When students are construed as 'bad' they are overtly blamed for their behaviour, which is seen as innate and deliberate. The teacher places him- or herself as a keeper of the rules and responsible for order. Students need to be controlled to maintain this order and if they resist they must be made to conform or punished.

When a student is given a psychiatric label, such as attention deficit disorder, there is an element of 'maybe s/he can't help it'. Teachers may place themselves as the victim of the challenging behaviour and refer to more qualified helpers to take responsibility for effecting change in the individual through drugs or therapies. In the 'sad' model someone is held to blame for the child's distress, usually the family. This student is also seen as needing outside help to cope with their difficulties, with social workers perhaps added to medical professionals. Teachers can maintain their position as caring educators but with no obligation to take any responsibility as the problems again exist outside their domain. All they need to do is find a way of managing in the classroom so that they are able to get on with the core business of teaching with minimum disruption.

Many schools use a model that asserts that behaviour changes with the offer of reward or the threat of sanction and that, if one sanction does not lead to improvement, punishments must be increased until the student 'sees sense' and buckles down. Current thinking is that behavioural change is far more complex (Bransford, Brown and Cocking 2003) and this simple behaviourist approach has only limited success with some individuals (Goddard 2003) and very little impact with those who are most distressed and difficult, who often end up suspended or excluded from school.

Despite the initial sigh of relief, excluding challenging students does not make schools safer or more effective learning environments. In 2006 the American Psychological Association published an evaluation of 'zero tolerance' policies in schools (APA 2006). This is the 'tough approach' to violence and drug abuse – one strike and you're out. The APA report concludes that such policies not only result in a 'school to prison pipeline' for individuals but also impact negatively on other students. Behaviour does not improve overall as an authoritarian ethos leads to little trust between teachers and students, and academic outcomes suffer. The report suggests that a 'community based' approach is more promising in both preventing and dealing with challenging issues.

An alternative theoretical position is based on the research on resilience and well-being, which acknowledges the fundamental importance of schools in providing protective factors for vulnerable and challenging young people. This interactive model positions students as an integral part of the school system where what they bring is either exacerbated or modified by what happens in the learning environment. Schools and teachers are therefore positioned as responsible for maximising these protective factors.

Choosing perspective and position

How challenging students and their families are positioned is not purely an individual matter. It is the socio-political context that determines much of what happens in schools and the emphases that are taken (Parsons 2005). A rule-bound, test-orientated discourse determines that 'good' teachers are constructed as those who keep discipline and get high grades. This may undermine the efforts of those who believe that student well-being is core business and integral to an effective learning environment.

When dominant discourses are negative, it is hard for individuals to counter with a more constructive view of a young person. In schools where an authoritarian ethos prevails, positive statements may be dismissed as evidence of a willingness to be soft on students rather than ensure that appropriate discipline is upheld. The accepted view may be that students who challenge the system need to adapt to the expected standards or be asked to leave to maintain the 'good' reputation of the school. However, where there has been conscious and sustained school development on well-being, respect and inclusion, the opposite may be true (Roffey 2008).

> Negativity about the kids is rare. It is taboo to talk negatively about the kids. When teachers do sometime say something negative others will give a different view. It is not seen as a cool thing to do.
>
> (School counsellor, in Roffey 2008: 5)

The vision of school leaders, the values that are espoused and practiced throughout the school and the conversations that occur within the school community contribute to the way individuals are conceptualised and hence the approach taken to behavioural issues (Roffey 2007).

School leaders are more likely to choose and activate a positive well-being discourse when this is the stated expectation of educational policy makers. When politicians have an eye to what is effective rather than expedient they are more likely to appoint school leaders with an educational philosophy which places value on the whole child and whole school approaches to well-being.

Resilience research

We have known for many years that exposure to negative life experiences, such as poverty, mental health difficulties, neglect, abuse, family violence, criminality and addictions, are risk factors for children and that, the more risk factors there are in a child's life, the more the likelihood of negative outcomes, in both the short and the longer term. Children may develop learning difficulties, be disengaged at school, become delinquents, be drug abusers, experience depression and become young parents themselves.

What has been illuminating and helpful, however, has been the research on resilience and the factors that inhibit what may seem inevitable outcomes of such risk and disadvantage. Many studies (e.g. Werner and Smith 2001; Benard 2004) have identified the personal and environmental factors that protect children and young people from these negative outcomes of risk. Schools have the potential to directly determine the extent to which the environment can support resilience in the following ways:

- the provision and promotion of caring relationships;
- high expectations: teachers not giving up on you; a focus on strengths and goals rather than an emphasis on deficits;
- a sense of belonging: opportunities to participate in and contribute to your community.

Schools can also influence the encouragement of a positive approach to life, the development of problem-solving abilities, a pro-social orientation and the skills to establish and maintain healthy relationships.

There is a growing body of research which says that those schools which are most effective are those which value the 'whole child', their potential and their well-being rather than focusing exclusively on academic outcomes (ASCD 2007). There is also increasing evidence that where schools emphasise relational values and quality there are fewer behavioural difficulties and more engaged students (Downey 2008).

Student well-being

Although there are differences between educational jurisdictions in different States and Territories there is an increasing interest across Australia in student well-being and how this can be maximised. The federal government has taken a lead in a number of related initiatives. These include the National Safe Schools Framework, the MindMatters and KidsMatter programmes aimed at raising awareness of and promoting mental health, the Framework for Values in Australian Schools, Drug Education and most recently scoping studies on student well-being and social and emotional learning.

There is a shift away from a 'welfare' conceptualisation targeting individuals to a recognition that universal well-being impacts on every level of the learning environment and each individual within the system, including the most vulnerable. The term reflects the inclusive nature of schooling and a whole school approach.

> The wellbeing of students in the school community is promoted through developing connectedness and social capital. Social Capital is a term used to describe the particular features of social relationships within a group or community. This includes such things as the extent of trust between people; whether they have a shared understanding of how they should behave toward, and care for one another.
>
> (Catholic Education Office Melbourne 2006: 1)

> An integral part of human health is social and emotional wellbeing, sometimes called mental health. This refers to people's thoughts, feelings, behaviour and relationships.
>
> (Hunter Institute of Mental Health 2007: 1)

Several educational jurisdictions have put considerable resources into schools to enhance this focus on student well-being.

The Department of Education and Children's Services (DECS) in South Australia has developed a Learner Wellbeing Framework for birth to Year 12 outlining five interconnected dimensions – cognitive, emotional, physical, social and spiritual – within four domains: the learning environment, curriculum and pedagogy, partnerships, and policies and procedures. 'What is learned through the curriculum will be practised in the learning environment, supported by partnerships with family and other agencies, and made explicit in policies and practices' (DECS 2006: 7).

Explicit within this framework is a culture of inquiry defined as 'a process of systematic, rigorous and critical reflection about professional practice, and the contexts in which it occurs, in ways that question taken-for-granted assumptions' (Reid 2004: 4). Examples of such reflections given in the Learner Wellbeing Framework include:

> When we explicitly teach about respect, will that lead to greater mutual respect between staff and students?
>
> Fregon Anangu School

> When we change the way in which we interact with students in the classroom, will levels of engagement improve?
>
> Mawson Lakes Primary School

When we introduce a variety of socially inclusive strategies and programmes, will this empower our children and families to be more socially inclusive?

Poonindie Community Kindergarten

One of the roles of Student Wellbeing and Inclusion Co-ordinators in South Australia is to support teachers in meeting the needs of students presenting with behavioural difficulties. This includes:

- Offering intervention based on identified needs of individual students.
- Brief intervention involving the design and implementation of student development plans, specific behaviour change plans etc.
- Consulting with school personnel in the provision of alternative strategies for individual students and/or whole class management.
- Observation of student behaviour and interactions in the school setting, including recommendations.
- Facilitating meetings with the family and school to foster cooperative planning and development of appropriate strategies.
- Supporting teachers to provide skills development programmes.
- Reintegration of students into school after exclusion.

(DECS 2006: p)

The Catholic Education Office in Melbourne (CEOM) has also been a front-runner in its emphasis on student well-being. Amongst other things it has made provision for a student well-being coordinator in each school. The thoroughness and professionalism of this initiative shows that this is no paper exercise. Since 1999 over 800 teachers have been sponsored to undertake a postgraduate course in student well-being at the University of Melbourne. As part of their studies they undertake research in the area, which is then fed back into the development of policy and practice. Inclusion is part of their mantra:

building supportive environments which are critical for the wellbeing, health, happiness and achievement of all students, but in particular for students who may have experienced trauma and disruption in their lives.

(Melbourne Graduate School of Education 2008)

Enhancing the quality of relationships

Relationships exist at every level within schools and each one contributes to the overall ethos. This includes relationships between school leaders and teachers, teacher colleagues, teacher and students, and students with each other. Where there is little emotional literacy or expectation of support, collaboration or consultation, and dominant cliques thrive, a toxic atmosphere can develop in which individuals and/or groups may be demonised, blamed or excluded. Negative communications can become the norm. This does little to promote pro-social behaviour in students or enhance well-being for teachers. It requires a positive vision with congruent policies and practices to change school culture over time (Roffey 2008). Where there is a well-being agenda within a school or educational jurisdiction the quality of relationships becomes a lynchpin for development.

Case study 1

Despite a lack of either pre- or post-service training, teachers are required to both manage a diverse range of conflicts in schools and teach students to manage conflict effectively. Part of the CEOM initiative is to carry out research projects to identify positive ways forward. The management of conflict in school is therefore an area for exploration. A three- to five-person core team incorporating school leaders and teachers, from each of twelve Melbourne primary schools, took part in a pilot project, working on conflict resolution and cultural identity. Schools were randomly assigned to either a full intervention group attending seven days of workshops over eighteen months and receiving periodic in-school support by project staff or a partial intervention group, attending two days of workshops with the same in-school support. Although both programme formats resulted in positive changes the full intervention appeared superior on a range of factors including teacher skill development and curriculum implementation. Findings include the following:

- School staff respond positively to the challenge of learning more effective ways of resolving conflict and examine their own assumptions and actions in relation to cultural diversity and enhancing relationships.
- The development of a skilled core team within each school provides an effective mechanism to foster relationship-enhancing approaches and embed these approaches in broader school structures, policies and processes.
- To promote positive relationships between all groups in school communities, not just to reduce existing conflict, requires investment in sustained, team-based professional development.

(ERIS 2007: 5)

Case study 2

In 1999, the Peer Support programme was introduced to Townsville Central State School, a government-run primary school in northern Queensland.

The programme sets out a series of steps in preparing Year 7 students to take leadership roles with younger cohorts at the school. Year 7 teachers support and prepare their Year 7 leaders to direct their group through a half-hour of activities, whilst other staff monitor these groups and support leaders if required. Critical reflection on personal attitudes and recognition of their implications in relationships are important aspects of applying the kinds of knowledge gained from involvement with Peer Support. However, the ultimate test of the value of such learning is in carrying these practices through into action. Students at Townsville Central have demonstrated high levels of communicative competence, for example by being able to communicate complex understandings clearly and articulately, in ways that reflect their own understandings. Teachers at the school have indicated that the programme has engaged the students in a richness of understandings, offering students the capacity to apply those understandings to their own lives and social relationships, specifically in relation to exhibiting values such as care, compassion, respect, responsibility, understanding, tolerance and inclusion. The school believes that their work with the Peer Support programme has represented one way in which state schools actively engage with the teaching of values and, in particular, how students can live and experience the values in the programme within and beyond the school itself (Curriculum Corporation 2006).

Teaching social and emotional skills

Teachers find students challenging when their social and emotional behaviour is uncontrolled, when young people do not seem to have safe ways of coping with their feelings and when relationships are threaded with negativity, manipulation and/or aggression. One answer to this is to help children and young people learn social and emotional skills in a structured way.

ResponseAbility is an organization set up by the Hunter Institute of Mental Health with the Australian Federal Government to provide mental health information for educators. They particularly target pre-service educators and suggest the following ways to help children and young people develop social skills and learn to manage their emotions:

- Invite children and young people to contribute to rules about treating each other with respect
- Develop games or activities that explore emotions, such as identifying feelings in yourself and others
- Promote empathy, take opportunities to ask how characters in stories, books or films might be feeling
- Teach skills for managing difficult emotions, such as going to a safe quiet place, relaxation or deep breathing
- Help young people to reflect on the behaviour or feelings that led up to time out or disciplinary action

- Build social skills, negotiation and communication skills using co-operative play and learning strategies
- Involve children or young people in planning out special tasks and solving practical problems
- Help children and young people to identify, articulate and work toward individual and group goals.

(Hunter Institute of Mental Health 2007: 2)

This same document gives teachers some strategies when they are concerned about possible emotional, behavioural or mental health programmes. They call this the GRIP framework. This is a sequence of actions, not all of which may be necessary. The following is a summary of this approach:

- **Gather** information, especially noting changes in the student or their circumstances.
- **Respond** by talking with the young person and their parent or carer, being calm, open and non-judgemental.
- **Involve** others who may be able to provide support – bearing confidentiality issues in mind.
- **Promote** a safe and supportive environment.

The context and pedagogy for social and emotional learning is crucial to its effectiveness. Programmes need to be embedded and multi-year with a congruent ethos and modelling from staff. A pedagogy that encourages discussion and reflection on the issues and gives students opportunities to practise what they are learning is more likely to produce cognitive and behavioural change.

Teaching resilience

Everyone needs to know how to cope with adversity – which is an inevitable part of life. Giving universal strategies in coping does not stigmatise those students who have the greatest struggles and also shows that others share some of the difficulties they face.

Eight out of the ten pilot schools for the KidsMatter mental health initiative adopted the Bounce Back programme to help children learn about resilience (McGrath and Noble 2006). This uses a range of tools, such as fiction, games, worksheets and Circle activities, to reinforce the Bounce Back acronym:

- **B**ad times don't last. Things always get better.
- **O**ther people can help if you talk to them. Get a reality check.
- **U**nhelpful thinking makes you feel more upset.
- **N**obody is perfect – not you and not others.
- **C**oncentrate on the positives (no matter how small) and use laughter.

- Everybody experiences sadness, changes, hurt, failure, rejection, and setbacks sometimes. They are a normal part of life. Try not to personalise them.
- Blame fairly – how much of what happened was because of you, others or bad luck or circumstances?
- Accept the things you can't change (but try to change what you can first).
- Catastrophising exaggerates your worries. Don't believe the worst possible picture.
- Keep things in perspective. It's one part of your life and doesn't have to spoil everything else.

Positive behaviour: focusing on what you want and where you want to go

There is an increasing interest in actively promoting positive behaviours within a whole school framework. The Whole School Positive Behaviour Support (PBS) in Queensland summarises this approach:

> 'Traditional' approaches to behaviour 'management' usually focus on students' problem behaviour, whereas PBS focuses on the needs that students are trying to meet by using the problem behaviour.
>
> 'Traditional' approaches focus on stopping student problem behaviour through the use of punishment or undesirable consequences whereas PBS focuses on actively teaching the student replacement behaviours that allow students to get their needs met in more efficient and socially acceptable ways, and on rewarding students for demonstrating appropriate behaviour.
>
> 'Traditional' approaches often leave alterations to the teaching and learning environment out of the equation, assuming that the student must change in order to accommodate the environment. In contrast, PBS focuses on changing the behaviour of adults, and on building environments that make the learning of replacement behaviours more effective and durable.
>
> (Education Queensland 2009)

In 2007 the implementation of Positive Behaviour for Learning (PBL) was investigated within the Greater Western Sydney area. It was found that student motivation and self-concept were generally more favourable and there was an impact on the attitudes of school staff leading to more positive and preventative practices within a systemic school-wide approach (Mooney *et al.* 2008).

Strengths and solution-based approaches

This is complementary to the positive behaviour approach in that it focuses on the existence and development of student competencies rather than on identifying and eliminating deficits. The South Australia policy statement on school discipline states that:

> responses to inappropriate behaviour will involve staff, students and families in partnerships which focus on student strengths and provide support for students in crisis while reinforcing the rights of other students to learn and teachers to teach in safety and without disruption.
>
> (DECS 2007: 3)

Solution-focused brief therapy is also having an impact on how some educators 're-frame' the difficulties they are having with some students (Ajmal and Rees 2001). For example, instead of asking 'When is this student most badly behaved?' you would want to know 'When is this student most cooperative and what is going on to support this?' Not 'What behaviour do we want to get rid of?' and 'What is most difficult?' but 'What behaviour do we want to see and what is most likely to change with minimum intervention – how can we get a quick success?'

Restorative approaches

Restorative approaches are increasingly in evidence around Australia and have been taken up with enthusiasm in some educational jurisdictions and individual schools.

In both public education in the Australian Capital Territory and Catholic education in Victoria restorative practices have been seen as congruent with values education.

Cameron and Thorsborne (2001) outline the way restorative justice in the school setting views challenging behaviour not simply as breaking the rules of the institution but as a violation against people and relationships in the school and wider school community.

The aim is to not to stigmatise offenders and place them outside the community but to facilitate their connection with those who have been harmed so that offenders can experience the impact of their behaviour and offer ways to 'restore' an equilibrium. Wrongdoing is not condoned but actively addressed as an interpersonal and community issue.

> Through taking responsibility for the wrongdoing and making amends, the shame can be acknowledged and discharged. Through this process, our feeling of connectedness to the community affected by our wrongdoing remains intact.
>
> (Morrison 2002: 2)

Connection and community: student voice, participation and agency

One of the most powerful protective factors for at-risk students is the opportunity to actively participate as a valued member of their group. Being connected with others is a fundamental need for human beings and makes a major difference to health, learning and life outcomes. As much of our society is geared to individualism rather than promoting a sense of community, children and young people may miss out on a sense of belonging unless this is actively promoted.

One way of doing this, increasingly in evidence around Australia, is Circle Time Solutions. Circles underpin restorative practices by increasing student connection to their class and school community. This framework for whole class interaction is based on the principles of democracy, respect, safety and inclusion. Its symbiotic aims promote a supportive class ethos along with the development of social and emotional skills for healthy relationships (Roffey 2006b). There are several versions of this pedagogy but there is evidence that a strengths approach with a focus on the positive, rather than using Circles primarily for problem solving, provides a place of safety, agency and positive change (McCarthy 2009). Playing collaborative games and other activities enables students to bond together in an enjoyable way (Hromek and Roffey 2009). The teacher is a participant, models what is expected and helps students make the connections between the activities and what they are learning about themselves and their class. Where facilitation is congruent with the philosophy students have opportunities to reflect on their behaviour and make more positive choices in their interactions with others.

> You think about bad things you've done and want to make up for it. (student year 5, in Roffey *et al.* 2004)

> We had a break through this week in Circle Time with a boy admitting bullying and saying he was sorry. We were blown away. (school counsellor, personal communication)

> It makes a difference to the way they (the students) relate to each other. (class teacher, in Roffey *et al.* 2004)

Case study 3

KIDSCAN is an initiative of the National Foundation for the Prevention of Child Abuse and Neglect (New South Wales). This offers children and young people opportunities and incentives to work collaboratively to develop projects to make their communities more child friendly. Although adults can be asked to help, they are supporters, not leaders. The many projects include a lunchtime camera club for non-sporty kids, building an indigenous garden, a one-day live music event, making books and DVDs about early settlement in their local area, setting up and recording a weekend camp with Darug elders, and a community arts project (http://www.napcan.org.au/kids-can).

Conclusion

There are still many schools who put all their efforts into identifying deficits and dealing with behavioural difficulties. Although understandable, the rise in exclusion rates indicates that something else needs to happen. This chapter summarises alternative ways of conceptualising students and challenging behaviour and offers a rationale for a focus on well-being, resilience and connection as being more effective and more ethical and having better outcomes for both students and teachers. This chapter also shares just a fraction of the many things that are happening in Australia to maximise the inclusion of our most vulnerable young people. It is possible to do things differently; it begins with the will to do so.

Bibliography

Ajmal, Y. and Rees, I. (2001) *Solutions in Schools: Creative Applications of Solution Focused Brief Thinking with Young People and Adults.* London: BT Press.

American Psychological Association (APA). (2006) *Are Zero Tolerance Policies Effective in the Schools? An Evidentiary Review and Recommendations.* Washington, DC: Zero Tolerance Task Force Report for the American Psychological Association.

Association for Supervision and Curriculum Development (ASCD). (2007) *The Learning Compact Redefined: A Call to Action. A Report of the Commission on the Whole Child.* Accessed 24 February 2009 at http://www.ascd.org on

Benard, B. (2004). *Resiliency: What We Have Learned.* San Francisco: WestEd.

Bransford, J. D., Brown, A. L. and Cocking, R. R. (2003) *How People Learn: Brain, Mind and Experience at School.* Washington, DC: National Academies Press.

Cameron, L. and Thorsborne, M. (2001) Restorative justice and school discipline: mutually exclusive? In J. Braithwaite and H. Strang (Eds) *Restorative Justice and Civil Society.* Cambridge: Cambridge University Press.

Catholic Education Office Melbourne (CEOM). (2006) *Student Wellbeing Research, Document 1.* Melbourne: CEOM.

Curriculum Corporation. (2006) *The Values Education Good Practice Schools Project – Stage 1.* Accessed 24 March 2010 at http://www.curriculum.edu.au/verve/_resources/VEGPS1_Final_report_Teach_1.pdf

Department of Education and Children's Services, South Australia (DECS). (2006) *Learner Wellbeing Framework.* Adelaide: DECS.

Department of Education and Children's Services, South Australia (DECS). (2007) *School Discipline Policy Statement.* Accessed 24 March 2010 at http://www.decs.sa.gov.au/docs/documents/1/SchoolDisciplinePolicy.pdf

Department of Education and Children's Services, South Australia (DECS). (2008) *Newly Appointed Leaders' Induction Handbook.* Adelaide: DECS.

Downey, J. (2008) Recommendations for fostering educational resiliency in the classroom. *Preventing School Failure,* 53 (1): 56–64.

Education Queensland. (2009) *Schoolwide Positive Behaviour Support*. Accessed 1 March 2009 at http://www.learningplace.com.au/deliver/content.asp?pid=40074

Enhancing Relationships in School Communities (ERIS). (2007) *Phase 1 Report (2004–2006)*. Accessed 27 February 2009 at http://www.education.unimelb.edu.au/swap/research/completed/downloads/eris_report_aug07.pdf

Goddard, A. (2003) The role of individual education plans/programmes in special education: a critique. *Support for Learning*, 12 (4): 170–174.

Hromek, R. and Roffey, S. (2009) Promoting social and emotional learning through games: 'It's fun and we learn things'. *Simulation and Gaming*, 40 (5): 626–644.

Hunter Institute of Mental Health. (2007) *Children and Young People's Wellbeing. An Educator's Guide*. Accessed 28 February 2009 at http://www.responseability.org/client/images/778595.pdf

Laws, C. and Davies, B. (2000) Post-structuralist theory in practice: working with 'behaviourally disturbed' children. *International Journal of Qualitative Studies in Education*, 13 (3): 205–222.

McCarthy, F. (2009) *Circle Time Solutions: Creating Caring School Communities*. Penrith, NSW: Report for the NSW Department of Education, University of Western Sydney.

McGrath, H. and Noble, T. (2006) *Bounce Back: Classroom Resiliency Programme*. Melbourne: Pearson Education.

Melbourne Graduate School of Education. (2008) Celebrating Inclusion within Catholic School Communities. Accessed 24 March 2010 at http://www.edfac.unimelb.edu.au/swap/wellbeing/teachers/environment/trans_eng.html/

Mooney, M., Dobia, B., Yeung, A., Barker, K., Power, A. and Watson, K. (2008) *Positive Behaviour for Learning: Investigating the Transfer of a United States System into the New South Wales Department of Education and Training Western Sydney Region Schools*. Penrith, NSW: University of Western Sydney.

Morrison, B. (2002) Bullying and victimisation in schools: a restorative justice approach. *Australian Institute of Criminology Trends and Issues in Crime and Criminal Justice*, 219.

Parsons, C. (2005) School exclusion: the will to punish. *British Journal of Educational Studies*, 53 (2): 187–211.

Reid, A. (2004) *Towards a Culture of Inquiry in DECS*. Occasional Paper No. 1. Adelaide: Department of Education and Children's Services.

Roffey, S., Jovanovich, M., Ioakimidis, C., Gunn, J., Woodward, J., Canales, G., et al. (2004) Evaluation of Circle Time in an Australian School. Penrith, NSW: Unpublished research, University of Western Sydney.

Roffey, S. (2006a) *Helping with Behaviour: Establishing the Positive and Addressing the Difficult in the Early Years*. London: Routledge.

Roffey, S. (2006b) *Circle Time for Emotional Literacy*. London: Sage Publications.

Roffey, S. (2007) Emotional literacy and transformation: the role of school leaders in developing a caring community. *Leading and Managing*, 13 (1): 16–30.

Roffey, S. (2008) Emotional literacy and the ecology of school wellbeing. *Educational and Child Psychology*, 25 (2): 29–39.

Werner, E. and Smith, R. (2001) *Journeys from Childhood to the Midlife: Risk, Resilience, and Recovery*. New York: Cornell University Press.

Chapter 20

Building on ideas and maintaining a dialogue for change

Richard Rose (University of Northampton, UK)

The commitment to working for a more equitable education system is evident in the writings of the authors who have contributed to this book. Although they write from a range of perspectives and certainly do not all interpret inclusion in exactly the same way, it is apparent that they have considered the many challenges and obstacles to inclusive schooling, which have resulted in marginalisation, and have endeavoured to find ways of overcoming these. However, although their commitment is assured, it is less easy to predict the responses towards educational reform from those politicians and policy makers who have it within their gift to implement change. We live in turbulent and fast-changing times during which national and international priorities shift, influenced by world events and the pressures exerted by socio-political and economic factors. Whereas in the wealthy countries of Europe, USA and Australasia inclusion has been a focus of attention for more than twenty years, elsewhere in the world priorities in this area have been less secure. In those countries where poverty and political instability remain a constant factor it is inevitably the most vulnerable members of society who face the greatest struggle to have their needs recognised or addressed. In such situations the need for advocacy is great and the responsibility upon all who are concerned for the achievement of greater social justice must be to look beyond their own situation and to join forces with others to promote change.

The chapters in this volume reflect many of the challenges which are faced by teachers, parents and pupils in schools across the world. Although some of the examples which they present are discussed in specific relation to an individual country, much of what the authors have to tell us will be familiar to teachers and others working anywhere. In highlighting the difficulties which individuals and groups face in their everyday lives, many of the writers articulate a struggle which will be familiar to many working in this field. By presenting examples of how some of the challenges are being addressed, others within the book are demonstrating the levels of innovation which are necessary to effect change. At no point is it suggested that an approach from one situation may be directly transferable to another. However, it is through the promotion of dialogue that we are most likely to gain new insights and to better understand how we might pursue actions which improve the lives of others and enrich the societies in which we live.

In bringing together researchers and writers from around the world this book has provided an opportunity for these individuals and for the reader of their work to gain some understanding of a range of approaches to addressing a common difficulty. That difficulty centres around the fact that many young people remain at a distance from those core features of education which others take for granted. The perpetuation of systems which continue to marginalise individuals on the basis of perceived difference is anathema in a world which has seen so much social, technological and scientific advance. However, the reality is that many of these advances, often casually referred to as 'progress', have become the exclusive property of those who are most advantaged within society. These writers demonstrate the importance of sharing ideas which may influence change in the lives of children. In reading their work it is important to recognise that the learning which is taking place is mutual and supportive in all directions. If we are to make progress in addressing complex educational issues it is essential that we recognise that, although the developments and advantages of economically advanced countries may have benefits which can be transferred to those in less advantageous situations, it is equally likely that we have much to learn from the approaches adopted in these same disadvantaged nations.

The importance of dialogue in promoting change cannot be ignored. The great Socratic tradition of dialectic, whereby the knowledge and interpretation of ideas is perpetually questioned and challenged, has provided the foundations of learning for many centuries. Effective classroom teachers know that not all pupils will respond to the same teaching approaches and that in some instances they will face difficulties in finding ways which engage their learners effectively. Such teachers question those conventions and simplifications which have come to characterise the ways in which education is perceived. Prescribed curricula and a focus upon narrowly conceived approaches to teaching have characterised the development of education in many countries. In such situations it has become the norm to label those individual learners who do not respond to the prescribed approach as divergent, troublesome or disaffected. Such an interpretation is limited in the extreme and is more likely perpetuate the distance between learners and the education process and to result in the imposition of negative labels being applied to young people who struggle to engage with the education system. Progress for many pupils is achieved when their teachers think beyond the imposed confines of standardised education approaches. However, to adopt innovative teaching approaches makes demands on teachers, not only in terms of their time and understanding, but also in respect of their confidence to challenge a system which fails to meet the needs of a number of their pupils.

The great Indian educator and Nobel laureate Rabindranath Tagore wrote:

> That education is a living, not a mechanical process, is a truth as freely admitted as it is persistently ignored.
>
> (*Advance*, lecture given in Calcutta, 10 February 1936)

Mechanistic approaches to education have been shown to fail many of the young people within our schools. A 'one size fits all' model is unlikely to yield the results which so many parents, teachers and young people desire. Yet the imposition of inflexible education systems appears to have become the norm in many societies. It has become clear that seeking a simple definition of inclusion which can be superimposed on a broad range of educational institutions and within diverse societies is unlikely to achieve the desired result of challenging exclusion. Multiple solutions are likely to be required. The maintenance of a dialogue which is conducted in a spirit of mutual respect and through which individuals are prepared to learn from the experiences of others is critical to an improved understanding of how education can change the lives of individuals. The authors within this book have demonstrated a commitment to such discourse and within their writings many have shown how a broadening of the conversation to ensure that those individuals who have been marginalised, their parents and their teachers are given opportunities to participate can have benefits for all.

Although considerable advances in our understanding of inclusion have been made, as has been demonstrated by the writers in this book, much remains to be achieved. The commitment to learning from all who are concerned to improve the educational opportunities for pupils who have been driven to the margins of our schooling systems needs to be maintained. Furthermore, it needs to be expanded in order to ensure that the voices of individuals can be heard and that those practices which are beginning to bring about change are shared. The contributions of teachers and those who are supporting them in their efforts to gain a greater understanding of how to ensure that all learners gain from a more equitable education system have implications well beyond the classroom. It is through these efforts and the maintenance of dialogue that inequalities may be challenged and change in the lives of individuals achieved.

Index

Please note: page numbers in *italics* refer to Figures and Tables.

eBooks – at www.eBookstore.tandf.co.uk

A library at your fingertips!

eBooks are electronic versions of printed books. You can
store them on your PC/laptop or browse them online.

They have advantages for anyone needing rapid access
to a wide variety of published, copyright information.

eBooks can help your research by enabling you to
bookmark chapters, annotate text and use instant searches
to find specific words or phrases. Several eBook files would
fit on even a small laptop or PDA.

NEW: Save money by eSubscribing: cheap, online access
to any eBook for as long as you need it.

Annual subscription packages

We now offer special low-cost bulk subscriptions to
packages of eBooks in certain subject areas. These are
available to libraries or to individuals.

For more information please contact
webmaster.ebooks@tandf.co.uk

We're continually developing the eBook concept, so
keep up to date by visiting the website.

www.eBookstore.tandf.co.uk